Nations by Design

ARNOLD RIVKIN was concernd with African affairs as a lawyer, United States aid official, research scholar, university professor, and economist. He was a pioneer in the development of multinational aid. He worked and traveled widely in some thirty African countries, where he headed special U.S. economic missions, particularly in Nigeria. In Sierra Leone he served as Economic Adviser to the Prime Minister. Mr. Rivkin authored *Africa and the West, The African Presence in World Affairs, Africa and the European Common Market,* and other works. He was Regents' Professor of African Studies at UCLA during the spring quarter, 1967, while on special leave from the World Bank, where he was Development Adviser for the African area until his death on September 19, 1968, of cancer.

Nations by Design

Institution-Building in Africa

EDITED, WITH AN INTRODUCTION BY

Arnold Rivkin

1968

Anchor Books

DOUBLEDAY & COMPANY, INC.
GARDEN CITY, NEW YORK

The Anchor Books edition is
the first publication of *Nations by Design*

Anchor Books edition: 1968

Contents

Preface

In keeping with practice and tradition the 1967 spring "Colloquium on Institution-Building and the African Development Process," sponsored by the African Studies Center of the University of California, Los Angeles, posed a good many questions. It also provided a few answers. The emphasis of the colloquium necessarily and by choice was exploratory and experimental. What have been the principal institutional patterns in Africa —before and after the major Eurafrican watersheds, the Act of Berlin of 1885, the Brazzaville Conference of 1944, and the Treaty of Rome of 1957? What are currently the nature and scope of "traditional," "modern," and "transitional" institutions in Africa? What is the link between institutions and African political, economic, and social development? What is the role of institutions in such development? What are the prospects for institutional development, transformation, and modernization? What are the possibilities for institutional transfers within Africa? For institutional transplants from outside? What are the prospects for institution-building as a useful technique in African development?

A core group of forty to fifty faculty members and graduate students, sharing a common interest in problems of institutional development as part of a larger concern with African development, convened once a week for ten consecutive weeks of scheduled three-hour sessions in the Regents' Board Room. Many sessions ran well beyond the scheduled time, and many were attended by additional visitors interested in the particular subject of the evening.

During each three-hour session the author of the paper under consideration, which had been reproduced and distributed a week or ten days before, presented, explained, elaborated, discussed, and, as need be, defended his paper. The participating interdisciplinary group of faculty members and graduate students—principally from the disciplines of anthropology, economics, history, law, political science, and sociology—explored, probed, queried, and at times attacked the paper under consideration, as well as their colleagues' comments and observations. Although occasionally heat rather than light was generated, the outcome was a generally positive contribution to the thinking of the group as well as to the authors of papers. There were two certain ways I had of knowing this in addition to the insights offered by my dual role as chairman of the colloquium and a contributing author. First, the colloquium papers were subjected to continuing scrutiny and analysis in a parallel graduate seminar on "Nation-Building in Africa" I offered as Visiting Regents' Professor of African Studies. (Students in the course were a selected interdisciplinary group of candidates for the M.A. degree in African studies.) Second, the authors made a good many revisions in their original papers in the aftermath of the respective colloquium sessions. The revised papers are collected in this volume.

The papers approach institutions and institution-building from many viewpoints. The historian is concerned with what has been; the sociologist with why and how institutions have been or are evolving; the political scientist with the way institutions have been or could be used to govern, to control, and to manipulate; and the economist with the importance and need for new or different institutions for inducing growth or restructuring the economy. All tend to assume or imply (a) a definition or concept of institutions, (b) the connection between institutions and African development, and (c) the possibility (or probability) that conscious programs of institution-building can be an integral part of national development efforts. In any event, there are few explicit definitions or stated assumptions relating to the three points in the papers.

The absence of such explicit definitions or stated assumptions I believe to be important. It demonstrates that, despite the absence of explicitly agreed definitions and individual differences in emphasis and nuance in the unstated assumptions underlying each paper (as well as the more explicitly stated differences which emerged during ten weeks of discussion), by and large it was possible to achieve a degree of consensus on the foregoing three key points (as well as several others). We were able to exchange views, and I further believe there was unspoken consensus on these principal points:

First, there seemed to be general recognition of the wide range and diversity of institutions in Africa, which incidentally make it most difficult and precarious (even if unavoidable) to generalize about the institutional framework of some forty independent states. Second, there seemed to be general agreement that institutions play an important, even a crucial, role in African development. Third, there seemed to be general agreement on the possibility (and for many the probability) that conscious efforts to build institutions could, would, and (except for some anthropologists) should proceed as part of the African development process. Fourth, the proposition that outsiders could contribute to the interrelated processes of institution-building and development seemed generally accepted, although the nature and degree of such contribution was much debated. And fifth, we recognized the need for a considerable amount of new, *interdisciplinary* research on the nature of the African development process, the role of institutions in the African development process, and the outlook for specific institution-building in Africa.

One explicit definition of institutions and institution-building in the collection is to be found in my own paper, which opened the series. The paper generally and the definition particularly were designed to establish a frame of reference and the interdisciplinary character of the colloquium's concern with institution-building and the African development process. The definition, I believe, encompassed most of the implied, assumed, and even stated definitions of institutions and institution-building the colloquium used. Despite its broad scope, I believe the definition may be useful: "Institution" and "structure" are used interchangeably. Both are taken to mean *organizations, arrangements, relationships* and *practices,* of an established nature, having political, economic or social purposes, and accepted as legitimate by the preponderant number of people affected or concerned. "Institution-building" is taken to mean the conscious, deliberate or studied attempt to develop new or to evolve existing institutions or structures in the given context to meet new or redefined needs.

As with any definition, particularly one so sweeping, there are inevitably problems of degree and emphasis. Adherents or practitioners of various disciplines would undoubtedly prefer to stress one or another aspect of the definition or would elaborate one or another aspect to the exclusion of others. However, I think, the definition provided a common meeting ground in the colloquium for interdisciplinary consideration of the complexities of institutions and institution-building.

If the colloquium's assumption that there is an important link between African development and institutions is correct, then institution-building becomes a central, even crucial task for all the new African states. Negatively, if not positively (and, I believe, positively too), the colloquium demonstrated not only the importance, of institutions *qua* institutions in the development process, but the over-all structural deficiency or "institutional gap" which exists in Africa.

Whether one talks of "traditional" and "modern" (and, as Professor Eisenstadt's paper suggests, the usefulness of this dichotomy increasingly is questioned) or of "underdeveloped" and "developed" sectors of African life, the point clearly emerges that in independent Africa there is a major discernible institutional gap between the new and the old, between market and subsistence organization of economic activity, and between national and tribal ways of life. It is strikingly clear that nationwide institutional frameworks or structures—to say nothing of specific national institutions—are absent from the political, economic, and social sectors of the newly independent states. The problem of developing national institutional frameworks has been accentuated by Africa's pervasive separatist and secessionist forces, on the one hand, and the vague, largely rejected, but still persistent dream of regional and continental "unity," on the other.

A possible role for outside institutions in African institution-building was generally thought by the colloquium to exist. There were, however, many reservations about how external forces and outside institutions might affect the problems of nation-building in Africa, and all types of constraining factors were recognized. Chief among these, in Professor Doob's words, was the general view that "no neocolonial attempt [should be made] to urge anyone to remake Africans in a Western image either effectively or rapidly, or not to do so." For the most part emphasis was on refraining from attempts to export Western institutions or models. Nonetheless, I believe it important not to forget Professor Doob's phrase, "or not to do so." In the same way that no attempt should be made to force Africans to "remake" themselves in a Western image, so too no effort should be made, as Frantz Fanon sought to make, to prevent or preclude Africans from "remaking" themselves by adopting or using such Western institutions as *they* might wish to take over. The decision after all is one for African countries to make in their own best interests. Presumably in a polycentric Africa the decision will vary from country to country. There is already a good deal of evidence to suggest that in Africa there will be, not only varying patterns, but also varying syntheses of Western institutions and existing institutions and institutions borrowed from other areas of the globe.

Finally, and probably inevitably, the collection of papers, and certainly the colloquium discussions, became involved with most of the major political, economic, and social issues of independent Africa in the late 1960s. This perhaps as much as anything else demonstrated the inescapable role of institutions in African development and the consequences of the institutional gap for it. It became clear that the endemic political instability, the widespread economic stagnation, and the epidemic of military *coups d'état* of the decade of the 60s are direct manifestations of the African institutional gap. They testify to the need for new institutions, or evolved or different institutions, to meet the problems of independence and development; they show what happens to both independence and development when such institutions are absent. There seems no detour around the gap; it must be bridged if development is to take place and if independence is to mean anything more to the nascent states than a seat in the United Nations. Institutional balance—of traditional and modern, of subsistence and exchange, of national and local, of public and private, to say nothing of political, economic, and social institutions—is an integral part of the problem of bridging the structural or institutional gap of independent African states. It may well prove to be the most intractable and difficult problem of all.

To the extent that the papers in this volume shed any light on the foregoing points, particularly on the relationship of institutions to development and the many problems of institution-building, they should serve to illuminate the relatively obscure and neglected structural aspect of the development process in Africa. To the extent that the papers effectively explore some of the complexities of institutions and institution-building from varying vantage points, they should provide some lines of inquiry and hypotheses, and hopefully of motivation, for the interdisciplinary research and study so urgently required.

It remains for me to express my sincere thanks and appreciation to the principal individuals and institutions which made it possible for me to take up the appointment of Regents' Professor of African Studies for the spring quarter of 1967 at the University of California, Los Angeles, and thus to co-ordinate and chair the colloquium. I owe thanks first and foremost to the Regents of the University of California, former Chancellor Franklin D. Murphy of the University of California, Los Angeles, and the three successive heads of the African Studies Center at UCLA, Professor James Coleman, founding director, Professor Benjamin Thomas, acting director, and Professor Paul O. Proehl, acting director, for their respective parts in honoring me with the invitation. I must also say a word of thanks to Professor Proehl for the many acts of personal friendship and professional co-operation he offered during my stimulating and enjoyable sojourn at UCLA, where he is now Vice-Chancellor. At the same time, I owe warm thanks and appreciation to Mr. Richard H. Demuth and Mr. Michael L. Hoffman, director and associate director of the Development Services Department, International Bank for Reconstruction and Development (World Bank), Washington, D.C., and to the bank itself, for their generosity and co-operation in making it possible for me to take leave from my post as Development Adviser in the Development Services Department, specializing in African affairs.

I owe a special note of thanks too to my wife, Jeanette Maling Rivkin, and my three children, Elizabeth Ann, William Mitchell, and Laura Maling for their good-natured pulling up of stakes and moving to Westwood Village, Los Angeles, in the midst of a school year and for adapting so well and agreeably to my temporary return to academia. In this connection, I also want to thank Mrs. Prue Baxter, a good family friend, who graciously took over running our home in Georgetown and looking after our oldest daughter, Elizabeth Ann, who could not leave National Cathedral School for Girls at the time we left for California in March 1967.

Finally, I should emphasize that my participation in the colloquium, including my role as editor of this volume, is my personal responsibility, and none of the materials, views, or judgments in the volume should in any way be attributed to the World Bank.

Arnold Rivkin

Georgetown,
Washington, D.C.
August 1968.

ARNOLD RIVKIN

The Role of Institution-Building in Africa

> *The direction of change remains undetermined. If we are to understand the variables that affect political growth more clearly than we do today, we must explore the relationships between political structures and the tasks that governments are called upon to perform in developing societies.*
>
> Aristide R. Zolberg,
> *One-Party Government in the Ivory Coast*

The relationship of structures and tasks is not only *the* critical factor, as Zolberg suggests, in understanding African political development; it is also critical in understanding African economic development. Further, the *building* of structures—institution-building—is the crucial factor in African political and economic development. This at any rate is the general hypothesis advanced in this paper.

Institution and structure are used interchangeably throughout. Both are taken to mean *organizations, arrangements, relationships,* and *practices,* of an established nature, having political, economic, or social purposes, and accepted as legitimate by the preponderant number of people affected or concerned. Institution-building is taken to mean the conscious, deliberate, or studied attempt to develop new or to evolve existing institutions or structures in the given context to meet new or redefined needs.

Although other factors have been singled out as crucial to development by one observer or another of the African scene, the cumulative African experience in the first decade of the African independence era suggests that in the absence of an appropriate institutional structure, and where other factors may be of varying importance, no one factor or combination of them has sufficed to sustain an integrated program of African political and economic development. We have seen too in one African country after another that none of these *other* factors alone or in combination has been sufficient to provide the impetus and momentum for a long enough period so that any of the new African states can be said to have been securely set on the path to political or economic development.

The most common factors thought crucial by observers have been the momentum deriving from the "struggle for independence"; the presence of a charismatic leader; the organization or apparatus of the independence movement, and of its common successor, the one-party system; the military, particularly in those instances where extended violence was involved in achieving independence, such as in Algeria; and the country's resource base, particularly in those cases, such as Congo (Kinshasa), Zambia, and Gabon, where there were known to be rich mineral resources, and in other cases, such as Nigeria and Ghana, which at independence had relatively well-developed agricultural exports. Other factors frequently cited as only slightly less crucial are the new national economic development plans adopted more or less universally soon after independence; the increased rate of investment effected in African countries which came to independence with substantial reserves, such as Ghana; the development of a new independent national currency not related to a European monetary area, such as in Guinea and Mali; the reorganization and redirection of inherited economic ties relating to investment, trade, aid, etc., such as in Guinea and Mali; the launching of new economic philosophies and programs under the banner of "African socialism" in a variety of African states, such as in Guinea, pre-coup Ghana, Algeria, Mali, and Tanzania; and the capacity for attracting large amounts of external financial and technical assistance from the West and the Communist bloc, such as in Algeria, Guinea, and Somalia.

At the political level various African states have had most of the crucial political factors alluded to by the various observers. By definition, all of the recently independent African states have had independence movements of one sort or another, ranging from the multiple, fragmented, embryonic political parties of Congo (Kinshasa) to the well-organized underground national party and guerrilla warfare units of Algeria. Also by definition, every newly independent African state has had at least one national independence leader who in his own local context had a touch of charisma. Some of these leaders exercised a considerable attraction for large numbers of people and countries on the broader African scene and beyond, e.g., Kwame Nkrumah, Ahmed Ben Bella, and Patrice Lumumba. So too, almost by definition, most of the newly independent states have developed their armed forces as national symbols. Increasingly in recent years

the symbols have translated themselves into active
participants, by seizing the reins of government in
one African country after another. One could go on,
but the foregoing illustrations serve to make the point
that African states have not lacked the presence of the
crucial political factors so often associated by students
of Africa with the requirements of national political
and economic development. Yet there has been little
or no development of accepted (legitimate) state
structures or political systems, and even less growth of
political stability.

At the economic level, too, Africa has had many of
the factors designated as crucial to its development.
Country after country has adopted a national development plan; some have had several plans since independence. Many have begun to develop and exploit
more effectively their resource bases. Those countries
fortunate enough to come to independence with substantial reserves or with access to significant external
aid have stepped up their rate of investment. Most of
the new states have increased the rate of investment
in particularly favored sectors, such as the industrial
and educational sectors. Some African states have
made major efforts to reorient the monetary, investment trade, and/or aid patterns of their economies,
away from those which existed during the colonial era
and toward the Communist bloc, or toward noncolo-
nial Western powers or other developed countries,
such as the United States, Canada, Scandinavia,
Japan, and even Israel. One could give further illustrations, but the foregoing enumeration should suggest
that African countries have not lacked the major economic preconditions thought necessary for African development. Yet there has been little actual growth,
and most often, even where growth has taken place,
little development.

Although the time interval between achieving inde-

pendence and the writing of this paper has been relatively brief for all the newly independent African
states (starting with the Sudan in 1956), it has not
been so brief that certain disconcerting provisional
generalizations do not emerge. It seems clear that, notwithstanding the presence and perhaps prevalence of
many of the major factors which have been thought
crucial for achieving political and economic development in new states, particularly those of Africa, their
presence alone has not been the touchstone to a desired state of political or economic development. In
fact, the African independence syndrome has been
characterized by the presence of many, perhaps
in some instances all, of the major factors often identified as crucial, followed by a longer or shorter time
interval during which the factors have been consumed, dissipated, or utilized without apparent result,
leading to stagnation, frustration, and even retrogres-
sion. For example, the major African state south of
the Sahara, Nigeria, had many of the prerequisites
identified as crucial for development, as summarized
in the following quotation, which also records their
fate:

> Nigeria contains about a quarter of Africa's total popu-
> lation. The federation is well endowed with natural
> wealth. At independence in 1960 it seemed certain that
> the country would become Africa's leading nation:
> Nigeria seemed to have everything—talent, resources and
> goodwill—and was set on the road to certain success.
> Everything, it seems now, except a leadership capable of
> giving the nation a sense of national unity and direction;
> and the deplorable tribal violence of recent months indi-
> cates that it may now be too late to save this potentially
> great country from disintegration.[1]

[1] "The African Giant," *New Africa* (London, November/
December 1966), Vol. 8, No. 11/12, p. 5.

Hardly a single African state has been able to come to grips with the problems involved in establishing any of the major preconditions for political and economic development, let alone with the problems for establishing all of the indispensable preconditions for such development. The independence-day agenda of preconditions required for development for most African states remains the same, one, two, three, five, and ten years after independence as it was on independence day. Most African states are still confronted with accomplishing five major tasks, the five preconditions for development: state-building, nation-building, economy-building, technological revolution, and social restructuring.

This paper maintains that what has been missing, and all too often overlooked, is the critically important institutional framework for development and the seminal institutions within that framework. We shall here be concerned with a schematic examination of the crucial role of institution-building in terms of establishing the five central preconditions for development set out in the preceding paragraph. We shall also be concerned in the body of the paper with the problem of institutional balance. In connection with the question of balance, we shall look at some of the consequences of the unbalanced growth of institutions in the many African states which have opted for a one-party structure as their route to development. This will also bring us to consider the role of the two organized institutions which have been stressed by the African leadership of most of the new states, the one-party structure and a national armed force. Finally, we shall try to develop at least a notional sense of the prospects of the new African states for successful institution-building, and thus in our view for success in their effort to achieve political stability and economic growth.

The Role of Institution-Building in State-Building

We of the Union Soudanaise affirm that the problem of Federation, the problem of Chiefs, etc., are but particular aspects of the single and same problem; the problem of the very conception of the structures of the Nation and of its framework, the problem of general political orientation in function of the economic and social organization of the state.[2]

In recent years it has been quite fashionable to denigrate the importance of the constitutional and governmental structures of newly independent states and to inflate the importance of the role of political leaders and political movements, but it seems quite clear that in Africa at any rate this has been a serious miscalculation. Without denying the relevance and importance of the roles of either political leaders or political movements, African experience in one state after another has suggested that the failure to resolve basic geopolitical structural problems has nullified or neutralized in significant degree the activities of both the political leader and the political movement. Failure to recognize the overriding importance in state-building of defining the physical and constitutional limits within which the state is to be built as the major physical and constitutional guidelines which are to

[2] *Essor* (Bamako), editorial, March 13, 1959, as quoted in William J. Foltz, *From French West Africa to the Mali Federation* (New Haven: Yale University Press), 1965, p. 128. To the same effect, see Crawford Young's *Politics in the Congo* (Princeton: Princeton University Press, 1965) especially Ch. XVII, wherein the author concludes: "The quest for political institutions that are at once stable and effective is far from over and is fundamental for the successful organization of independence."

control and orient the state-building effort, has resulted in a good deal of wasted, unfocused effort; in
a dissipation of leadership prestige, popular enthusiasm and scarce resources; and in a growing disillusionment with the promised glories of independence.

At the most fundamental level, the question of
physical and constitutional limits within which the new
states are to be built has hardly been identified, let
alone emphasized, by commentators on the African
scene. Yet until the physical boundaries are determined
and the constitutional limits are established, it would
seem all but impossible to focus national efforts to
build a state. At independence, every new African
country is a state in the limited sense only of having
acceded to international sovereignty, i.e., general recognition by the community of international states and
membership in the United Nations. Beyond this nominal quality of statehood, the new African countries
came to independence with the shell rather than the
substance of statehood. In the words of President
Houphouët-Boigny of Ivory Coast:

> Independence has only bequeathed statehood to us; it
> remains for us to create nations transcending the tribal
> level, which is what I believe we are doing in the Ivory
> Coast.[3]

Physical Boundaries

To start with the physical boundaries problem,
there are a variety of actual, and an even larger number of potential, situations which inhibit effective state-
building. In its clearest form the lack of definition of
boundary lines for many African states creates an at-

---

[3] As quoted in *Cahiers de l'Afrique Occidentale et de
l'Afrique Equatoriale* (Paris, No. 337, July 22, 1967), p. 15;
translation from the French by the author.

mosphere of uncertainty which in more acute cases has already caused serious dispute, occasional hostilities, and several actual outbreaks of conflict. The most serious cases have arisen in the Horn of Africa and in North Africa. In the Horn of Africa, Somalia and Ethiopia have been engaged in more or less unremitting border warfare in the Haud and Ogaden areas, which has diverted a good deal of both countries' national energy and resources from the basic problem of building states. Both of these poverty-stricken states with per capita income levels among the lowest in the world (of the order of fifty dollars per annum) are allocating increasing amounts of their scarce resources to military purposes. Both may be allocating as much as 35 per cent to 40 per cent of their annual budgets to military purposes.

Closely related to the Somalia-Ethiopian conflict is the running conflict of Somalia with its neighbor to the south, Kenya. Here again the national energy and resources of the two states have been seriously diverted. Until the three countries in question establish defined boundaries, the distortions in and distractions from their state-building efforts will remain substantial and will constrain the effectiveness of their efforts. Will the new Somali state contain all, a significant part, or any segment of the old Northern Frontier District of Kenya? All, a significant part, or any segment of the Haud or Ogaden areas of Ethiopia? And until the status of French Somaliland, claimed by both Somalia and Ethiopia, is resolved, there is still another important element of uncertainty in the picture. Will the state of Somalia encompass all, a significant part, or any of the area which is now French Somaliland? Will the Somali peoples and other tribes in the contested areas be Somali, Ethiopian, or Kenyan citizens? Alternatively, with respect to Kenya and Ethiopia, one must pose the same range of questions. Will the states of Kenya and Ethiopia be built within their present geographic borders, or in some lesser areas, following a possible cession of territory (and/or population) to Somalia?

In North Africa the irredentist claims of Morocco have already given rise to one armed engagement with Algeria. Although hostilities have abated, the underlying border dispute remains to fester unresolved. The Algerian response to the tension and uncertainty has been a major arms buildup, including Russian-supplied tanks, artillery, jet fighters, and bombers. The Moroccan riposte has been to turn to the United States for military equipment, particularly aircraft and antitank weapons "to balance" the Algerian expansion of forces. All of the ingredients of the Middle East arms race are present, with the concept of "maintaining a balance" between the Arab states led by the United Arab Republic and those led by Saudi Arabia, as well as between the Arab states and Israel. Both Algeria and Morocco are devoting increasing segments of their annual budgets to military purposes, perhaps as much as 25 per cent.

Morocco also claims all of the area of Spanish Sahara, which is simultaneously claimed in toto by Mauritania. With a Spanish withdrawal from the area sooner or later likely, this tends to be a sore spot between the two countries. The unresolved pending claims of Morocco vis-à-vis her two neighbors, to say nothing of Morocco's territorial claims on Mauritania itself, remain a diversion for Morocco from its central focus on state-building within the given territory it now occupies. The Moroccan claims also create an element of uneasiness in the neighboring states of Algeria and Mauritania, which could only adversely affect their respective state-building efforts.

Although a separate issue, the question of possible political unions and federations can be closely related to problems of physical boundaries. Since before independence Kenya has been concerned with proposals for the development of an East African federation to include Kenya, Uganda, and Tanganyika (now Tanzania). On the one hand, the possibility of the founding of such a federation could not help but have an important effect on the state-building efforts of the three proposed component states. Should the state-building effort in each of the three independent states maximize the sovereign status of each of the components, or should the state-building efforts minimize the sovereign status of each of the components, with a view to facilitating a loss or diminution of the components' sovereignty through a merger or union into a larger political unit? This dilemma can be seen most clearly in the swings of the nationalist pendulum in Tanganyika from ardent federalist agitation to narrow, almost xenophobic, Tanzanian nationalism. (We shall return to this point later on in this section.) On the other hand, Kenya and, perhaps to a lesser degree, the two other proposed components of an East African federation, have been tempted to resolve the apparently intractable triangular problem of establishing boundaries between Somalia and Kenya and between Somalia and Ethiopia, by expanding the proposed East African federal political union to include, *inter alia*, Ethiopia and Somalia. The logic seems to be that if the boundary problem cannot be resolved directly between the parties, somehow, by incorporating all of the parties and their problems into a larger context, the problems will disappear or fade away.

So too in North Africa the concept of a political union of North African states under the banner of Maghreb has long been present. Morocco, Algeria, and Tunisia are always put forward as the three prospective candidates for membership; sometimes Libya is included along with her three neighbors to the West.

The Maghreb solution has frequently been pressed as a way to resolve the Moroccan-Algerian boundary dispute, to say nothing of lesser boundary claims of Tunisia on Algeria. A Maghreb union has also been urged from time to time, quite independently of boundary issues. In any event, it overhangs the efforts of state-building of the North African countries, one or another of which, whenever the internal going gets rough, has recourse to this Maghrebian possibility as a diversion.

Apart from the boundary disputes and irredentist claims, there have been any number of proposals, plans, and projects for political unions and associations of independent African states. As we have already suggested, the East African federation proposals and the Maghreb proposals have an impetus which exists apart from the claims and counterclaims involving the boundaries of one or more of their prospective members. There are many reasons for the propensity of various African leaders to sponsor occasionally projects for African political unions or associations of one sort or another. The maxim "in union there is strength," the political counterpart of the economic doctrine of economies of scale said to result from producing for larger markets thought to result from an association of states, is frequently a principal motivating factor. So too are expansionist drives, Pan-African doctrines, historical factors, cultural affinities, economic advantages (presumed or real), tribal connections, and external diversions from internal problems.

The political union of Senegal and Soudan in the Federation of Mali on the eve of the two territories' achieving independence, served, during its short life and bitter aftermath, to becloud the focus for state-building of the two units, and to disperse energy and resources. Given the interdependence of state-building and economy-building, this could only have had negative effects on both. The unconsummated union of Tanganyika and Zanzibar in the United Republic of Tanzania has not only introduced unresolved constitutional and political complications but also an atmosphere of serious uncertainty into the state-building and economy-building efforts of both states. Tanganyika has done all it could do to build the state, nation, and economy of Tanganyika. Its efforts simultaneously to build the state, nation, and economy of Tanzania may well prove to be not only beyond its capacity, but also self-defeating.

Is the constitutional and governmental structure of Tanzania to encompass both members of the "union"? If so, what kind of reconciliation of the fundamental differences between the two will be sought? Will there be a single Tanzanian nation? Or a mainland Tanganyikan nation and an island Zanzibari nation? Will there be one integrated economy, or two separate economies? In outward form, the answers to those and many other related questions have been one state-structure, one nation, one economy, and so on; in practice, frequently, the answer has been two separate units or goals behind a façade of union. Thus, there is a shared president, at least constitutionally, but quite separate constitutional and governmental structures and parliamentary institutions; travel and trade between mainland and the islands is in many ways more difficult than between independent states; the economies are basically separate; nation-building is basically separate in the two areas; military, police, "foreign" policies, etc., are also more or less separate. So too are the two "one-party" structures, the Tanganyika African Nation Union and the Afro-Shirazi Party. Both are exclusive and monolithic in their respective domains. Are two such separate parties *cum* governments compatible with the concept of an integrated, centralized unitary state structure?[4] In this geopolitical miasma, it is not at all surprising that institution-building in Tanzania has not evolved to a degree that one could say the union of the two states has been integrated, let alone consummated or securely launched toward development.

Even where there are no external boundary issues and no political union proposals to deflect attention from the formidable constitutional and legal problems of state-building, there are, at least in the larger states—Nigeria, Congo, the Sudan, Ethiopia, Algeria— serious *internal* borderline or boundary issues. In Nigeria and the Congo, the constitutional problems are tightly interwoven with those of the boundary lines demarcating regions or provinces. In the Sudan the constitutional crisis between north and south also involves the drawing of at least constitutional lines to delimit, in effect, the areas in which the competing racial/religious groups will have regional ascendancy. In Ethiopia, the still-undigested absorption of the former Italian colony of Eritrea involves not only constitutional but also internal boundary line problems. And in Algeria, the constitutional issues at heart of the country's political crisis interact with the problem of integrating the large desert wastelands to the south with the Mediterranean provinces of the country; the problem reflects the country's colonial legacy, which treated the Mediterranean coastal area as an integral part of metropolitan France.

Thus, in many ways the physical limits for state-building are the starting point for the constitutional

---

[4] Apparently in the Federation of Mali the answer was "no." The *Union Progressive Sénégalaise* (UPS) and the *Union Soudanaise* insisted on not only supremacy or primacy but also exclusivity in their respective areas. This was particularly true of the UPS, which felt threatened by the incursions of the *Union Soudanaise* into Senegalese politics. See Foltz, *ibid.*, p. 170.

framework and institutions which must be developed in every new African state. The constitutional structure and institutions require territorial definition, and with it, accompanying substantive definition of state-building objectives and scope, e.g., reconciliation or incorporation of disputed areas and populations.

Constitutional Frameworks

The geopolitical issues of external physical boundaries and internal physical guidelines, within which to build a constitutional structure to shape and form the new states, have plagued a large part of the continent. Related to the basic institutional problem of physical boundaries are the constitutional problems. What kind of state structure should be built? Should states seek to develop one-party unitary structures, federal structures, likely to be multiparty in nature, modernize an existing monarchy, or seek stability and growth with types of military state structures? How centralized or decentralized should the state structures be? How much devolution of power should there be to the regional, provincial, and local governmental levels? What should be the role of the military? These and many more problems infuse the constitutional dimension of state-building; all must be faced in establishing the constitutional framework for a state, and in devising its basic institutional pattern—the roles of the executive, legislative, and judiciary, the relationship of state and party or parties, and the role of the individual.

Whatever constitutional institutions are chosen, the problem of governmental structure remains. What type of public administration should be developed? Size and status? Should it be impartial and above, or at any rate out of, politics? What should the civil service's relationship be to the one-party in a one-party state? To the military in a military-state structure?

The problems of state-building and the institutions

to be built to give shape and meaning to the state structure are, clearly, closely interwined. Together they raise problems, the successful resolution of which is the first precondition for development.

The problem of institution-building has been complicated in any number of African states by the constitutional dilemma of the institutional relationship to be established between state institutions and party institutions. Which is to be supreme, state apparatus or party machine? The doctrinaire one-party states in pre-coup Algeria, Guinea, Mali, pre-coup Ghana, Congo (Brazzaville), and Tanzania have had little difficulty in deciding—the one-party apparatus was to be supreme. And any number of other one-party states have sought to follow suit. In practice this has meant that state-building—the problems of boundary lines and constitutional structures—has passed into the province of the single party, which, no matter how massive or democratic in its centralism, means the state institutions are not for *all* the people of the country. The judiciary, the civil service, the universities, even the military—all are subordinated or will be subordinated to the party. The party test of loyalty (of necessity in the exclusive one-party state) is to the party apparatus, its principles, dogmas, and leadership cult; not to the state and nation, which are larger, more universal units. The opposition, the nonconformists, the bourgeoisie, the dissenters, etc., are still part of the state and nation, even though they are excluded from the single party. In the words of Dr. Foltz, contrasting the patterns in the defunct Federation of Mali—Senegal and Soudan:

In a certain sense, the Senegalese view of unity is an inclusive one, based on acceptance of a few rules of the game, e.g., tolerance of a national political opposition but not one in the service of a foreign power, while the Soudanese view is exclusive; one is a complete member of the club, or one is cast out from society in the African tribal tradition.[5]

Institution-building, then, in this context, has meant dependent, circumscribed, and controlled institutions. The history of universities, courts, civil services, parliaments—to say nothing of private or theretofore private voluntary groups—in Africa has been one of subordination, take-over, and destruction by the one party. The implications of this institutional pattern for state-building have been serious and direct. It has made it all but impossible for truly national institutions representative of and responsive to the total nation to develop and grow. It has also made the formal constitutional structure meaningless, as the party structure (notwithstanding propaganda to the contrary) has generally been a tightly held monopoly of a relatively small controlling group who can play musical chairs with formal constitutional institutions—consolidating ministries, dismissing ministers, and disregarding legislative prerogatives. When the uncertainties of geography are added, the result has been a façade of institutions which have not been able either to command support or to induce participation by an ever-increasing part of the public. The measure of the failure is the plague of military coups sweeping Africa—and the general popular acceptance of the coups, which have more often than not overthrown the "independence" leaders of their countries—Olympio, Nkrumah, Ben Bella, Youlou, Yaméogo, Maga, Apithy, Dacko, Kasavubu, et al.

[5] *Ibid.*, p. 211. In practice, in so far as the federal union of the two states was concerned, the proviso attached by the Senegalese to their view of "unity," excluding political opposition "in the service of a foreign power," meant rejection of the activities of the *Union Soudanaise* in Senegal, as by definition the party was "in the service of" the Soudan. The federation was foredoomed from its inception. See footnote 4.

Another facet of the constitutional conflict between state structure and party apparatus has been the insatiable appetite of the controlling single party for unqualified power. All other institutions—public and private—irrespective of constitutional provisions and structure had preferably to be taken into camp, or at a minimum "guided," manipulated, or controlled. Thus, in Tunisia, one of the most effective and "permissive" of the one-party African regimes, "party control sapped their [voluntary national institutions, e.g., trade unions and agricultural organizations] vitality and tended to divorce them from their members."[6]

All public institutions clearly were subordinated, with one important exception. All private institutions—trade unions, newspapers, youth groups, women's clubs, trade associations, farmers' groups, co-operatives, cultural societies, and even in some instances religious societies—were absorbed directly by, or grafted on as auxiliaries to, the party apparatus. Only one public institution escaped the one party's embrace—the military—and herein lies the African tale of two institutions—the one party and the military, which sooner or later must have a confrontation. In country after country, the one-party state has attempted to subordinate and control the military through its party machinery, its control of the state apparatus and the state's budget, its monopoly over the means of communication, its capacity to bestow prestige, honors, patronage, and other rewards. When these levers of power failed, as they must sooner or later, the one party has had recourse to a countervailing force, the creation of a party or people's militia, which has been done in Algeria, Ghana, and Congo (Brazzaville), *inter alia*. In the first two cases when the confrontation came between the party and the military, the regular military

[6] Clement H. Moore, *Tunisia Since Independence* (Berkeley and Los Angeles: University of California Press, 1965), p. 159.

prevailed and took over. In the last case, the foreign-dominated party militia held fast and prevailed for the moment over the faction-ridden military. Guinea and Mali bear close attention on this score. Both heap great praise and honors on their military. Both report plots and conspiracies to overthrow the government, particularly Guinea. Whether these two tendencies will continue along parallel lines, or at some point intersect, remains to be seen.

The Role of Institution-Building in Nation-Building

Once the physical and boundary problems are met, or at least confronted, another problem arises. What sort of political structure and system is to be built to operate the state structure, to relate the population to the state structure, and to breathe life into the independent state?

For the most part African states have chosen centralized, unitary state structures *with* authoritarian political structures and systems. The growth of authoritarian institutions has been almost a natural concomitant—a reflex action—to the highly centralized constitutional structures and the ascendancy or domination of the apparatus or machinery of their *de jure* or *de facto* single parties over them. Coercion, ranging from social ostracism for nonconformity to manipulation of the state structure through preventive detention and forced compliance, has come to be the rule. Persuasion and participation through unrigged, competitive, free elections, voluntary political and economic interest groups, and freedom of speech, assembly, and petition have been the exception.

Institution-building, then, for the largest part of Africa has had two complementary goals—one, to concentrate and control power through the authorized set of institutions, and, two, to liquidate and prevent the growth of institutions outside the establishment. The political structures and systems have been shaped with this dual purpose in mind.[7]

Election districts and voting systems have been designed to gerrymander actual or potential opposition out of the race. The military, police, paramilitary forces, party militias, Workers' Brigades, party thugs, etc., have all been used to protect the monopoly of the one party and its state structure against all who remain recalcitrant or outside the direct orbit of party control.

Military regimes too have based their political structure and systems on coercion rather than persuasion and participation. None has succeeded, and few have been able or even willing to try systems based on voluntarism. The decree and the force to impose it have determined, more rather than less, the capacity of military regimes in Africa to survive, let alone govern.

In those few instances where democratic or quasi-democratic approaches have been tried by new states in Africa, they too have had limited success in developing institutions through which voluntary participation could voice its views and exercise its will. Nigeria has been the prime example of an effort to build relatively open and responsive political institutions to give mean-

[7] Moore, *ibid.*, p. 205, characterizing the "permissive one-party state in Africa" concludes that the leader in such a state, deliberately as well as inevitably, "inhibits the development of institutions that might help to keep the system open after his departure." Thus "no institution may develop while the leader, to maintain his supremacy, fragments any countervailing centers of power." (*Ibid.*, p. 204.) The author believes the same result is reached in what Moore classifies as "neo-Leninist" one-party states in Africa, e.g., Guinea, in which the cult of the party's supremacy prevails and prescribes doctrinaire views to guide party action, including, at least in theory, those of the leader(s). See the author's discussion of economy-building in this paper, and in *The African Presence in World Affairs* (New York: Free Press of Glencoe, 1963), pp. 13–14, pp. 21–32, and pp. 35–47 for a fuller treatment of the subject.

ing to its constitutional structure. It has come to grief in large part because the basic approach and ultimate goal were not widely enough shared in that large, plural society. On the other hand, the determined attempt to preserve democratic and representative institutions and procedures in the midst of the agonizing series of political crises and intermittent turmoil the country has been caught up in ever since independence in 1960 is a lasting tribute to the commitment of an important segment of the Nigerian leadership to the political concepts of persuasion and voluntary participation. The testing of the new Nigerian fabric of democratic social and political order at the hands of those agitating for a centralized unitary political structure came much too soon and much too abruptly; it will be remarkable if it shows the resiliency to spring back into shape rather than give at its most vulnerable points—the tribal, separatist flaws in the cloth, which in time (had time been available) might have been reinforced or covered over with usage and reweaving.

Related to the means—authoritarian vs. democratic approach—is the question of goal. Should the political system seek to achieve uniformity or ensure diversity amid a larger over-all constitutional unity? Most African states have opted for uniformity. Although not necessarily inevitable, in practice one-party state structures in Africa have meant authoritarian political systems with uniformity as their goal. The combination has meant, as we have seen with state-building, dependent, circumscribed, and shadowy institutions. Legislatures without power, judiciaries without independence, newspapers, radio, and television without news or views beyond the party line, trade unions, cooperatives, farmers' associations, women's clubs, youth leagues, etc., without independence or functions beyond the buttressing of the one party's monopoly of power, universities without academic freedom, elections without choice, public meetings without freedom of speech or dissent, laws without the rule of law, economic development plans without incentives, entrepreneurs or innovators, and party cells without a channel to the top—all have appeared in country after country in Africa to coerce performance and impose uniformity. These are state and political institutions without roots—and in country after country in Africa the experience has been the same. Right, left, or center—these institutions in the one-party state structures and systems have, in their inherent weakness and failure to gain popular acceptance, made inevitable the military coup which has become an integral part of the African independence syndrome.

Sterile institutions, which use the vocabulary of mass participation but in fact exclude meaningful participation by the masses, under pressure tend to collapse before military takeovers. The only uncertainty in the calculation has been the time factor: how long can regimes of the sort described tread water and survive? How long can they defer the take-over state of the type which has taken hold in Algeria, Ghana, Upper Volta, Central African Republic, Dahomey, Togo, and Burundi, and came close to power in Congo (Brazzaville) and Gabon?

Elsewhere in Africa too the military has been active, in the absence of the resolution of state-building and nation-building problems, in taking over governmental power—in Nigeria, Congo (Kinshasa), Sierre Leone, and on-again, off-again in the Sudan, and in the UAR. There have also been limited abortive military uprisings in Tanganyika, Kenya, and Uganda. In Uganda, there was also a "preventive coup" in 1966 in which the prime minister with support of a purged military ousted the president and turned the quasi-federal multiparty state into a one-party unitary structure.

All of which leads us to ask—philosophy and principles aside—can the authoritarian *cum* uniformity approach to political (and, as we shall see, economic) institution-building, as a practical matter, succeed in Africa? In our view it clearly cannot. The very qualities, elements, factors—particularly the institutional gaps—which are by definition the state of being underdeveloped, make it improbable and probably impossible for an effective authoritarian regime to evolve, which will be able to do very much more than perpetuate itself in power for a longer or shorter period. It seems most unlikely that such regimes will be able to resolve satisfactorily the state-building and nation-building problems already discussed, to say nothing of economy-building, through the use of coercion, exhortation, and incantation. It seems most unlikely that institutions of the required efficiency could be developed to force the indispensable participation of the mass of the population or impose the uniformity, which has been equated by these regions with unity, on the plural, disparate populations of every independent African state.

For the most part, state- and nation-building remains for African countries five and ten years after independence the unfinished task it was at the moment of independence.

Economy-Building

Almost more than state and political institutions, modern economic institutions have been lacking in Africa. Although various subsistence societies in Africa had evolved "state" and political institutions with which to govern themselves and maintain relations with neighboring subsistence societies, very few had developed until recently, under the pressure of outside stimuli, economic institutions which consciously sought to induce greater production of a wider variety of commodities and products for more than direct, immediate subsistence of the producing unit, the family. There has been traditionally little impetus for market production—for an exchange economy—except at a local level, and then, more often than not, largely as a matter of chance or for highly circumscribed and limited purposes.

The problem of monetizing the economy or modernizing the subsistence economy so that a modern market economy evolves is the critical structural problem for all the independent African states. Crucial institutions for economic planning or programming are needed—statistical services, research bodies, geological and topographical units to map and explore the resource base and test the soils, meteorological and hydrological services to record rainfall and locate surface and subsurface water, etc.; crucial institutions for transferring data to producers and potential producers are needed —agricultural extension services, industrial advisory services, manpower training institutions, etc.; crucial institutions for carrying out the physical elements of development projects are needed—public works departments, soil conservation units, reforestation units, training institutions for surveyors, designers, architects, engineers, etc.; crucial institutions for mobilizing internal resources, savings institutions, commercial banks, development banks, home loan and mortgage institutions, domestic money markets, stock and bond markets, etc.; crucial marketing institutions—commodity markets, trading centers, storage and grading centers, credit institutions, etc. The list is almost endless. The gap between what exists and what is needed is tremendous. The capacity to develop the institutions is limited. The traditional subsistence society and its cultural milieu did not provide the incentive or create the need for the type of individuals or institutions that economy-building now requires. There is a desperate race in Africa to throw up institutions and create the skilled and semiskilled cadres needed to span the gulf between subsistence and market production. A handful of African states—pre-coup Nigeria, Ivory Coast, Kenya and Tunisia—have taken important strides in this race. Others such as pre-coup Ghana, Guinea and Mali, have tried to erect patchwork façades which look like the finished product, but without solid foundations, which have collapsed under the inescapable pressures of economic reality—world market prices and competition, inflation, international trade requirements for convertible currency, the cost of living beyond a country's means, and so forth.

Aside from establishing the concept of production for the market and housing it in appropriate institutions, it is vital to restructure the economies so that they are not exclusively export-oriented. Although overseas exports must continue to grow, production for the internal market and for inter-African exchange is a high priority. The starting point for industrialization is the processing of locally grown agricultural and forestry commodities for food, beverages, clothing, and housing. Sensible import-substitution too is a factor to be considered in developing an industrialization pattern and in using foreign exchange in the most productive manner. All of this restructuring involves the development of many of the institutions already enumerated in this section. In addition, it requires export promotion, transport, packaging, shipping, insurance, financing institutions, and much more, to determine market demand, tastes, and local needs, and to bring production and markets together in a systematic, rational way.

In addition to production, financing, and marketing, the institutional framework for the economy at large must be put in place and developed. Is there to be a predominant state sector and a small or nonexistent private sector? Is there to be a large private sector and a relatively limited state sector? Is the economy, like the polity, to be highly centralized? In fact, can you

have a decentralized economy within a highly structured centralized constitutional and political setup?[8]
Is the economy to be decentralized, with a large area
reserved for individual and voluntary nonstate sector
decision-making? For entrepreneurs? Trade unions?
Producer-co-operatives? Trade groups?

The proclamation of African socialism without the
institutional infrastructure such a system presupposes
has led a fair number of African states down the blind
alley of investment without growth, and of growth
without development. Plants have been built in the
public sector which are idle or underutilized for lack of
machinery, or spare parts, or managers or raw materials, or markets. The capital output ratio has been high.
Jobs have not opened up to any significant degree.
Monetization of the economy has not been markedly
encouraged. New institutions have not been built.
Only the gloss of industrial production, represented by
the bricks and mortar of new plants and the intermittent emission of smoke, has too often been the output of important amounts of capital investment in
public sector industrial undertakings. The "sick industries" of Algeria, Ghana, Guinea, and Mali, and many
others, who for doctrinaire or other reasons have invested heavily in public sector producing industry
without building the institutional framework indispensable for sustaining such industry, dot the African
landscape.

More than a few African development plans in the
one-party states and beyond have had their greatest

[8] More than likely, it would be incompatible to have vigorous
and flourishing centers of private economic power outside the
control of one-party state structures and systems in Africa. In
practice, the tendency has been increasingly for the one party to
seek to enlarge the public sector, and *pari passu* its direction of
and control over the public sector. Independent economic institutions have tended to disappear in these circumstances.

difficulties and failures in the publicly financed industrial sector. Investment in industry has tended in these
instances to precede the institutional infrastructure
without which industry cannot operate successfully or
profitably.

Technological Revolution

Intimately related to economy-building in Africa is
the associated problem of technological modernization. Africa has the most striking incongruities—the
most modern, automated equipment and the most
primitive and backward technology—at one and the
same time. Hence, side by side, one finds the machine-
drawn plow and the crude digging stick, the dial telephone and the talking drum, the modern hospital and
the witch doctor, and the jet airplane and the human
beast of burden.

Africa lacks a hierarchy of technology. It lacks a
technology developed in response to its needs and purposes. It lacks the supporting institutions for adapting
imported technology, for rationalizing and developing
the imported technology, and for training staff to use
and maintain the imported technology. Thus, often, on
a continent with allegedly surplus or underutilized manpower, one finds no particular philosophy or system of
labor-intensive investment and production. At the same
time, on a continent with scarce capital resources, one
finds no particular philosophy or approach to capital-
intensive investment and production.

The broken machine, the broken-down truck, and the
rusting tractor—for lack of mechanics, spare parts, and
basic maintenance—are a sad tale of investment without growth. Although investment rates creep up, or
even spurt, one has to ask, with what results? The
high-cost steel mill may have an import-savings effect.
It will also have ramifying effects throughout the

economy, as one plant after another has to pay too much for its steel—and hence, for its buildings. High amortization charges mean higher, noncompetitive tariff-protected prices. Industrial output is encumbered and handicapped by this sort of built-in high-cost base. There is also the direct cost to the budget of production subsidies for high-cost steel, as well as loss of revenue from customs duties on imported steel products.

There is major need for institutions, for manpower training, for market studies, for project preparation, for technological research, for appraising investment opportunities, for designing technological systems appropriate in African circumstances, for systematizing, rationalizing, and expanding the technological base of African economies. So far the response has been relatively limited. Few African countries have identified the problem, and fewer have done very much about it; so too, few external aid-giving institutions have identified the problem or done very much about it.

Social Restructuring: "Things Fall Apart"

It is a commonplace to talk of the European impact on Africa and its subsistence society, and the wreckage and confusion left in the wake of the European presence. Without attempting to refine or assess the degree of truth in this frequent generalization, it seems quite clear that Western culture, with its technology, statecraft, and production for the market has disrupted the closed-circle existence of a good many of Africa's subsistence societies. The classical production cycle was obviously disturbed and in some places disrupted by commercialization of crops, introduction of export crops, enticement of male labor to plantations and mines, urbanization and its attendant factors. The welfare pattern or subsistence life was impaired first and then broken in place after place, as money rather than relationships, duties, and tokens of fealty and esteem became the medium for discharging and regulating social obligations. Chinua Achebe, in his novels, *Things Fall Apart, Arrow of God,* and *No Longer at Ease,* graphically depicts the process of subsistence societies giving way to the force of the European presence and the fluid, uneasy aftermath which ensued in Nigeria.

Capital accumulation needs interfered with normal extended family duties. Or the other way round, as reflected in a recent warning of President Kenyatta of Kenya, the impoverished relative who leaves his *shamba* in the country to live idly off the bounty of his wage-earning relative in the city interferes not only with production on the farms, but also with savings and productive investment by urban dwellers, and inflates unnecessarily the already overwhelming demand for more and more expensive urban facilities and housing. President Kenyatta said this was a "social waste" that would not be tolerated. The unemployed would be rounded up and sent back to their *shambas*. Countless European colonial administrators before him in tropical Africa failed to cope effectively with this most common dislocation of modernization. The Belgian authorities in Leopoldville planted the seeds of their own undoing in 1957 and 1959 by shipping such discontented unemployed or unemployables back to the countryside.

The social structures of all African states are in a fluid state. The old, the traditional, the customary structures, on the one hand, have collapsed or yielded without replacements ready at hand; yet on the other, although shaken and badly impaired, various elements and practices are tenaciously hanging on. In some instances, African states have been attempting to synthesize a concept of African socialism with a new view of traditional communal or tribal social systems—sometimes referred to as communalism. The attempts vary remarkably from President Léopold Senghor's attempt in Senegal to launch a type of moderate Christian socialism to that of President Julius Nyerere's in Tanzania to initiate a type of radical nationalist socialism.

Many African states are seeking to build modern social structures as an inevitable concomitant of economy-building, nation-building, and state-building. Those that are committed to centralized states, nations and economies, such as Guinea, Mali, Tanzania, and Congo (Brazzaville), have been seeking to build egalitarian "classless" societies. Others have been seeking to build a new middle class as the backbone and springboard of their development, as in Nigeria, Kenya, Ivory Coast, and Sierra Leone. Still others have yet to perceive clearly what sort of social structure they seek beyond modernization of the traditional subsistence society. One has consciously sought a religious identification, the Islamic Republic of Mauritania. Another, the soon-to-be independent self-governing island of Mauritius, is committed to building a multiracial society because of the strangely mixed population it has inherited—Hindu and Muslim Indians, Goans, Muslim Pakistanis, Ceylonese, Chinese, "black Africans," "creoles" (i.e., those of mixed French-"black African" lineage), and French-descended whites.

In the absence of an established or accepted social structure and in light of the erosion of subsistence society as political and economic change and development continue, the context for all institution-building, including social institutions, is anything but clear. It is not surprising then that the military looms larger and larger in country after country as the one oasis of definitive, organized power in an otherwise unstructured and unfamiliar national arena. The one party in its insistence on monopolistic control of *all* organized activity has not only precluded opposition political organizations from emerging, it has also resisted the growth of independent economic power, academic institutions, and cultural and social bodies. Can the state in Africa be all things? Can it decree and then build an approved social structure? Only the Communist Chinese in the underdeveloped world persist in this effort, and twenty years after the assumption of power, it seems clear that mainland China still faces an uphill struggle to establish a controlled social structure with uniformity at its core.

In Africa, it seems most doubtful, for the same reasons discussed above with respect to nation-building and economy-building, that institutions can be established which will produce centralized, highly structured, culturally uniform social systems. The attempt to do so in Algeria and Ghana has certainly been an important reason for military take-overs in those two countries.

There can be little doubt that the absence of accepted social structures, and institutions to give them shape and direction, has been a vital factor in the political instability and economic stagnation common to today's Africa.

A Concluding Word

This paper has tried to redress the balance somewhat. Obviously, institutions alone, no more than any other factors alone, will not launch, sustain, and advance African political and economic development. But equally clear, the absence of at least minimal institutional development, has been and will continue to be a critical deficiency in African development efforts. Such an absence has distorted, retarded, and forestalled African development. To return to the quotation from Zolberg at the heading of this paper,[9] the African countries will not and cannot achieve the minimal base for carrying out their development tasks with "talent, resources and goodwill," plus the missing ingredient, "leadership," identified in the quotation relating to the "African Giant," Nigeria, unless and until these and other qualities are consciously directed, on a systematic and urgent basis, to evolving an appropriate set of complementary institutions. The geographic boundaries, the constitutional structure, the political structure and system, the economic structure and system, and the social restructuring—all must be resolved or decided upon, designed, built and actually put in operation, if the new African countries are to become viable political and economic units.

Unfortunately the outlook for successful institution-building is anything but bright. It will be done because in the end it must be. But the record to date shows little reason for optimism about the speed or the effectiveness with which it will be done.

Unfortunately, too, a large part of Africa is only beginning to approach the problem, and then all too often in a spirit of St. George slaying the dragon; rather, the new independence must be consolidated by building viable institutions in the *given* African circumstances. Thus we find the Minister of State for Economic Development of Zambia inveighing against institutions built on principles of the market place and profitability in a 1967 statement about the need

[9] Samuel P. Huntington makes the same connection between political structures and tasks confronting developing societies: "Writers on political development emphasize the processes of modernization and increasing political participation. A balanced view of the politics of contemporary Asia, Africa and Latin America requires more attention to the 'art of associating together' and the growth of political institutions." ("Political Development and Political Decay," *World Politics,* Vol. XVII, No. 3, [1965] p. 386.)

for destroying old institutions, presumably as a precondition to building new ones. In the Minister's pungent words:

We have to destroy the old structures, in which the un-
bridled forces of *laissez-faire* were let loose in Zambia,
in which the market principle was the dynamo or the
compulsive engine. Government, people, the business
community, and the Press, and all the political institutions, were all conditioned by the sordid force whose
logic of economic calculus is to maximize the benefits or
minimize the loss.[10]

Africa is thus in flux. Almost thirty years ago, Joyce
Cary wrote of the European impact, symbolized by a
new road in Northern Nigeria, leading to the imagi-
nary town of Fada:

The road itself seems to speak to him. 'I'm smashing it
up the old Fada—I shall change everything and everybody in it. I am abolishing the old ways, the old ideas,
the old law; I am bringing wealth and opportunity for
good as well as vice, new powers to men and therefore
new conflicts. I am the revolution. I am giving you plenty
of trouble already, you governors, and I am going to give
you plenty more. I destroy and I make new. What are
you going to do about it? I am your idea. You made me,
so I suppose you know.'[11]

The situation for the most part remains the same
today. The impact of outside cultures; the unsettled
"revolutionary" aftermath; the need for social, politi-

[10] Mr. U. G. Mwila, Minister of State for Economic Development, Zambia, as quoted in *Rhodesia and Eastern Africa*
(London, Vol. 43, No. 2206, January 19, 1967), p. 280.
[11] Joyce Cary, *Mister Johnson* (London: Penguin Edition,
1962), p. 186.

cal, and economic institutions—new ones—to control, regulate, guide, harness, and channel the "idea" and the goal of development; and the forces which they let loose, "which will maximize the benefits or minimize the loss"—not necessarily for the few but for the many—all remain the problems and tasks of the new African states.[12]

[12] See Chinua Achebe, *A Man of the People* (New York: Doubleday Anchor Books, 1967), which vividly illustrates this point in telling the story of Chief Nanga, the postindependence embodiment of Joyce Cary's earlier Mister Johnson.

S. N. EISENSTADT

Reflections on a Theory of Modernization

S. N. Eisenstadt is Chairman of the Department of Sociology at Hebrew University and a fellow at the Stanford Center for Advanced Study in the Behavioral Sciences. In 1964 he won the MacIver Award of the American Sociological Association for The Political Systems of Empires, *one of his many publications.*

1.

Since their beginnings in the late eighteenth and early nineteenth centuries, modern social thought and analysis have been greatly concerned with the nature of modern society as a distinct type of social order. It was but natural that this concern was transformed very quickly into the confrontation between modern and nonmodern, modern and premodern society. Given the conception of modern society as a society oriented toward "progress" or "change," this confrontation tended very often to become defined in terms of modern vs. traditional society.

This confrontation of modern vs. traditional society in the history of modern social analysis initially took the form of depicting both as more or less completely "closed," dichotomous types. These types were described in various ways, among the most famous of which were Tönnies' distinction between *Gemeinschaft* and *Gesellschaft* and Redfield's later, more anthropologically-oriented distinction between primitive, folk, and urban societies.

Whatever the methodological and substantive criticism raised for decades against these and similar typologies, they dominated the thinking on this subject for a very long period of time and they inspired many researches and investigations. Out of them emerged the picture of traditional and modern societies which prevailed in sociological thought for many years.

In this picture, traditional society was depicted as a static one with little differentiation or specialization, with a low level of urbanization and of literacy. Modern society, on the other hand, was seen as a society with a very high level of differentiation, or urbanization, literacy and exposure to mass media. In the political realm, traditional society has been depicted as based on a "traditional" elite ruling by virtue of some Mandate of Heaven, while modern society is based on wide participation of the masses who do not accept any traditional legitimation of the rulers and who hold these rulers accountable in terms of secular values and efficiency. Above all, traditional society has been conceived as bound by the cultural horizons set by its tradition while modern society is culturally dynamic, oriented to change and innovation.

It was only in the forties and fifties of this century that this view became undermined and more refined analytical approaches, as well as new *Problemstellungen* with regard to this whole area, began to develop. True, the conception of modern society in terms of opposition to traditional society and the sharp dichotomization of the two has become even more pronounced with the great upsurge of interest in the breakthrough of non-Western societies into modernity, with the so-called underdeveloped or developing countries, "new states" and the like, which have emerged since World War II. Yet the convergence of this growing interest in underdeveloped societies with the growth of analytical tools in sociology gave rise, first of all in the late forties and early fifties, to an analytically more refined and differentiated approach.

2.

In the first stage of this new approach the differences between modern and traditional societies were analyzed in terms of the "pattern variables," in which traditional societies were conceived as characterized by the predominance of particularistic, ascriptive, and diffuse orientations as against the universalism, specificity, and achievement orientations of modern societies.

Somewhat later, with the development of various conceptual and methodological tools in the social sciences, a much more diversified search for the indicators or indices of modern societies was undertaken. At this stage of the research on the basis of extensive researches two major types of such indices—namely the sociodemographic and the "structural"—emerged as the most indicative of these differences between modern and traditional societies.

The best over-all summary of the sociodemographic indices of modernization has perhaps been coined by Karl Deutsch in the term "social mobilization." He has defined it as the "process in which major clusters of old social, economic and psychological commitments are eroded and broken and people become available for new patterns of socialization and behaviour." He has indicated that some of its main indices are exposure to aspects of modern life through demonstrations of machinery, buildings, consumer goods, etc., response to mass media, change of residence, urbanization, change from agricultural occupations, literacy, growth of per capita income, etc.

Similarly, the major structural characteristics of modernization have been identified as the development of a very high extent of social differentiation, of free resources which are not committed to any fixed, ascriptive (kinship, caste or territorial) groups, the development of specialized and diversified types of social organization, and the concomitant development, in all major institutional spheres, of wider regulative and allocative mechanisms and organizations—such as market mechanisms in economic life, voting and party activities in politics, and diverse bureaucratic organizations and mechanisms in most institutional spheres.

But side by side with these methodological and conceptual advances there developed also some new *Problemstellungen* of the contrasts between traditional premodern and modern societies.

First, instead of concentrating on the distinct characteristics of each of these types of societies, there emerged a growing interest in the *conditions of emergence* of modern societies; instead of taking the emergence of these institutions, of a viable modern social order, for granted and concentrating on the analytical description of the nature of such an order, the growing concern with the possibility of relatively unsuccessful transition of these societies into modernity gave rise to asking about the *preconditions* of such successful "take-off" into modernity.

Second, given the conception of modern society as a society oriented toward change and having to deal with continuous change, there developed also the search for the conditions of such continued, sustained growth in modern societies.

In the initial stages of these researches relatively

little analytic distinctions between these different *Problemstellungen* was made. Thus, initially, in many of the works which dealt with this problem, the preconditions of emergence of modern societies were very often described in the very same terms which denoted their characteristics (e.g., in terms of universalism, achievement orientation, etc.), thus in a way neglecting the more specific questions about the conditions of emergence of modern societies, of the processes through which they emerge—or fail to emerge—successfully from within the premodern societies.

Moreover, many researches starting out from the preceding considerations, led to or were based on the —usually implicit—assumption that the conditions for *sustained growth,* for continuous development and modernization in different institutional fields are dependent on, or tantamount to continuous extension of these various sociodemographic and/or structural indices. According to this view the more a society exhibits or develops the basic characteristics of structural specialization and the higher are its various indices of social mobilization, and structural specialization, the better it would be able to develop continuously, to deal with new problems and social forces, and to develop a continuously expanding institutional structure.

This view assumed that the conditions for sustained growth, for continuous development and modernization in different institutional fields are dependent on or tantamount to the destruction of all traditional elements in modern life.

Closely related to this there prevailed also the view that continuity of modernization, of "sustained growth," of continuous development in any institutional sphere—be it economics, politics, or in the sphere of social organization—is assured after the initial "take-off," after the initial transition from a premodern to a modern society, by the very fact of this take-off.

3.

Against these approaches and assumptions there developed several criticisms, which gradually tended to
converge in what amounted to an almost total denial
of the whole dichotomy of modern and traditional,
virtually refuting entirely the validity of any such
distinction.

The accumulation of research in this field has shown
that although some minimal development of various
sociodemographic indices within a society can be seen
as a necessary condition for the development of any
modern structure, yet the further extension of these
indices does not necessarily assure the continuous extension of modernization, i.e., the creation of a viable
social, political, or social structure which is capable of
sustained growth, of dealing with continuously new
social, economic, and political problems.

In many cases—such as several Central and Eastern
European, Latin American, and Asian countries—a
negative correlation has developed—at certain levels—
between a high degree of development of various sociodemographic indices like the degree of literacy,
spread of mass media of formal education or of urbanization, and the institutional ability to sustain
growth.

Thus the implicit assumption that existed in many
of these studies—namely that the less traditional society is more capable of such sustained growth—has
been proved incorrect. The various sociodemographic
or structural indices of modernization indicate only
the extent to which traditional, self-contained societies
or communities become weakened, or disintegrated,
the extent to which—to paraphrase the title of Daniel
Lerner's book, traditional society is passing. But they
do not in themselves indicate the extent to which a
new viable, modern society which is capable of such

continuous growth may develop or exactly what kind of such a society will develop and what its exact institutional contours will be.

Similarly, it became clear that the mere destruction of traditional forms of life does not necessarily assure the development of such a new viable, modern society. Very often the disruption of traditional settings —be it family, community, or even sometimes political settings—tends to lead more to disorganization, delinquency, and chaos than to the beginning of a viable modern order.

There was a continuously growing awareness of basic historical facts that in many countries modernization has been successfully undertaken under the aegis of traditional symbols and even traditional elites. In such countries as Japan, or even England, many of their traditional symbols—be it the Japanese emperor, the crown or the symbols of aristocracy in Britain or the traditional symbols of provincial life in Holland— were retained. In many cases when the initial impetus to modernization was given under the aegis of anti-traditional elites—there soon followed an attempt, even if in a halting way, to revive some of the traditional symbols.

All these considerations have also contributed to undermining the assumption about the assurance of continuity of growth after the take-off. In both the economic and the political spheres it became quite obvious that no assurance of such continuity exists. Argentina in the economic sphere, Burma or Indonesia in the political sphere are among the most pertinent examples of the possibility of breakdowns after some initial—or even sometimes relatively advanced—stages of modernization have been reached.

These examples, however, have also shown that the relation between processes of change which tend to undermine or destroy traditional societies and the development of a viable modern society are not simple.

The one does not always necessarily lead to the other. The awareness that a great part of contemporary history in general and of contemporary international relations in particular, is in a way the history of breakdowns or of stagnation of political regimes or economic systems—which have seemingly "taken-off" into modernity but yet have been unable to continue to fly at all or to attain higher altitudes—slowly became accepted as fact.

But the more paradoxical outcome of these processes was that such breakdowns or stagnations did not necessarily lead to the total collapse of these new regimes or to their return to some traditional social and political form. Such polities and societies certainly differ in many ways from the "older" (Western) modern ones and they do not necessarily develop in the direction of these "older" societies. Yet they are by no means any longer simply traditional societies. Moreover, however stagnating or unstable these regimes are, they evince some capability of reorganization and continuity and they develop various internal and external policies which aim at assuring for themselves the conditions of such continuity.

Closely connected with the preceding considerations was also the growing recognition of the structural diversity attendant on modernity. It became accepted fact that the concrete structural contours of different modern societies tend greatly to vary and that they certainly will differ from those of the first, i.e., European, modern countries.

4.

All these developments gradually converged into what may seem a total rejection of the whole dichotomy between traditional and modern societies and of the usefulness of this whole approach in understanding of the processes of change in the contemporary non-Western societies.

Several recent works—of a sociologist, of a historian of Southeast Asia, and of an anthropologically oriented Indologist—may serve as appropriate illustrations for the new stage of this discussion and as starting points for its revaluation.

Gusfield, a sociologist who has recently worked in India, has listed, on the basis of the Indian situation, the following objection to the view polarizing traditional and modern societies. His main arguments may perhaps be best presented by the subheadings of his paper and by its concluding paragraph.

These subheadings read:[1]

"Traditional Culture Is Not a Uniform and Consistent Body of Rules"

"Traditional Society Is Not a Homogeneous Social Structure"

"Old Traditions Are Not Misplaced by New Changes"

"Tradition Adapts to Modernization in Specific Contexts"

"Tradition and Modernity Are Not Unidimensional"

"Modernizing Processes May Revivify Traditions"

"Tradition, Ideology and Nationhood"

He sums up his argument in the following way:

"The linear theory of social change, as a model for understanding change in the new nations, hides the ambiguities of modernity and ignores the need for tradition as a foundation to the social solidarity of national units. We cannot easily separate modernity and tradition from some specific tradition and some spe-

---

[1] Joseph R. Gusfield—*Tradition and Modernity in India: Misplaced Polarities in the Study of Social Change* (tentative draft). Presented at the Annual Meeting of the American Foreign Association (Chicago), September 2, 1962.

cific modernity, some version which functions ideologically as a directive.

The modern comes to the traditional society as a
particular culture, with its own traditions. In this respect it has been impossible to divorce modernization
from some process of Westernization. McKim Marriott
has made this point most vividly in analyzing the reasons for villagers' rejection of Western and Westernized doctors. The role of the doctor, as a technical
expert, grants him authority in modern culture but not
in the Indian village, where technical and commercial
skills receive low approval. Efficiency and thrift, those
two great Western virtues, are not such in the eyes of
the peasant in Utter Pradesh.

. . . it is important to note that a distinction can
be made between 'Western' and 'scientific' medicine.
Westerners conceive of a Western medicine as a system of curing based on 'rational' techniques and 'scientific' concepts of cause and effect. But this characteristic . . . only partly determines the total range of
practices involved in treatment and cure. Treatment is
bedded in a social as well as a scientific matrix, and
many practices of the Western doctor are based on
cultural values and ideas of personal relationships that
are peculiar to Western society . . .

The social scientist's designation of specific institutional forms as modern may also function as ideology
and as aspiration, specifying what it is in a particular
culture which is emulative. The concept of political
development is far more difficult and culture-bound
than that of economic development. Even with the
latter we clearly recognize a diversity of institutional
routes to industrialization and higher incomes. To label, apart from a specific context, either a capitalistic,
socialistic, or communist approach to economic growth
as antithetical to economic growth would certainly
seem fallacious to the economist. Similarly, the industrialized and egalitarian societies of the West have

by no means demonstrated either a uniform or an un-changing form of polity. The Soviet Union, France, Germany and the United States (and we might well include Japan) are hardly a single form of political structure and each of these has in turn undergone many changes during its history. They are all national polities, to be sure, and all ones in which the popula-tion is mobilized, to a degree, to political participation and loyalty. These facts, however, state problems in a wider fashion, without specific institutional directives.

To conclude, the all too common practice of pitting tradition and modernity against each other as paired opposites tends to overlook the mixtures and blends which reality displays. Above all, it becomes an ide-ology of anti-traditionalism, denying the necessary and usable ways in which the past serves as support, espe-cially in the sphere of values and political legitimation, to the present and the future. We need a perspective toward change which does not deny the specific and contextual character of events . . ."[2]

We may now pass on to the other scholars—Harry Benda, a historian of Southeast Asia (Indonesia) in general and of Islam in that area in particular, has developed arguments which are seemingly similar to those of Gusfield, especially in their strong polemics against the Western-centricity of most contemporary analyses of the situation in Southeast Asia.

To quote from one of his recent articles:

"Decolonization bears a qualitative significance whose manifold ramifications we have been very slow to apprehend. So firmly were we in the grips of the rectilinear fallacy that we confidently expected the democratic—some of us, indeed, the Islamic—consum-

[2] In several of the details and especially in the general tenor of his arguments, Gusfield has come very close to several other scholars who addressed themselves to this problem, especially to Milton Singer, David Apter, and Bert Hoselitz.

mation of the Indonesian Revolution once it was freed from the shackles of an authoritarian Japanese militarism. We applauded the return to democratic 'normalcy' in 1946; we expectantly hailed the free elections of 1955; and we were stunned when democracy, having been successfully put to the test, evaporated three years later. We were agonized to watch increasing political and ideological polarization pitting party against party, orthodox Muslim against syncretically nominal Muslim, if not against anti-Muslim, and finally Outer Indonesia against Java. And with increasing alarm we have seen the economic indexes of Indonesia's prosperity decline after the expropriation of the foreign, capitalist economy and its subjection to bureaucratic-military controls, amidst the unabated forward march of agricultural involution and rising population pressure. The portents of imminent catastrophe multiplied when fratricidal war threatened Indonesian unity and when subsequently Guided Democracy flexed its muscles in international confrontations.

But essentially what we have witnessed is the agonizing, difficult adjustment of Indonesia to its own identity. It is not, of course, anything quite as simplistic as a return to premodern, pre-Western continuity. It is, rather, a selective process of adapting resurgent continuity to a changing reality. It may be suggested that, substantially, the Java-centric—or really Djakarta-centric—polity is recapturing some of the political facets of the past, some of them in Western eyes distinctly less palatable than others. If it is intensely bureaucratic, cavalierly disdainful of economic rationalism, vengefully repressive of Islamic competition, jealously assertive vis-à-vis the Outer Islands, and, finally, grandiosely exuberant in foreign affairs, it is in the final analysis only acting out its own logic. If its charismatic President has shed constitutional restraints and surrounded himself with a glittering palace entourage in the midst of accelerating poverty, if he is seeking ideological, magical formulas to restore the realm to harmony and balance, he is surely less Machiavellian than Javanese. And what is true of him is by no means true of him alone; it may in paradoxically equal measure even apply to such outwardly modern dramatic personae as the Indonesian officers corps.

Whatever Guided Democracy may be—and it has had more than its full share of adulation at home and vituperation abroad—at least it is undeniably Indonesian, for better or worse. One by one, most of the artificial dams, economic, political, but above all psychological, of foreign overlordship are breaking down. The Indonesian river is flowing more and more in an Indonesian bed; the game being played is, once again, Indonesian. This, though it may smack of historicism, may well be the true meaning of the first phase of decolonization in Indonesia."[3]

Last we come to Jan Hesteerman—a Dutch Indologist with a very strong orientation towards sociological and anthropological studies. In an article dealing with recent, modern changes in Indian society he states:

". . . In recent times, especially since the Second World War, a new image of India has come to the fore, an image in which the emphasis is on rapid change, on development and transition from tradition to modernity. It seems, however, justified to ask whether this new image of India is again influenced by our own outlook, that is by the avidity for change that is proper to western civilization. This avidity for change is coupled with the idea of simpler harmonious societies apparently free from the strains and stresses

[3] See Harry Benda, "Democracy in Indonesia," *The Journal of Asian Studies*, XXIII, May 1964, pp. 449–50. Idem, "Decolonization in Indonesia—The Problem of Continuity and Change," *American Historical Review*, LXX (New York, July 1965), pp. 1058–73.

that are believed to be the almost exclusive privilege of our own changing society—in short the Paradise lost. This dual attitude can not but have an impact on our thinking when we contrast tradition and modernity. We are prone to overstress the stability of traditional society and the upheaval caused by modernization. On the other hand we are apt to play down the capacity of tradition for internal change and accommodation to modern circumstances. This readily leads us to the foregone conclusion of an all but unbridgeable chasm between tradition and modernity. . . .

". . . Modern developments more often than not go to strengthen tradition and give it a new dimension. To take a well known example: modern means of mass-communication such as radio and film give an unprecedented spread to traditional culture (broadcasting of Sanskrit *mantras* or of classical Indian music, films on mythological and devotional themes). At the same time the traditional cultural performances have not lost their importance as is shown by the fact that the government as well as the political parties try, often successfully, to enlist dance drama, storytelling and such like traditional media for their propaganda. . . ."

He then continues:

". . . It is clear that in this way the *samnyasa* ideal was stretched too far, it tended to absorb life in the world. This may have been possible only because the counterpole, i.e., worldly life, was represented by alien rule. When alien rule fell away the original polarity re-established itself; a polarity as between 'Saint and Secretariat.' A 'saint,' like Vinoba Bhave, whose land redistribution campaign and similar undertakings are based on the renunciation ideology; on the other hand the 'secretariat,' the governmental machinery with its modern planned economy.

"Their respective ideologies are diametrically opposed to each other. Bhave—like his master Gandhi—

aims at the 'change of heart' and their ideal for India is in fact the asram, the self-sufficient hermits' colony based on the ideology of renunciation, the government on the other hand aims at worldly goals with worldly means. The central point, however, is that both respect and accommodate each other and try to collaborate in steering India's course.

"The interplay between these two poles of India's tradition has been decisive for the changes and developments that Hinduism underwent in the course of its history.

"In the past it has enabled Hinduism to remain vital and to renew itself. Under modern circumstances it has found new ways and opportunities to express itself. Perhaps we may say that this interplay holds the secret of India's continuity, the retentiveness and the capacity for absorption that is so striking a feature of India's civilization. There is no doubt that today India and its tradition are changing. This process to all appearances will again be determined by the interplay of the two poles of Hinduism, as has been the case in the past. This means that we will have to think of Indian modernity in terms of the continuity of India's ever-changing tradition. . . ."[4]

5.

At first glance it may seem that the approaches of these scholars—Gusfield (and to some extent Singer and perhaps Apter) on the one hand, Benda and Hesteerman, on the other—are identical in their rejection of the dichotomy between traditional and modern societies, in their emphasis on the Western-centeredness of the prevalent definitions of modernity

[4] Jan Hesteerman, *Tradition and Modernity in India*, Bijdragem Tot de Taal, Land en Volkenkunde, Deel 119, 1963, pp. 237–53.

in the stress of the importance and persistence of traditional forms of life in Asia, and on the fact that whatever changes occur there take place in basically traditional frameworks.

But a closer glance will show that in fact these approaches are, from the point of view of our discussion, diametrically opposed. This may perhaps best be seen if we examine closely one of the central areas of this seeming agreement—namely their common emphasis on the persistence of traditional forms of social organization and cultural orientations and on the relation of these to the development of modernity in these societies.

Hesteerman and Benda claim that, in a sense, the whole impact of modernity, of modern social forces, on Indian or Indonesian society has been rather superficial or a passing phase. It is their contention that it did not really change the basic traditional central frameworks, orientations, symbols, and self-identity of these societies.

It is true that this impact, which came about mostly under colonial rule, has implanted in these societies many new types of organizations or of institutions such as industries, schools, and universities, which are historically derived from modern (Western) societies and which, in these societies of their origin, do indeed function within a framework of an over-all modern society.

Moreover, the impact of modernity has greatly changed the international setting within which these societies functioned and brought them into much closer interaction with modern, industrialized societies.

But once the colonial regimes collapsed, the over-all modern-oriented institutional frameworks which they imposed on these societies crumbled, giving rise instead to some new types of central societal framework—close to and derived from—their previous traditional setting, even though, of course, they have undergone considerable change.

Within these new frameworks in the independent states of India and Indonesia many of the more modern or Western organizations—schools, industries, or some modern associations—which were implanted during the colonial regime have indeed continued to exist and function. But whatever the success of these organizations within the limited scope of their operation, they became more and more oriented toward the new "traditional" setting, thus changing not only their over-all orientations but probably, of necessity, many of their own internal structural characteristics also.

If we look closely at Gusfield's analysis we shall discern there a rather obverse approach. Unlike Benda or Hesteerman he seems to assume that Indian society has, in its over-all, total frameworks, in its central institutional core, acquired some of the characteristics of a modern society or at least basic, central orientations to modernity. He does however stress that within the framework of these new orientations not only do many traditional, "premodern" forms of life persist, but very often they may indeed greatly facilitate the transition to modernity or even the continuity of viable modern settings.

Thus in one sense these two approaches are diametrically opposed in the evaluation of the situation. Gusfield assumes that the transition to modernity has taken place (at least in India) even if the modernity differs in structure and character from the forms known in the West. Benda and Hesteerman, on the other hand, assume that any such transition is rather superficial or transitory and that the older, traditional central orientations tend basically to prevail in India and Indonesia.

Thus, although these scholars might certainly agree about many details of this situation, such as the changes in the analysis of the structure of many concrete organizations and institutions, or the persistence of traditional forms of social life and of organizations, they differ greatly with regard to the evaluation of the degree to which Asian societies will or tend to acquire some of these basic characteristics of modernity.

Yet paradoxically enough they all assume that—at least implicitly, and in a way against their own explicit argument—neither the term "modern" society nor the dichotomy between traditional and modern societies is necessarily meaningless. Both their implicit disagreements with regard to the evaluation of the situation in Asia as their polemics with the older ways of defining the differences of "traditional" and "modern" societies would be meaningless if they did not assume, in one way or another, that the distinction between a modern society, a modern social order, and other types of societies or of social order is meaningful—although they certainly do not define the nature of this order.[5]

And yet these various considerations do indeed necessitate a redefinition of the nature of the distinction between traditional and modern sociopolitical and cul-

[5] An interesting—and perhaps paradoxical—illustration of the way in which the criticism of the current applications of the dichotomy between traditional and modern societies implies the acceptance of the legitimacy of this distinction can be found in their allegation that all the definitions of modernity are Western-centered. Thus, for instance, Gusfield implies that most of the scholars who have emphasized the distinction between modern and traditional society are necessarily Western-centered and assume a unilinear evolutionary path which all societies have to cross, a path culminating in a Western-like modernity. It is, however, interesting to point out that, whatever correctness of this general allegation may be, parallels most of the concrete historical illustration used by Gusfield—or others—could easily be found in the history of European experience of modernization itself. Thus, they support this claim by pointing out the structural diversity of the so-called modernizing societies in general and the great preponderance of various traditional forms of social organization and of cultural orientations in particular.

tural orders. Such a redefinition can be attempted both on the basis of the various criticisms brought out above and by referring to the numerous new studies which have been undertaken by social scientists in the last decade, in the wake of the great upsurge of interest in these problems.

All these factors seem to point out that within the sociopolitical order the distinction between a traditional and a modern political or cultural order does not lie in the development within any institutional sphere, of the specific structural characteristics which have been often identified as modern—be it industrial labor force and free markets, in the economic sphere, or of a centralized administration and unified legal system in the political sphere. Rather it may be seen from the extent to which the basic *symbolic* and *cultural* premises of traditionalism, with their structural and cultural limitations, are, or are not, maintained on the central levels of the societal and cultural orders.

The most important among these premises in the political field are the continuing symbolic and cultural differentiation between the center and periphery; the concomitant limitation on the access of members of broader groups to the political center or centers and on participation within them.

Premises were, in traditional regimes, in turn, closely connected first to the fact that the legitimation of the rulers is couched in basically traditional religious terms, and, second, in that there was the lack of distinction of basic political role of the subject societal roles, such as, for instance, membership in local communities; that it was often embedded in such groups, but the citizens of subjects did not exercise any actual direct or symbolic political rights through a system of voting or franchise.

In the cultural sphere the basic premises of traditionality, common to all "traditional" societies—however great the differences between them—seem to be the acceptance of tradition, of the "given-ness" of some past event, order, or figure (whether real or symbolic) as the major focus of their collective identity, as the scope and nature of their social and cultural order, as the ultimate legitimizer of change, and as the delineator of the limits of innovation. In traditional societies tradition serves not only as a symbol of continuity but as the delineator of the legitimate limits of creativity and innovation and as the major criterion of their legitimacy—even if in fact any such symbol of tradition might have been forged out as a great innovative creation which destroyed what till then was perceived as the major symbol of the legitimate past.

These cultural connotations of traditionality had definite structural implications. The most important of these was first that parts of the social structure and some groups were—or attempted to become—designed as the legitimate upholder, guardian, and manifestation of those collective symbols, as their legitimate bearers and interpreters, and hence also as the legitimizers of any innovation or change. In the more differentiated among the traditional societies these functions became crystallized into the symbolic and institutional distinctiveness of the central focuses of the political and cultural orders from the periphery. Here this symbolic and institutional distinctiveness of the center in traditional societies was manifest in a threefold symbolic institutional limitation. The three aspects of this limitation were: a) limitation in terms of reference to some past event of the scope, contents, and degree of changes and innovations; b) limitation of access to positions the incumbents of which are the legitimate interpreters of such scope of the contents of the traditions; and c) limitation of the right to participate in these centers and in forging the legitimate contents and symbols of the social and cultural orders.

Whatever the extent and scope which the various traditional forms of life in various spheres of society persist, it is then in so far as such changes in the connotation of tradition on central levels have taken place that—to our mind—we witness the breakthrough—which may be gradual or abrupt—to some sort of modern sociopolitical or cultural order. On the contrary, in so far as such changes in the connotation of tradition on central levels have not taken place, whatever the extent of structural changes or of possible transformation of tradition in different parts of the society, then, to our mind, we still have before us some type of traditional order.

It is such changes in the connotation of tradition and of their major structural implications that provide the impetus to continuous processes of change and to the perception of change as a positive value in itself, and which create the problem of the absorption of change as the major challenge of modernization.[6]

The preceding analysis has dealt mostly with the distinction between traditional and modernity in the sphere of sociopolitical and of cultural order and by implication it points out to an important point, namely that it is necessary to distinguish between such distinction in the different institutional spheres of a society. Both the preceding discussion and the materials on which it was based point out that there may indeed develop within any institutional sphere of a society some "modern" organizations without the whole sphere becoming modernized; and moreover—and more important—that the prerequisites of modernization in the different institutional fields are not the same and they need not develop simultaneously in any given, fixed sequence.

Of special interest in this context is that the charac-

[6] See on this in greater detail S. N. Eisenstadt, *Modernization, Protest and Change,* Prentice-Hall (Englewood Cliffs: 1966), especially chapter III.

teristics and prerequisites of modernization, of sustained growth in the economic-industrial spheres are not necessarily the same as those in the sociopolitical and cultural spheres and that they need not develop simultaneously.

The available data indicate that they develop in different temporal sequences and that such different temporal sequences may greatly influence the whole process of change and modernization of a society.

6.

Although the preceding analysis seems to show that the distinction between traditional and modern societies is still valid, it not only points out that this distinction has to be defined in a new way, but—and this is probably much more important—it raises a whole series of new approaches to the problems of modernization and development.

It necessitates the reformulation of some of the assumptions which have guided the approach to these problems and of some of the questions which we asked in this framework.

Perhaps the most important insight which can be derived from the preceding discussion, and which calls for re-examination of the contrast or dichotomy between modern and traditional societies, is first the fact that it is wrong to equate any far-reaching change in traditional societies with modernization. Not only does quite a lot of change indeed take place within traditional societies, but also some patterns of change which destroy these traditional societies may nevertheless not lead to the crystallization of viable modern societies. Secondly, it necessitates the re-examination of the relations between the persistence of certain traditional forms of social organization on the one hand, and the development of new over-all—whether traditional or modern—social frameworks, on the other. Third, it means we must re-examine the relations of tradition to change and analyze those forces within a given tradition or traditional society which help or facilitate the process of change as against those which hinder it.

It points out the need to examine the characteristics of those processes which may help in the transition to modernity as against those which may hinder it, and those which lead to the development and continuity of modern frameworks as against those types which impede the viability of such frameworks once they are established. Last, it points out the necessity to relate all the preceding problems to that of the great structural variety attendant on modernization.

In order to be able to approach these problems we have to distinguish between several aspects of modernization.

We have to distinguish first among the impingement of forces of modernity and the consequent undermining of the existing traditional settings, second, the "breakthrough" to modernity on the structural and cultural levels, and, third, the ways in which the new emerging social systems tend to deal with these problems, and their capacity to deal with them.

Given the historical spread of modernity from the seventeenth and eighteenth centuries until today, almost all traditional societies have been, or are being, caught up in it, in the sense that modern forces "impinge" on them, undermining their existing settings in at least three different ways.

First, they impinge on many of the bases of the various existing traditional institutional spheres—economic, political, or community life or social organization—make various new demands on them, and open up new vistas to their members. There obviously exist very great differences among various modern and modernizing societies with regard to the intensity of this impingement and its specific institutional location.

Second, these forces create a new international system within which differences in strength in modern (economic or political) terms is a major determinant of relative international standing. Here too, however, great variations exist in the extent to which these international forces impinge on different traditional societies and in the extent to which they are exposed to them.

Third, the forces of modernity tend to impinge on many traditional societies in creating the vogue or demand for a growing participation of the citizens in the center, most clearly manifest in the tendency to establish universal citizenship and suffrage and some semblance of a "participatory" political or social order.

These different forces may impinge in varied constellations in different historical cases. Each of these constellations tends to create different types of breakthrough to modernity and institutional and cultural problems with which these societies and their new emerging structures have to deal.

Such transition or breakthrough to modernity may take place under a variety of conditions. It may, of course, first of all take place under different structural conditions, different types of impingement of modern forces on the basic institutional spheres—the economic, political, or in the sphere of social organization and stratification.

Such transition or breakthrough to modernity may take place in societies whose groups and elites evince different degrees of adaptability or resistance to change, different degrees of erosion of wider normative commitments, and of transformative capacities, and where the new centers evince different degrees or kinds of strength or weakness.

It may take place under different degrees of structural differentiation with broad strata evincing a relatively high level of resistance to change in the new setting, and of erosion of normative commitments, or conversely a high level of adaptability to it; with secondary elites and especially with more central elites which may be resistant to change—"traditionalistic" in a militant or an erosive way; with elites which are highly adaptable to the new settings, with only a few transformative orientations; with elites which have transformative orientations; or with elites which have transformative capacities—either in a flexible or in a coercive way.

It may take place under different temporal sequences of development in different institutional spheres and such different temporal sequences may greatly influence both the problems which these societies had to face and the responses that they develop to them.

These various structural and temporal differences greatly affect the nature of the concrete problems which arise within these societies—the levels of aspirations and conflicts of various groups as well as some aspects or conditions of the ability of the central elites to deal with these problems—and especially the level of economic, organizational, and educational resources available for the crystallization of new institutional settings.

Each constellation of these processes tends to create the impetus for a breakthrough to modernity in the sociopolitical and cultural order and the concomitant impetus toward intensive continuous change. But each such specific constellation tends also to create different types or patterns of such a breakthrough, different types of institutional and cultural problems with which these societies and their new emerging structures have to deal, as well as the patterns of institutional response to the problem of continuous change, different degrees and types of ability or lack of ability to deal with these problems.[7]

It is the different constellations of these various

[7] For a preliminary statement of this problem see also S. N. Eisenstadt, *Modernization, Protest and Change*, especially chapter VIII.

forces which create the crises specific to each type of modern or modernizing societies.

The number of such types of cases evincing specific characteristics, problems, and crises is, of course, very great. It would be beyond the scope of this essay to attempt even a preliminary survey of them all. We shall only briefly mention some types which are of special interest from the point of view of African problems.

Of special interest in African settings is the possibility of development of what may be called a situation of ineffective transition from traditional to modern society, and especially of the development of so-called weak, ineffective centers. Such weak centers may develop when the undermining of traditional frameworks and the erosion of traditional commitments result in nonadaptive traditionalistic attitudes which are, however, virtually shorn of any commitment to accepted, meaningful traditional order, or in unregulated demands for various new modern goals. These attitudes may then give rise to a much wider scope of apathy and withdrawal from participation in broader settings, on the one hand, and to a growing level of unregulated conflicts among them, on the other.

The specific crises or problems which these regimes face are, first, their effectiveness on the new modern international scene; second, the upsurge of unregulated demands of various broader groups which are very often fostered by these elites and the concomitant waste of resources. They are confronted with potentially continuous conflicts within the elite and the new centers. The crises and problems that may develop out of the great intensity of the conflicts between traditionalistic and more modern elites, the new modern ways in which the claims of many of these groups are being made, and in the contradictory assumptions of these groups about the nature of the center itself and the bases of its legitimization may minimize the possibilities of establishing new, stable, and viable centers of any kind.

The common denominator of such centers is what may be called pure patrimonialism, i.e., the establishment or continuation of new political and administrative central frameworks, which have a tendency to maintain the external contents of traditional or of modern symbols without simultaneously maintaining any strong commitments to them. At the same time the center displays almost exclusive concern for the preservation of the existing weak frameworks of power—giving thus rise to a continuous succession of weak centers.

One of the major problems of research on modernization and development in general—and in Africa in particular—is the search for the conditions and policies through which these tendencies that result in the development of weak centers may indeed be overcome.

WILLIAM B. HARVEY

Democratic Values, Social Change, and Legal Institutions in the Development Process

William Burnett Harvey is currently Dean of the Law School at the University of Indiana. From 1962 to 1964 he served as Dean of Law and Director of Legal Education at the University of Ghana.

The subject of this paper may be formulated as a question: What role can law and legal institutions play in inculcating or preserving democratic values, while stimulating and guiding the modernization of economies, of social structures, and of political processes? I have been careful to frame the question in terms of the role that *can be played,* rather than the role that *is being played.* To answer the latter question would invite, indeed require, far more empirical data than I or anyone of whom I am aware now possesses. This essay, therefore, is analytical, not descriptive. As the reader will detect, I am acutely and uncomfortably aware that analysis also needs an empirical base and that thus far legal scholarship has provided a relatively inadequate one. Arguably, however, analysis responsive to the "can" question may proceed on a narrower factual base than description would require.

The question utilizes three key concepts that call for analysis: first, values, and more specifically "democratic values"; second, law and legal institutions; and third, "modernization" as a particular kind of social change. Adequate analysis of any one of these concepts is too large a task for this paper, even if I were competent to undertake it anywhere. Therefore, I shall indicate only briefly, with little supporting analysis or argumentation, the meanings I shall ascribe to these key concepts in the later discussion. In this way, I hope, in Lon Fuller's neat phrase, that, even if I am clearly wrong, I will be wrong clearly.

I use the term "value" to mean merely a specific focus of human desire that may be, and often is, manifested objectively through a claim or demand advanced by an individual or a group. If there exists, aside from such values, an order of true or real values, these are deemed irrelevant and beyond the range of human cognition other than by intuition or charisma. Such routes to knowledge, however significant they may be to those with the advantage of intuition or charismatic gift, share the critical limitation that the knowledge to which they lead may not be transmitted to others in any reliable way. When my intuition conflicts with yours, how can you persuade me, or I persuade you? We tolerate each other or we fight.

It often is useful to distinguish between ultimate (immediate) and instrumental (mediate) values. Roughly corresponding to the two categories are the concepts of ends and means. At the level of instrumental values or means, there may be a basis for resolving conflicting desires through scientific inquiry and rational discourse—if we can agree on an ultimate value to which the instrumental value, as means, is related. Important though the distinction may be, it is not the universal solvent of conflict or competition among values. Almost always a particular choice of value is both ultimate and instrumental. Illustratively, we may desire something as a means to a further end, while also attaching to it certain ultimate or non-instrumental preferences. Similarly, in human experience, it rarely is entirely clear that a particular value, though *prima-facie* immediate, is not in some measure a means to an end only dimly perceived. Consequently, while certain value judgments may be moved within the range of cognition by resolving them into choices of instrumental values, that is, by making them questions of fact, the fact that the means-ends categories are not mutually exclusive prevents in many cases a fruitful resort to factual inquiry and rational discourse.

Within this axiological framework, "democratic values" are viewed as only the preferences or desires of some men in certain times and places. Were it possible to consider them as common to all men, they perhaps would acquire a special order of importance. There is, however, no clear factual support for such a premise. Nevertheless, though validated only as desires, claims, or demands, democratic values may appear more important by reason of the fact that at certain times and places a large number of men have thought them desirable enough to risk all, including life, to preserve them.

Beyond the general status that can be ascribed to "democratic values" under the noncognitivist and relativistic axiology presented here, what further elucidation of them is possible? For the purpose of this essay, I shall take "democratic values" to comprehend the claim or demand that government find its validation in the consent of the governed. An effort to particularize beyond this fundamental claim—to inquire whether the consent must be manifested in a particular way, whether it may be granted once for all time or must be renewed periodically, whether it also must involve continuing active participation by the governed in the affairs of government, and what concept of man himself is implicit in the basic claim—such an effort involves an infinite diversity of detail and innumerable subtle gradations. Acknowledging the risk of gross oversimplification, I will restrict the concept of democratic values to the fundamental claim, recognizing a variety of approaches to its realization.

The only justification for this summary statement of value theory is that it confronts directly, and at the start, a concept of law that must be examined briefly and laid aside. This is the natural law view or, actually, views that over the centuries have appeared in innumerable guises. I am not concerned here with that variety of natural law thinking that invokes a higher law merely as a standard of justice, a means of identifying the unjust law. Some natural law philosophers have held, however, that a certain irreducible value content must be found in any norm for it to qualify as law. If the adherent to such a natural law position is also a democrat, he is able summarily to avoid or dispose of much of the discussion in this essay by the mere assertion that the implementation of some minimum of democratic values is essential for the achievement of law. Nondemocratic enactments, irrespective of any effect given by attendant sanctions, he simply would not regard as law.

While I share the value preferences of many who hold a natural law view, I regard most natural law thinking as a snare and a delusion. I find no contribution to clear thought in an insistence that law, in order to be law, must adopt any particular value content. To me, law is merely one among many techniques for ordering, controlling or channeling human conduct; it requires no commitment to any particular values. This is not an appropriate occasion to analyze extensively this one technique, though some brief comments on it will be offered later. Nor is it, in fact, necessary to press to its ultimate conclusion the view that law, as technique, is neutral toward values. One might agree with H. L. A. Hart that any discussion of law presupposes a social arrangement for continued existence, not a suicide club, and that law therefore necessitates a minimum commitment to the value of survival. Such agreement, however, would not involve the further view that law has any irreducible content of *democratic* value. In so far as that value is concerned, law may be regarded properly as a totally value neutral technique. An understanding of law's relation to democratic values must depend, therefore, on a study of the value preferences of those persons in a society who are in a position to utilize the legal technique, and of the ways in which their preferences are introduced into the legal order for implementation. Such a study necessarily comprehends both the rules of law and their administration, both the law in the books and the law in action.

One further distinction must be suggested in this abbeviated analysis of the concept of law. The most characteristic expression of law is the norm. Following Kelsen, we may regard the legal norm as a hypothetical judgment—a coupling of a conditioning circumstance with a conditioned consequence: if and only if A, then B—if one takes another human life with malice aforethought, then he shall be hanged. The coupling of circumstance and consequence is not causal but purposive, dependent upon the intervention of human agents who, it is contemplated, will intervene to produce the consequence in order to accomplish the purpose implicit in the norm. The norm is not realized most fully, however, when the conditioned consequence results. For the purpose implicit in the norm is not primarily that the murderer be hanged, but that human life not be destroyed. That purpose is achieved most fully by the forbearance from murder by all members of the society. In a stable and successful legal order, that forbearance is induced, not only by the legal norm, but by religious, ethical, and social standards as well.

The norm, traditionally the most characteristic expression of law, remains of central importance today. Over the last century or so, however, changes of profound significance have occurred in virtually all societies. These have affected the expectations men direct toward government, and in consequence are reflected in the roles of official actors within the legal order. From the traditional roles of norm creation and execution, that is, of defining the norm and on the happening of the conditioning circumstances intervening to produce the consequence, official actors in most societies have come to assume more pervasively active roles. Instead of relying on private conduct induced by general norms for securing desired actions and for achieving their purposes, the manipulators of the legal technique now frequently address norms to official actors so as to pattern their conduct for the actual doing of desired tasks. This manifestation we may denominate as the law as "institution." It is not novel. A court, for example, is the expression of law as institution. In contemporary societies, however, this manifestation of law occurs much more often; it involves official actors in a far wider range of tasks, e.g., the provision of social services such as transportation or the planning and implementation of economic development.

This preliminary sketch of concepts would be incomplete without a brief discussion of development. This concept is invoked by two terms in my subject—"social change" and the "development process." Presumably the first encompasses more than the basic premise of social fluidity. No society is absolutely static. Change occurs everywhere, though vastly important differences in the rate of change may appear in different times and places. The term "social change" is relatively ambiguous as to the direction or quality of the change, and on this ground alone we might prefer different and more precise terminology. "Development" enjoys an aura of approbation and might serve to suggest the kind of values or claims now being advanced in many parts of the world. It also may suggest, however, a teleological view of social movement that many would reject, and on that ground I have rejected it in favor of the concept of "modernization."

In the present discussion, I take modernization to encompass a technique involving the purposive employment of scientific method to achieve knowledge of physical and social causality in order to design means rationally related to achieving satisfaction of values, that is, of human desires, claims, or demands. These values may cover the whole broad spectrum of human wants, and the means for satisfying them may involve social structures, economic arrangements, and political processes.

In the light of this statement of the conceptual apparatus, the initial question may be broken down in more precise and possibly useful components. Three questions emerge. 1) What role can the value-neutral technique of law, manifested as both norm and institution, play in satisfying the claim of men in society that their government be validated by the consent of the governed, or in stimulating the advancement of such a claim? 2) What role can law, so conceived, play in stimulating and guiding modernization in the social, economic, and political life of a society? 3) To what extent are these two roles compatible?

It is probably now evident and will become increasingly clear that theorizing about law in relation to human values has both an affirmative and negative thrust. The affirmative presses the question: How can law be employed to maximize the realization of values? This question may be put either from the perspective of a governing elite that wants to use law to realize its own values or from the perspective of the governed. The negative, on the other hand, usually emphasizes the problem of controlling law, and ultimately its manipulators, so that it does not serve to deny or defeat the values of the governed. The latter question has been considered often in the long history of political and legal philosophy. It is the central theme of much of the contemporary concern about the "Rule of Law." Without denying the importance of the negative thrust, however, I believe it desirable to accord equal attention to the affirmative. Hence the following discussion considers both.

On turning to the first question, it is necessary to sketch briefly a set of factual hypotheses to relate the analysis to contemporary Africa. Many of the indigenous peoples of Africa lived under traditional governmental and legal orders that had a fundamental democratic underpinning. This often was obscured by a tendency to combine in the same functionary the roles of priest and secular ruler and by the restriction of eligibility for chiefly office to certain royal lines. Very commonly, however, each royal line presented a number of eligibles, and choice among them was expected to result from pervasive consultation. Further evidence of democratic tendencies in traditional systems was the possibility of removing from office a traditional ruler who failed to perform to the satisfaction of his people.

While it is hazardous to generalize about traditional African law and legal-governmental institutions, there is no need to encounter such hazards. Our concern is with modern African government and law. The extent to which democratic values were implemented in traditional institutions is irrelevant, since these institutions are in no meaningful sense the antecedents of most governments and basic legal orders of postcolonial Africa. Most of the independent national governments of sub-Saharan Africa are the progeny of colonialism, not the successors to traditional groups and their governmental arrangements. An African government that received the imperium from the departing metropolitan power cannot, therefore, derive its legitimacy from the consent accorded to traditional regimes. Each new national unit usually comprised an aggregate of traditional units or fragments of units with disparate governmental and legal orders. If popular sentiment could have been gauged accurately on the eve of independence, it is doubtful that significant agreement would have been found on the scope of the society to be organized into a national state, on any order of unifying values within the new national group, or on a set of useful symbols for those values. On occasion, independence was preceded by a plebiscite or election, and the colonial apologist might contend that this act provided democratic validation for the new regime. More realistically, however, the results might be regarded only as a manifestation of desire for the departure of an alien power, not as a truly consensual grant of power to a new government. I doubt, therefore, that most of the legal-governmental orders in Africa even at their inception stood on democratic values.

Even should it be assumed that the constituent elements of the new nations were democratically united at independence, it seems quite clear that most of the evolving legal-governmental orders cannot claim continuing validation through democratic choice. The hallmark of postindependence Africa has been frequent change or merely abrogation of constitutions. In most states progressive efforts have been made to concentrate the power to manipulate the techniques of law in the hands of elite groups, civil or military, whose claim to govern by consent can hardly be seriously advanced. It is not surprising in these circumstances that the new national governments of Africa have been extraordinarily fragile.

It has been fashionable in many quarters to justify this movement toward government by nondemocratic elites on the ground that it was essential to achieve modernization. Certainly few Africanists, if any, would contend that the traditional authorities, whatever their democratic support, could have been relied upon for successful, modernizing initiatives. Stimulation of and guidance for modernization had to come from and through new governmental agencies and laws. Yet surely experience is now sufficient to indicate that authoritarian government by an elite provides no assurance of modernization—of rational, scientific efforts to satisfy the desires, claims, and demands of the people. Although the sacrifice of democratic values does not assure modernization, it may in the circumstances of contemporary Africa be an essential prerequisite to *achieve law* at the level of the new nation states. In many of these states, opening the door to democratic choice could loose such an array of centrifugal forces, oriented toward traditional groupings, that the fragile structures of the new nation states could not survive. The question whether new and more viable groupings, with governments validated by democratic choice, would emerge from the breakdown of the nation states spawned by colonialism, and if so when, leads to speculation too extreme for useful pursuit here.

The analysis set out earlier indicates that the fact that a legal order does not rest on consent and thus does not implement democratic values will not deprive its enactments of the character of law. Thus, an elite group within a certain territory, able to monopolize sufficient sanctioning force for its enactments to make them generally effective, is entitled to insist that they are law, even if it candidly admits what no elite is likely to concede—that in no sense is its power to rule grounded on the consent of the governed. As long as its power remains intact, the elite is able to make law and to accept for attempted satisfaction in the legal order whatever values it chooses. It is possible, though not likely, that an elite without democratic support would opt for democratic values, thereby risking the possibility of its ouster and the fragmentation of the entire order. Should such an elite be unwilling to open the door to democratic choice, believing such a move would imperil the entire governmental and legal order, but nevertheless be committed to an ultimate satisfaction of democratic values, we may ask what contributions its legal norms and institutions might make toward that long-range end. Though the factual premises may and probably do forsake reality, the question deserves serious consideration.

A nondemocratic government that values and aspires to democratic legitimization might gain it or open the possibility of gaining it by successful efforts to maximize the realization by its people of their nonpolitical desires, claims, and demands. Thus, success in maintaining the public peace and rendering human life more secure, in furthering economic modernization and improving the standards of life and health, and in dealing with citizens generally as if their interests are worthy of respect would be contributive factors. Coupled with such activities might go educational programs designed to cultivate citizen perception of a community wider than traditional groupings, encompassing the entire nation, and of an identity of interests that can be furthered adequately only by a governmental and legal system comprehending the nation. Important in this effort is the discovery or development of symbols of national cohesion, some of which might be "legal." In the United States, for example, the unifying symbolic value of the Constitution is recognized widely, even though many people would dispute or reject certain specific interpretations when they are known. Finally, even within the political arena, democratic choice and participation might be nurtured at the level of local government under constitutional or statutory delegations of limited power to be exercised under supervisory control at the national level of government. Many of these efforts obviously involve the use of law as a tool for modernization, and this point will be considered later.

A governing elite with ultimate democratic aspirations also might further its aims by the ways it structures and exercises its own power. One persistent danger in all elitist regimes is the progressive concentration of significant power in fewer and fewer hands. Such a progression in the allocation of power usually seems to be paralleled by two phenomena: a deterioration of the commitment to ultimate democratization of government and the denial of a wider range of human values. An elite without democratic support that desires to arrest this progression or, for that matter, a democratically chosen government that seeks to impede any movement toward undemocratic usurpation of power has available a number of legal techniques that human experience has shown to be useful in achieving these ends. Whether or not the effort is described in the traditional American terminology of checks and balances, it is prudent to disperse governmental power widely enough that the individuals and groups sharing power may impose mutual restraints. Equally wise is an insistence, vigorously implemented, that official actors find their authority to act in clearly and precisely articulated norms. Such an insistence does not preclude official discretion, but it counsels against the grant of unlimited discretion. Where grants of discretionary authority are needed, as will often be the case, discretion should be limited by well-defined standards and purposes, by reference to which the conduct of the official actor can be reviewed. Values of great importance to individuals may be defined in and their greater protection assured by a bill of rights buttressed against easy revision and enforceable against executive or legislative action by an independent judiciary.

Such techniques are familiar. Experience in many societies has found them useful. It bears emphasis, however, that they are only techniques, not guarantees. Rarely will they be utilized by an undemocratic elite, for they impede the augmentation and perhaps the preservation of its own power. Even when adopted and entrenched by a democratic government, they may be and frequently have been subverted by elites able to array an overriding power. The effectiveness of all legal techniques must be assessed, therefore, by reference to the power ratios within the society.

In brief summary of the argument thus far, we may say that the implementation of democratic values is not a necessary condition to the achievement of law. On the contrary, in the social fragmentation of contemporary Africa, the achievement of law by the new nation states actually may require substantial rejection of democratic values if such values require the consent of the governed to render legitimate the power of government. It is theoretically possible, but factually improbable, that a nondemocratically chosen but democratically inclined elite may take certain steps leading toward an infusion of democratic values in the legal order and an ultimate democratization of government. Thus far, the brief experience of independent governments in Africa justifies scant optimism for this development, but the longer experience of the Soviet Union may provide a thin basis for hope. In the final analysis, the greatest and probably the sole effective assurance of democratic government is the strongly and persistently advanced claim by the people of a society that government and law be validated only by their own consent. The prevalence and vigor of that claim in

Africa today are justifiably subject to dispute. Where the claim has been advanced and implemented, it frequently has focused on a level and form of government that cannot respond effectively to public demands for the fruits of modernization. To those claims, which probably are asserted in Africa today with more vigor than the claim for democratic government, we now will turn.

I will assume that the desires, claims, or demands for the fruits of modernization—particularly more and better food, health, and material well-being—are widespread among the people of Africa. A similar assumption with respect to modernization itself, as an instrumental value, does not appear warranted. Among the African governments we will assume not only a desire for the fruits of modernization but also some degree of commitment to the technique. The latter assumption may, of course, be seriously questioned. Too frequently the new African governing elites seem committed primarily to the increase and preservation of their own power and prerequisites, to conspicuous consumption in the midst of general privation, to prestige expenditures rather than productive investments, and to settling old accounts arising from actual or imagined wrongs rather than to the construction of a new social cohesion and co-operation.[1] In the present discussion, however, we will assume an enlightened government, firmly committed to modernization. The question may now be posed, what role can the legal norms and institutions of such a government play in stimulating and guiding modernization?

In this part of the discussion, the distinction suggested earlier between law as norm and law as institution becomes especially relevant. The effectiveness of

[1] This statement has reference to the top political leadership whether it be civil or military. In many parts of Africa, the civil service deserves a much more favorable judgment.

law as general norm depends on communication of the norm to and understanding of it by the persons whose conduct it is intended to affect. Perhaps more importantly, it depends in large measure upon their internalization of the law's implicit values so that compliance is, in the majority of cases, not the result of threatened sanctions. If such internalization is absent, the effectiveness of the norm depends heavily on how immediate and certain is the occurrence of the conditioned consequence following the conditioning circumstance. Consequently, for the law manifested as norm to have significant effect, one of two situations must exist: either substantial internalization of the values implicit in the norm and thus voluntary compliance by most people or assured and probably frequent resort to the ultimate sanctioning force behind the norm. For the effectiveness of law as institution, both voluntary compliance with desired standards of conduct and efficient and forceful organs of government are relevant. It seems clear, however, that understanding and co-operation of the people are less critical, if effectiveness for the law is sought primarily through the conduct of official actors charged specifically with the actual doing of the desired acts. An oversimplified illustration may clarify the point. A government desiring to improve transportation facilities between two large towns might consider at least two expedients: first, a general norm imposing a fine if any driver of a private vehicle between the two towns did not stop at a central depot and load his vehicle with passengers and goods waiting there for transportation; second, establishment by the government itself of a bus and truck line to provide the needed service. The second approach obviously depends less on widespread private action and therefore less on official policing.

The significance of the foregoing distinction emerges clearly in the light of two factors: 1) the enclave phenomenon that characterizes African societies, and

2) the relatively sophisticated action required for modernization. We will consider each briefly.

A characteristic feature of African societies, one consequence of the colonial experience, is the existence of a relatively advanced enclave within or, perhaps more nearly accurately, *on* the more numerous, less advanced society. Typically, the latter depends on subsistence agriculture or pastoral activities, has a minimal level of education or even literacy, is relatively static, and has most of its significant relationships governed by customary law. The enclave, comprising the expatriate community and a thin stratum of more affluent Africans, tends to be urban, better educated or at least literate, engaged more frequently in salaried employment, business or a profession, more mobile, and governed either entirely or in a broad range of its relations by metropolitan law and modern local enactments. This is the enclave phenomenon in its most obvious form. In reality, however, the broader, less advanced society itself is an aggregate of often highly disparate ethnic enclaves, each differing from the others in aspects as profound and significant as their collective differences from the Europeanized enclave.

Little discussion is required to make the point that modernization requires action usually more extensive, sustained, complex, and purposive than traditional forms of social organization and control could or would have stimulated or perhaps even tolerated. Consider the well-documented efforts in West Africa to clear tsetse-infested bush. Failure to understand the purpose of the action, doubt of its effectiveness, and superstition combined to place even this modest program well beyond what could be achieved along traditional routes and almost beyond the capabilities of colonial agencies.

Against this background, assessment of the role of law in stimulating and guiding modernization suggests the following conclusions. Within the advanced enclave, law as norm often can be a reasonably effective tool for modernization. Communication of the norm, understanding of its purposes, and acceptance of its objectives frequently will induce a wide range of compliance with relatively modest official interventions to secure enforcement. Outside the enclave, however, the problems of effectuating law as norm tend to become too great when the norm is innovative and geared to the needs of economic or social modernization. It is true that this same segment of the population accepts and hence renders effective many norms of the customary law. As has been suggested, however, customary law and the institutions through which it is applied are rarely functional to the needs of modernization.

Even within the advanced enclave, where economic activity is above subsistence levels, conduct required for modernization often cannot be induced and guided simply by general norms. For example, saving for reinvestment, rather than consumption, or choosing the type of investment for any surplus earnings requires far greater planning and co-ordination of action than a general norm usually can induce. Consequently, law as institution, frequently manifested as an official planning agency, is required, even though its actions and decisions may ultimately need the support and sanctions of legal norms as well.

If the analysis above is correct, law's most fruitful role in modernization processes within the broad social group may involve its manifestation as institution. Thus, in Africa this role has been and will continue to be reflected in government schools, state corporations, and planning commissions—that is, agencies created by law and staffed by public agents charged with the responsibility to organize and frequently carry out modernizing activity. While emphasizing the central role of law as institution, however, I do not intend to minimize unduly the importance of the legal norm. Reliance upon the latter manifestation or technique of law is preferable when there is a prospect of reasonable effectiveness, since the burden it imposes on scarce public manpower and other resources is lighter than a public institution would impose. Furthermore, even when an institution is necessary or desirable, its activity usually needs the support of norms, some directed broadly to the social group but many directed specifically toward other officials. For example, the work of a planning commission can be defeated unless other officials are required to supply it with reliable data and to implement its decisions within the sphere of their own activity. For these purposes norms addressed to officials play an indispensable supporting role to the institution.

The view advanced here on the role of law in modernization involves substantial reliance on public activity in many aspects of social and economic life that we in this country remit to the private sector under varying degrees of regulation. I hope to make clear, however, that this view is grounded entirely on functional considerations related to existing circumstances in Africa, not on any doctrinaire preference. I would hope that the modernizing activities of the various institutions created by law would be the means to move the general population toward levels of understanding and value agreement that would permit greater reliance on modernizing private activity guided and regulated by general norms. If modernization is the assumed objective, however, it seems essential to rely primarily on those persons committed to the objective and to the relevant technique, those possessing the requisite knowledge and other resources. At this stage of African development, such persons and resources are concentrated overwhelmingly in the public or governmental sector.

A heavy reliance on the law as institution carries with it a potential for democratization that deserves brief mention to re-emphasize a point made earlier. Consolidation of governmental power in a single leader or a compact elite presents the maximum risk that democratic values will not have been satisfied at any time or that initial democratic legitimization will be eroded through increasingly authoritarian action. It is very difficult for the people who lack organization or resources to effectively assert a claim to be governed only by their consent. As a leader or elite creates institutions, however, some dispersion of power among them is inevitable. In theory the various institutional power centers could maintain full cohesion and mutual support for the preservation of an undemocratic and repressive regime. In fact, however, a new institution that shares governmental power is potentially a competitor for a larger share. Institutional competition may introduce patterns of mutual restraint, and, as such competition develops, popular support may be sought by one or more of the institutions simply to improve its own competitive position. It appears possible, therefore, that institution-building may not only impose restraints on the broader elite among whom power is dispersed but also contribute indirectly to democratization of the regime.

Indispensable to progressive modernization—whether by unregulated private activity, by the general guidance of legal norms, or by the activity of public institutions—is the basic requirement of a peaceful society in which, as a minimum, human life is relatively secure. Beyond that, some security of property, both public and private, and of expectations induced by promises is probably essential. Unless one imagines a utopian society, peaceful and secure by reason of its inherent homogeneity and coherence, the postulated requirements necessitate a government, an identifiable group of actors, with sufficiently monopolized force to impose peace, assure the requisite degree of security, enforce its norms when they are breached, and organize and staff the required legal institutions. Obviously the existence of such government is doubtful in many parts of contemporary Africa.

With this consideration our discussion has completed its circle; we are brought back to the interrelation between the implementation of democratic values and the achievement of law. The general lack of social homogeneity and coherence in Africa today makes difficult or impossible in many places the organization of national governments based on democratic choice. With increasing frequency, therefore, one encounters elites, civil and military, with no plausible claim to democratic support, seeking a sufficient monopoly of force to secure their own positions and achieve a legal order of national extension. Even the assumption that such elites (or some of them) are committed to the values of modernization leaves the nagging question of their ability to achieve the law required for minimum social peace and security, let alone for active modernizing efforts. Without the support of democratic consent, the monopolization of force for the achievement of law and effective legal action is an awesome task.

I would be happy to conclude on a more hopeful note. Examples like Nigeria, however, do not stimulate optimism about the prospects for reconciling democratic values, national legal institutions, and the processes of modernization. On a relatively short-term basis, I am not optimistic. For the much longer run, without assurance or even great optimism, I would suggest that the basis for continued effort is the hope that through the cycle of social upheaval, official corruption, governmental collapse or overthrow, and new gropings for power there will come some halting progress toward social cohesion and mobilization. If a government proves itself capable of governing and is committed to modernization, it deserves support and assistance whether or not it rests on democratic consent. If modernization does occur, the government in time may receive such consent. And if the people continue to withhold their consent, modernization may help them ultimately to replace an undemocratic government with one of their own choice.

OJETUNJI ABOYADE

Relations Between Central and Local Institutions in the Development Process

Ojetunji Aboyade is Chairman of the Department of Economics at the University College of Ibadan. He has worked with the Federal Government of Nigeria as Adviser to the Ministry of Economic Development and served on national committees of both the Western Nigerian and Federal Governments. His publications include Foundations of Nigerian Economy: A Study of Investment Growth in Nigeria.

1. Introduction

The main problem of planned development can be stated broadly in terms of the conflict between the use of resources for present-day desires and the increasing needs of tomorrow. The first is manifested in the enormous pressure for increased consumption by the mass of the population. The second is reflected by the efforts of developers to increase productive investment and preserve the balance of payments. Theoretically, the two forces need not conflict. But in many developing countries, both the character of government and the pattern of economic organization are such that the conflict is in fact intensified. In the last decade or two, the notion of planning has been invoked in many of these countries to resolve the conflict, but with little or no visible evidence of success. It is the contention of this paper that one major explanation of this failure lies in the tenuous relationship existing in practice between central and local developmental institutions. It is suggested that an effective resolution of the conflict lies, not in the rejection of planning, but in the evolution of an institutional machinery that recognizes the social and administrative realities of each country.

Stated differently, the process of planned development can be described as a massive struggle against free market forces by changing through time, the prices of both products and factors into new equilibrium channels that are judged to be more socially desirable. If this statement is correct, then the only admissible pattern of economic organization is that which allows a uniform reading of the free market signals and a uniform corrective reaction throughout the whole system and at each point in time. In practice, an organizational structure that aims at such synchronized policy formation process by all decision units in the economy is the one most likely to achieve success in resolving the inherent conflict in people's time preferences.

Historically, the development of industrial capitalism was not concerned with whether or how any such conflict was resolved. The three basic problems of what to produce, how, and for whom were settled more or less automatically by the free market forces with varying degrees of social satisfaction. Today, the story is different, for better or for worse. There are still a handful of economists whose prescribed road to the salvation of developing countries lies in their making the market forces purer by minimizing or indeed eliminating all kinds of public policy intervention. But most development economists, especially in the developing

countries themselves, tend to see the matter differently
—more and not less public control, provided the controls are socially relevant, politically acceptable, and
administratively efficient. No doubt these are important qualifications; but they form the acid test of good
or bad planning. A consideration of the relationship
between central and local institutions offers an excellent opportunity for evaluating the chance that planned
development might or might not succeed.

2. Some General Principles

In any human organization, the degree of harmony
achieved among the different units will depend on a
number of vital factors. Apart from any peculiarities of
the organization (its ethos, norms, beliefs, and value
system), we should expect its historical evolution to
mold its present character and affect in varying degrees its internal relationship and general efficacy. We
cannot, for example, develop an adequate grasp of
Nigeria's planning organization without considering
the administrative legacy bequeathed by the British
colonial system. Historically, British colonial governments were never geared to planned development of
the colonial economy, at any rate not in the way we
think of dynamic general equilibrium planning today.
The role of government was clearly less ambitious;
and the administrative machinery handed over at the
achievement of political independence was generally
unsuited for any serious planning.

This historical antecedent also affects the attitudes
of those in authority. Unless the objectives of planned
development are clearly specified, understood, and
accepted by all units in the organization, it is difficult
to see how harmonious co-ordination can be achieved.
Now, the objectives of development as seen by a high
official behind a desk in the national headquarters may
be different from how the peasant or petty trader sees

them in the village or how his local official sees them. Without common objectives and a common approach to achieving these objectives, it is futile to expect consistent or meaningful planning. Where the organization has never even bothered to make a conscious effort to define a realistic set of objectives, planning may be worse than a farce—it may become positively dangerous. And there is little doubt that many developing countries have accepted planning only as a matter of nationalist fashion or as a façade for the foreign-aid donor or the peddler of questionable projects on short-term, high-cost credits.

Usually, where a society has a clear leader with some ideological posture, it may not take long to evolve a set of coherent objectives of development policy. But it needs more than charisma to avoid a socially sexy but economically wrongheaded approach to planning. Highly risky social experimentations derived from defective interpretations of economic history or from naïve international parallels can quickly generate social frustrations and an eventual demise of the leadership. But where the leadership maintains and develops its grass roots, keeps its ears firmly to the village ground, and is socially relevant in its policies, it can gradually improve the capacity and extend the complexity of its inherited administrative machinery. No matter how great a leader, the ultimate success of his social reforms depends on the efficacy of the administrative network he develops and controls.

Given these basic principles, it is easy to appreciate the task of a smoothly co-ordinated, planned development in a country like Nigeria. There has been scarcely any clear, strong leadership that is widely acceptable politically. The colonial heritage has itself intensified social stratifications and ethnic conflicts. Developmental policies have only been superficially relevant to the real problems of the people, dictated as they have been by short-term party political exigencies. The party game quickly bred corruption, nepotism, and unconstitutionalism. The intensified pace of economic differentiation, by fair or foul, pushed the political class and the bureaucracy further from proper appreciation of the developmental needs of the masses. Given the large size of the country, the poor system of communication, and the relatively small size of the bureaucracy, effective and rapid feedback throughout the organizational hierarchy is scarcely feasible. Compounded by the low level of skills of the bureaucratic personnel, not much could be expected by way of administrative efficiency and hence of harmonious co-ordination. As a small illustration, there is evidence that in some parts of the country, the rate of income tax evasion varies directly with the size of the administrative unit!

All the foregoing factors must therefore be taken into account in proposing administrative reforms. Appropriate responsibilities must be given to appropriate authorities considering their respective capacities to discharge those responsibilities. Suitable devices must also be introduced to harmonize and streamline the activities of different units with a common goal. Discussion of this problem usually revolves, at this point, around the familiar golden mean between centralization and decentralization. But in a proper planning context, the choice is not really between one or the other or of necessarily striking a unique mean between the two. For planning to succeed well in a developing country with inadequate administrative machinery, the organizational device must simultaneously centralize *and* decentralize. In addition, there must be both vertical *and* horizontal co-ordination, involving especially the full integration of the private sector at all levels of policy formation in the development process.

The irony about the Nigerian case is that, in spite of appearances, neither centralization nor decentralization has so far been given a fair trial in the planning process. But now more than ever, it is necessary to have both if planning is to be meaningful. Furthermore, it is essential that each organizational directive be pursued with greater vigor. As a prerequisite, however, the administrative framework for planning must be overhauled and a start made with improving the quality of its personnel. It is not easy to see how planning can be meaningful without a central articulation of national development objectives, manifested for example in a common investment, industrial, fiscal, and pricing policies, or without ensuring that the activities of the private enterprise sector are indeed complementary and not competitive to the social objectives. Centralization does not necessarily involve giving detailed and specific bureaucratic instructions, or rejecting indirect policy instruments and reducing all other units in the organizational hierarchy to decision executors. But unless the strategy and tactics of development are centrally defined *and* controlled—as in any modern large-scale business enterprise—decentralization itself will be useless.

The case for greater decentralization is probably much easier to make in the Nigerian context. Below the regional governments, the local communities sometimes (indeed, often) have superior knowledge of their potentialities. Given the right stimuli and the right challenges, they might throw up more imaginative programs and be more truly development-conscious—not simply demanding social-welfare facilities. Greater mutual confidence could be promoted with the higher levels in the organizational hierarchy by fostering a stronger sense of social identity. Another consideration that is easily overlooked is the fact that, in spite of the administrative bottlenecks, the local communities are sometimes in a position to undertake vital development projects at lower costs, in shorter periods, and with higher social satisfaction.

A planning organization cannot be said to be optimum unless it can ensure mutual consistency of goals as well as of the mechanics of achieving the goals. And the real test of consistency does not lie so much in the formal organizational chart as in the dynamics of the actual and informal relations among the different cells of the social organism. Therefore, in evaluating the real relations among different units of an organization for planned development the foregoing principles can be reformulated into a few specific questions. First, are the objectives of social policy clearly stated, communicated to, understood, and accepted by all units in the system? Second, is every unit in the chain of authority fully involved in the process of policy formation affecting it within the framework of accepted goals? Third, how are the final decisions to be executed or communicated to all units for sociopolitical consensus; and if consensus is impossible or difficult how are those whose interests may be hurt (or who may consider their interests hurt) to be palliated and kept in the game? Fourth, with what economic and administrative efficiency are these decisions being implemented; and how adequate is the over-all administrative machine for the increasing complexities of planned development? Finally, how does the system as a whole adjust to unpredictable changes in circumstances; and how sound is its network of social communications and feedbacks? In succeeding paragraphs, I shall attempt to answer these questions in the light of experience from the Nigerian case.

3. Setting the Goals

Under the civilian government, the highest formal authority for decision-making in the development process was the National Economic Council, chaired by the Prime Minister. An examination of the records of its actual working reveal, however, that if it had any role in the formulation of social goals, its function was in fact exercised by a subordinate body of officials—the Joint Planning Committee. From its very conception, it was doubtful that the council was in fact expected to indulge itself in what was probably regarded as an academic exercise—defining the objectives of social policy. The council was a platform of permanent consultation and bargaining, consisting of four ministers from each of the governments and the Federal Economic Adviser. Since responsibility for economic development is a concurrent subject under Nigeria's inept constitutional arrangement, the right of each government to pursue its own development policies was recognized in the very design of the council. The council was to provide a framework of intergovernmental dialogue without encroaching on the duties and responsibilities of the respective governments under the Constitution. But in the typical ambivalence of the country's constitution makers, it was also to provide maximum encouragement to the development of national economic policy and to close economic cooperation between the governments in the federation.

At the seventh meeting of the council in August 1958, it gave approval to the composition and procedure of the Joint Planning Committee. One of the central terms of reference of the committee was to prepare a statement of fundamental objectives to guide the planning committees of the different governments in the formulation of their development plans for each succeeding period. The creation of the committee, no doubt, came from increasing realization by the council itself that it was little more than a talking shop. There was also probably the psychological factor of a propensity to pass the intellectual buck on the part of the pragmatic politicians. As long as the country was politically stable, sidetracking potential or actual crises, and as long as no government touched on the financial buoyancy and tight executive capacity of any other government, as was true through most of the 1950s, all was well with development policy in the mind of the council and it seemed superfluous to evolve a social policy.

At its first meeting in October 1955, the council merely noted the plan of the federal government for preparing its own economic program as well as noting that other governments were making plans along "similar lines." In retrospect, these programs cannot be described as development plans; they are more correctly thought of as forward statements of capital budget. But as early as April 1958 at the sixth meeting of the council, at least one member government on the council was already applying pressure for more vigorous developmental leadership from the center. It reminded the council of the stress laid in the earlier years by both the British Secretary of State for the Colonies and the International Bank for Reconstruction and Development on the need for a central planning machinery to co-ordinate economic planning among the different governments. The earlier pious hope that the attendance of all premiers at the council's meetings would make the council's recommendations more authoritative and accelerate their execution had not been borne out by experience. The final offshoot of this pressure was the creation of the Joint Planning Committee.

It is easy to confuse institutional reforms with the need for a clear formulation of social objectives. No doubt, the two are interrelated, the one reinforcing the other; but they are in fact conceptually different. When the magazine *West Africa* wrote in 1957 (issue of September 28) on "Development Without Coordination," the author was pointing out the difficulties that were arising in Nigeria from the absence of a proper Economic Secretariat. But the difficulties probably arose equally (indeed, initially) from the absence of a coherent and consistent objective of social policy. It was, therefore, not surprising that with all the paraphernalia of economic institutions and the network of co-ordinating committees created through the late 1950s, the council was still, as late as its thirteenth meeting in February 1962, bedeviled by how to achieve effective co-ordination and direction of economic development in the country. In fact, as recently as its seventeenth (and final) meeting in August 1965, the council was still frantically but unsuccessfully searching for the institutional formula that would enable leaders of opinion in government, universities, agriculture, commerce, and industry to exchange views and consult on development problems in order to make an impact on public policy.

What was amiss all along was not so much the absence of a statement of social objective. The Joint Planning Committee duly produced one which was duly blessed by the council. But designing an objective of developmental policy involves more than putting vague platitudes on paper. The statement or statements must be unambiguous, reflect the social realities and cultural aspirations of the country, embrace all units in the development process; the sentiments expressed therein must be sincerely and manifestly held by the political leaders, and their general acceptance must be actively promoted by the administrative machinery—whose bureaucratic leaders must themselves be dedicated to those goals.

The only written official statement of social policy in Nigerian planning experience is that formulated by the Joint Planning Committee at its second meeting in October 1958. It recommended to the National Economic Council that the fundamental objectives of national economic policy should be

the achievement and maintenance of the highest possible rate of increase in the standard of living and the creation of the necessary conditions to this end, including public support and awareness of both the potentialities that exist and the sacrifices that will be required.

The committee itself helped to give an operational interpretation of these fundamental objectives. It had no doubt that the whole purpose of planning was to raise and maintain a high living standard; but it was silent on the need to reconcile the inherent conflict in peoples' time preferences in a development process. It was also clear that the expansion of the economy was to be expressed in terms of an increase in the national income; but there was no reference to the need for institutional reforms. Targets are to be quantitatively formulated; but there was little awareness that, even if achieved, these targets may not bring social progress. A development plan can scarcely be socially satisfactory if it does not go much deeper than aggregate economic growth and recognize the necessity for qualitative transformation in social relations. In a country like Nigeria, profound institutional reforms are needed in the political, social, and cultural spheres as well as in economic organization; and these reforms must precede or operate concurrently with the growth in per capita incomes. The targets must not be limited to raising people's incomes but directed at creating a new and better social order, with special reference to the distribution of income and of productive wealth; the attainment of intergenerational equity; the active involvement of the masses in the development process by tapping all potential human resources of the nation; the containment of the exercise of private economic discretionary powers for narrow personal gains; and the minimization of social and political tensions in the process of economic growth.

The weakness in the fundamental objectives set by the Joint Planning Committee lies not only in its banality but also in its narrowness of focus. And it is a kind of narrowness which may negate the very principles of planning. As the Nigerian experience has shown, a statement of fundamental objectives that is devoid of political and social equities may in fact harm the growth process in the long run. Unless the social objective is designed to answer the difficult but fundamentally important question of "For whom?" those responsible both for making the plan allocations and for implementing them (i.e., politicians and bureaucrats alike) will try to use their leverage in the process to twist the distribution of benefits to themselves. The eventual social repercussions may deter and not accelerate the very economic growth the statement of objectives was supposed to promote.

It should now be easy to understand that the quality and character of the social goals will affect the relations between central and local planning institutions in the development process. They may, as indeed they do in Nigeria, also determine the very character of those institutions as well as indicate whether or not particular vital institutions exist in the first place. In spite of the recent macroeconomic framework, planning in Nigeria has in fact been partial and half-spirited. The planning institutions have remained heavily skewed toward the regions, weakening both local involvement as well as central direction. With the lukewarm indirect policy instruments, the private enterprise sector has also been developing along its own orbit without any guarantee that its objectives are in fact always consistent with public pursuits. It is difficult to establish that all basic objectives of policy in all sectors of the Nigerian economy, whether explicitly stated or implicitly derived from behavior patterns, are fundamentally coherent or mutually consistent. If indeed they are, this must be so more by accident than by design and cannot be attributed to the organizational structure of the planning institutions. If the fundamental objectives of polity are themselves neither clear nor adequate, it is difficult to see how they can be communicated to, understood, and accepted by all decision units to guide national economic performance and social change.

4. Involvement in the Planning Process

The principle of representation in tax decisions has become so ingrained in democratic institutions that it is now taken for granted as an automatic right of the citizen. Historically, the development of parliamentary government was fought on the battle cry of "no taxation without representation." Planning decisions involve far more than tax decisions and touch the lives of citizens at almost all points. They affect their future even more than the influence of tax measures. It follows therefore with greater force that all those who will be affected by any planned implementation—and that means practically every citizen under comprehensive planning—must be actively involved in designing the plan. This is especially important in a democratic society where coercion is rejected as an instrument of social participation in governmental processes. So that if the plan is to be freely accepted and implemented by the mass of the community, they must be represented in the process of decision formation. But since planning has a technical dimension (a good plan should be far more than an elegant technical paper) and since every single individual cannot directly participate in running a central planning office, the social institutions for planning must be organized for the maximum possible public consultation by the bureaucracy. One good administrative design is to have a series of planning committees, both horizontally and vertically placed throughout the whole economy, with the central planning office as its nerve center.

The Nigerian organizational format is not wanting in committees. There are in fact (or there used to be) so many committees. The National Economic Council had directed at its eleventh meeting, in September 1961, that the Joint Planning Committee should examine and report on reorganization of the council itself. The committee submitted in June 1962 proposals designed to make the council speed up its work. It may be noted in passing that meetings of the council were few and far between, partly but not wholly due to the way the council was originally designed: it was left to the chairman to decide when meetings were to be called after he had consulted the respective governments; and except when occasion demanded, there were to be no more than two meetings held in a year. The Joint Planning Committee's approach to making the council's work more effective was to propose a series of committees (of the council) charged with specific problem areas, to examine in depth papers put up to them by the Joint Planning Committee, such that discussions at the full council's meeting would become easier and faster. The number of committees initially recommended were six, but the general approach was one of flexibility and adaptation to changing circumstances.

In December 1963, at its fifteenth meeting, the council went beyond the recommendations of the Joint Planning Committee. In addition to a number of committees which had been administratively established earlier (e.g., the National Committee for External Finance and the Co-ordinating Committee for External Aid for Education), the council established a committee in each of the following problem areas: fiscal and monetary affairs; trade, industry, and power; natural resources; education; plan co-ordination; works, communication and transport; scientific research and statistics. An earlier decision to set up a Manpower Committee was rescinded in the light of this new arrangement and especially the creation of plan co-ordination and education committees. The council also decided that the various committees could exercise decision-making powers on behalf of the council and that the Joint Planning Committee could deal directly with the various committees.

We may note that, although this arrangement widens the scope and frequency of consultation by the various governments at the ministerial level, it came rather late in the day to have much institutional impact on the design of the first "national" plan. Furthermore, by its very ministerial nature, it could not provide the wide degree of social participation necessary for a successful comprehensive planning process. It is therefore not surprising that at its seventeenth and last meeting, in August 1965, the council was considering another proposal for reform—this time for a Consultative Committee on National Economic Development. The proposal had not come to fruition before the fall of the civilian government, so it is impossible to evaluate its practical value. It did offer some promise of wider participation (even if only consultative) at the highest level of policy decision-making, for it would have brought together major economic interests in industry, commerce, agriculture, trade unions, public utilities, banking, universities, and the various governments.

The Joint Planning Committee itself adopted the method of functional committees to carry out its assignment. There were at least two standing committees, one on statistics and the other on agricultural policy (which also services the Council on National Resources). A subcommittee on external aid was later added. But the committee as a whole made greater use of the idea of working parties and *ad hoc* study groups than of the functional standing committee system. At different stages in its life, the committee made use of working parties over a variety of subjects— economic survey, external aid and technical assistance, industrial policy, etc. On the whole, the Joint Planning Committee was probably more effective than the National Economic Council, to which it was advisory and responsible. It held about fifty meetings in its seven years of existence and exhibited a high standard of debate on economic development and planning policy. But in the unique political situation of Nigeria, there were serious limits to the committee's influence over final policy formation. Outside pure debates, the committee in its decisions often reflected the uneasy compromises and political bargainings that were the hallmark of the council.

The Joint Planning Committee was at least able to provide a working platform for policy consultation (and to a less degree, policy co-ordination) at the senior official level. But by way of wider social participation in the process of decision-making, it was not—and maybe could not be, by its very structure— able to offer much opportunity. True that its constitution allowed it, *where desirable,* to co-opt persons with specialized knowledge or experience, whether official or nonofficial, to assist the committee and its working parties. But the scope of consultation invited by the committee was very narrow. The matter was extensively debated at the fifteenth meeting of the committee, in May 1960, partly from the need to improve communication with professional economists in the country, and hopefully reduce the intensity of professional criticism of government policy. The machinery of using outside opinion was considered at length; but there was little doubt that the committee guarded its privileged position very jealously and resisted any formal or extensive consultation. It regarded the duty of giving advice to ministers as one belonging to public officials alone, which could not be delegated even in part. But as a nodding concession to the principle of seeking outside objective comments, it invited the then Director of the Nigerian Institute of Social and Economic Research (who also happened to be the Professor of Economics) and the Director of Extramural Studies (also a professional academic economist), both of the University of Ibadan, to take part in the discussion of certain items at the committee's meetings. In years subsequent to this debate, the range of invitees was widened as both the composition of leading officials changed and the body of outside professional economists expanded. But the general feeling of a nodding concession persisted; and as a group there was no doubt that the influence of outside objective opinion on the deliberations of the committee was minimal.

The chance for a professional economist to make an impact on planning decisions was considerably increased when he succeeded in getting inside the administrative machine as a full-time official or full-time consultant. As it happened, most of those who were able or willing to do this were foreigners from one kind of technical assistance program or another. Whatever the technical contributions of these foreign scholars to the technical quality of decision-making—and they are indeed many—they were no substitute for the kind of wider indigenous social participation and public involvement discussed above. The motivations may or may not differ from those of the nationals; their aims may even be nobler and their relative competence unmatched. But the real test of a good plan, and the criterion of its chances for success, is its general, enthusiastic acceptability.

The same stories of decision-making and of decision-makers told so far about federal institutions can be translated without significant modification to government at the regional level. The most important modification lies in the national composition of the group who worked the institutions—a larger or smaller proportion of Nigerian officials and larger or smaller proportion of outside (i.e., nonofficial) Nigerian professionals. But the narrowness in over-all numbers and class orientation is similar for the federal and regional levels alike. Even if all the various committees had opened their doors to all nonofficial professional participation, there would still remain sizable sectors of the economy excluded from the process of policy formation. The private enterprise sector was substantially left alone. The big and crucial rural sector was more strikingly neglected. It was, in the eyes of the policy makers, too large, too illiterate, and too complex for involvement in the process of social participation. It was best treated as an undifferentiated mass in national income projections! Other groups—vital ingredients in the development process—such as traders, transporters, workers, and the growing band of petty bourgeoisie, were thought of as media of plan implementation and not as essential agents in the process of plan design. With "appropriate" indirect policy instruments, and given the well-known responsiveness to economic incentives, the question of wider social participation was supposed to take care of itself.

The weakness in this approach should be evident from our earlier discussion. First, comprehensive planning means full, explicit social participation to increase the chances of successful implementation. In carrying out a plan, it should be easier to enlist the enthusiastic support of someone who has participated in one way or another in the task of decision-making. Second, we know very little about the real efficacy of indirect tools (especially of monetary and fiscal policy instruments) in developing countries with inadequate and ill-developed economic institutions. Third, knowledge of available real resources, and especially of the limit to which human effort can be strained in the development process, is considerably enhanced by full social involvement. To ignore mass participation is to sacrifice much potential capacity of a people for better results in economic growth and social change.

5. Conflicts in Plan Implementation

The dynamics of the relations between central and local institutions in the development process are best exemplified by the way a plan is implemented. All the weaknesses, both technical and organizational, in plan design begin to show up rapidly. If the need for full social participation has not been recognized, then enthusiastic, widespread acceptance of the plan becomes doubtful, generating latent social frustrations and group conflicts. Such conflicts can be minimized where the general population has understood the real meaning of planning and accepted its implications and where the process of plan design has recognized explicitly the social, political, and administrative problems of plan implementation.

If the central government was inept, it did in fact have much potential economic power to achieve better co-ordination if the political leadership had been more purposeful, dynamic, and development-conscious. As it happened, for purposes of planned development, there was not so much a government as a collection of regions at the center. The federal government did succeed in wielding some influence in the foreign sector and preventing the balance-of-payments problem from running out of control. It also succeeded in getting some rational program of public utilities, even though at costs inflated by all kinds of administrative corruption and political kickback. Otherwise, it was caught in the continuous struggle for regional economic advantage, especially as the resource picture became less promising as the years rolled by.

This struggle for regional economic advantage— known in Nigerian journalistic parlance as "sharing the national cake"—provides the key to understanding the planning strategy and plan implementation. The energies of the people were consumed by the politics of regional rivalry; and since local planning institutions were practically nonexistent below the regional level, the political game at the center received more than usual prominence among all communities. The party and electioneering systems had themselves contributed in no small measure (through two decades of wild promises) to the ingrained expectation of the people that a good plan meant the maximum possible welfare amenities for their own village in the shortest possible period. Political success was then judged by the ability of the representative to deliver the goods. And since politics itself was a richly rewarding pursuit for its practitioners, it was worth all the effort to associate with governmental power by any and all means. There were political plums to be picked in the regions (and the same parallel applied to intercommunity politics with lesser severity, given the slightly more homogeneous structure of regional societies), but the prize plums were in the center. In any case, in terms of political arithmetic, having both sets of plums was always better than having one—at least in the short run.

One project which well typifies this intensive conflict is the iron and steel industry that never was. This notorious project in the Nigerian development plan has been variously described as the symbol of national disunity. Records show that the National Economic Council debated this project from as early as 1959 and never reached a conclusion until the council disappeared with the fall of civilian government in 1966. Some staff of the United Nations Technical Assistance Administration had written a definite report in December 1958 (the report itself being a climax of several reports) showing a prima facie economic feasibility case for establishing an iron and steel industry in the country. But for location, it suggested two alternative places, Enugu (in the east) and Lokoja (in the north) with a third possibility, Onitsha (again in the east). From the federal elections of late 1959, both the northern and eastern political powers dominated and ran the federal government, which was to establish the industry; each side knew and wanted the potential economic advantages of such a basic industry in its own area and in no other.

All kinds of arguments were invoked by each side at both the National Economic Council's and Joint Planning Committee's meetings to buttress its case and undermine its rival's; and each succeeded in getting some technical expert to back its claims. There were complaints that the ferrous content of Enugu ores was low and included a high phosphorus element; that the costs for necessary infrastructure were much higher at Idah than at Onitsha; that particular expert reports were falsified through inflated costs; and that particular steel-making processes recommended were ill suited to available raw materials or scale of operation. It must be admitted that the foreign technical consultants—and several were appointed at great costs—were not always consistent and did not manifest objectivity on relative location costs. The situation became further confused in 1964, when the discovery of iron ore deposits was announced for Ikare (in the west) and the possibility of incorporating ancillary industries based on the deposits of limestone in Ukpilla and lignite in Asaba (both in the midwest) were broached by some technical consultants.

It was not entirely clear that the industry would be profitable using any of the known steel-making processes. What seemed to be agreed was that the profit would drop (and indeed almost disappear) if the plant was to be split between two sites. A report had definitely shown that the idea of splitting the works into different stages at two different sites should be rejected as uneconomical. Yet, at its sixteenth meeting, in May 1964, the National Economic Council went even further than splitting the works by adopting the principle of two separate integrated mills (one in the north and one in the east). Not to be completely left out in the bargain, it was also agreed at a later meeting that consideration should be given to establishing a third one, in the west, as soon as the ore situation justified it. They were, of course, all to be federal responsibility.

Although the iron and steel story may be the most dramatic example of the futility of Nigerian planning, it is by no means the only indication of regional rivalry, political bargaining, and costly economic compromises that characterized much of the country's decision-making process. The uneasy, ineffectual relations between the central and regional institutions can also be demonstrated by the stories of the national population census, federal aid to agricultural development, education and manpower program, to mention only a few. The census question is too well known internationally to warrant any elaboration. Suffice it to say that the country now has no fair idea of such a basic statistic as its total population, and that the explosive consequence of that series of exercises is at the root of the nation's political troubles today. The census question also influenced and ruined the fine principles designed in 1962 for using federal aid to influence regional agricultural programs and thereby to promote a coherent national agricultural policy. On manpower, regional self-interest and mutual suspicion had not helped to create a truly national market with complete labor mobility; and there was little that the federal government could do otherwise. In spite of the terms of reference of the National Manpower Board (which explicitly mentions the co-ordination of the policies and activities of the federal and regional ministries primarily concerned with manpower problems), there remained almost as many variations in education programs, curriculum, educational finance, scholarships, training, administration, and employment policy among the regions as before the board was created.

It will be seen, therefore, that the so-called Nigerian ingenuity for compromise was only a farce. There were many areas where the compromises were not sensible and were actually self-defeating from a developmental standpoint. There were other areas where the compromises were only negative in the sense of leaving the different regions to follow their own paths, whose goals might be competitive rather than complementary. There were still other vital areas where the compromises were far from being national consensus, especially when decisions were against politically important groups who were outside the main stream of governmental power. Soon, there developed an increasing dichotomy between "insiders" and "outsiders," both in the sense of social stratification and regional participation. Not being broadly based, the decision-making institutions had no means of palliating growing political resentment, or even of warning of such resentment before it was, politically, too late. With no clear goals or social objective, the political class had become too immersed in its preoccupation with power, pomp, and personal gain to evolve a more purposeful compromise through full social participation. Even the rules of the game—a set of carefully designed control mechanisms for implementing the plans—became mostly paperwork to impress foreign donors. In the end, the social conflicts became too intense and the fragile institutions simply cracked under the growing upsurge of economic frustration and political bitterness from below.

6. Administrative Framework

Attention has been drawn to the character of the administrative machinery bequeathed by the colonial government and to its basic unsuitability to the task of planned development. The narrowness of number and quality of the bureaucratic class has also been indicated. At its best, especially in one or two of the regions, it was able to resist and delay some of the antidevelopmental excesses of the political bosses. But it was unable to do so with much concerted effort or over a sustained period. It had a basic weakness of its own. With no clear-cut, effective leadership, it was difficult to ensure even dedication to a common objective. It was torn by its own internal rivalries for power and personal career and soon succumbed to these pressures. Indeed, at its worst, it even actively encouraged and sometimes initiated some of the political mismanagement of which the bureaucracy itself now bitterly complains with indecent self-righteousness. Apart from the questionable integrity of some high officials, they were scarcely qualified to provide the continuous expertise required for sustained co-ordination in the development process.

Consider the Joint Planning Committee indicative of the changing composition in bureaucratic personnel; few participants in its activities were there under the same schedule for more than two years running. From its very conception, although it was left open to the different governments to send different officials to different meetings of the committee, there was no doubt from the record that continuity of membership was held to be expressly desirable. In a way, the high rate of turnover in the committee's membership is a reflection of the high mobility on the bureaucratic ladder created by the unique promotion opportunities of a newly independent country. But it was also due in no small measure to the colonial administrative notion of intelligent amateurism, which held that anybody in the administrative class could handle any schedule at any time in any department of government. Whatever the merits of this belief in the metropolitan country, it scarcely encouraged the high-level, sustained professionalism which a planned development process requires in a country with scarce manpower and few bureaucratic traditions.

The Joint Planning Committee by March 1965 was no doubt getting worried about its own increasing ineffectiveness. The chairman then made a passionate appeal for member governments to take a stronger interest in the committee's meetings. Even permanent secretaries in the federal service who should themselves have attended meetings were becoming regularly absent and sent their deputies or sometimes even relatively junior nominees—a habit which started in 1962 and gradually deteriorated with time. Yet the committee was supposed to be the highest official organ of coordination on all economic and financial matters; and given its special responsibilities to both the National Economic Council and the various governments, one would have thought that representation at its meetings would be at the highest possible official level. In the relations at official level, some personal sentiments probably played a part as a psychological background. On balance, the regional officials were older, more experienced and nearer the source of party political power; and it was possible this generated some resistance against the initiative and leadership which their younger and more junior federal officials were expected to give. In terms of personalities, the situation was parallel to the political relations—a case of the tail wagging the dog.

If co-ordination is taken at the level of interministerial relations, either within the same government or among different governments, the situation was not fundamentally different. The Economic Planning Unit of the Federal Ministry of Economic Development was established specifically to provide a general administrative framework of national planning targets and plan implementation. But co-ordination at the national level must presuppose effective co-ordination within each government. As late as July 1965, a meeting of the (national) Ministerial Committee on Plan Coordination was still recommending the setting-up of a working party of designated senior officials, especially those of the respective Ministries of Finance and Economic Development, of each government to provide more effective co-ordination. The problem areas identified by the authorities themselves were the preparation of suitable lists for external finance; the periodic revision of project lists competing for available domestic resources; the difficulty of applying external finance to high-priority sectors in the plan (e.g., primary production); the adaptation of preinvestment studies to the requirements of various donors; and negotiation exercises with the foreign Consultative Group on the National Plan.

But even within a given government itself, co-ordination was not easy among different ministries and agencies concerned with development. Within the federal government, it was possible in practice to by-pass the Economic Planning Unit to get funds for a particular project, as long as the Ministry of Finance and the Economic Committee of the Council of Ministries were prepared to play ball. It was not until 1964 that a Coordinating Committee of high-level officials in which the Economic Planning Unit was strongly represented, was established to oversee whether or not the project was ripe for execution before it went to the Economic Committee of Council.

With little executive power of its own, the Economic Planning Unit had little direct means of ensuring compliance with its own conclusions. The relationship between it and the executive ministries or agencies has remained always vague and tenuous. The old idea of departmentalisation under the colonial administrative machine died hard. If it was so difficult to achieve co-ordination within the federal level, how was the Economic Planning Unit expected to be the central technical planning organization for the whole nation? Furthermore, when one looked at the personnel strength—in size and quality—of the unit itself, it was indeed a marvel of ingenious personal relations that it could even achieve the modest success it had won.

Within each government, power over developmental matters was diffused among the Cabinet Office, the

Treasury, and the Ministry of Economic Development.
The uneasy relations among them often depended
on the kind of leadership which the bureaucracy could
provide, on the one hand, and the character of development strategy adopted by the political class, on
the other. Most of the governments in the country,
however, tended to treat their Ministry of Economic
Development as the academic arm of the administration, politically unrealistic and not to be taken too
seriously in deciding action. Here, political and bureaucratic tactics in the development planning conflict
found common ground in co-operating to isolate as
far as possible the "idealistic" rules of administrative
behavior demanded by the professional planners. Ten-
dering procedures were stage-managed, especially under the ubiquitous and growing system of contractor
finance and supplier credit. Costs were distorted and
the timing and phasing of projects departed from their
predetermined sequence.

It is however fair to admit that in the Nigerian case
the fault has not always been with the nonplanners.
Part of the problem arose initially from the plans
themselves. Typically, the group of foreign experts
who designed them would disband after the documents
were approved and published. And the rules of the
game—the control mechanism for controlling the plans
and their implementation—often came as a separate
exercise after a sizable time lag. Appreciable components of the projects were often not phased and the
aggregate financial figures entered for them in plan
documents often represented nothing more than highly
preliminary guess-estimates of their approximate costs
deriving from tentative preinvestment studies. Thorough project evaluations were often carried out only
after the plans had been approved in the first instance.
All these tended to intensify the clash of interest between the political class and the bureaucracy, on the
one hand, and among different arms of the administra-

tive machine, on the other, especially between the executive ministries and the planning offices.

But by and large, the structural defects in the plans themselves cannot fully explain the actual defects of their implementation. Even if the plans had been technically perfect in all respects, the chances were great in the Nigerian case that their execution would still have run into administrative problems. We have seen from our earlier analysis that the propensity to distort was already inherent in the country's development process, latent in the nature of the decision-making institutions. This latent propensity could not be contained. Apart from the politically compromising position of some of the senior officials and the absence of a concerted bureaucratic leadership, there were problems of a more routine, but no less important, nature. The top officials often lacked relevant supporting staff, especially at the intermediate grades—a good secretary, clerk, or storekeeper. The ancillary or auxiliary services which are taken for granted in the advanced countries are simply lacking in the administrative machine of a developing country with ill-developed manpower. The result is a very defective system of communication and administrative feedback.

The slow and uncertain system of communication was reinforced by the poor quality and inadequacy of statistical information. Memoranda were late in preparation, not only because of personnel bottlenecks, but also because of perennial difficulties in getting the timely, relevant statistical intelligence essential to any planning operation. Even where memoranda were submitted, debated, and approved, the resulting recommendations could be ignored by the appropriate higher authorities; partly because of infrequency of co-ordinating meetings, but mostly because of the slow nature of the bureaucratic machine itself. Take, for example, the case of Ministerial Committees set up on a number of subjects by the National Economic

Council in 1964. The chairmen of the respective committees were asked in July 1964 to call inaugural meetings of their committees. There was no reply, and so reminders went out in September, twice in October, November, and the following January. It was obvious that throughout the whole country the preoccupation was then with the federal elections and few could spare any thoughts for the less politically exciting problem of development planning and plan administration. But this was not all, because the records show that, even within the federal government itself within the same city, some of this correspondence took a very long time indeed to get to the appropriate officers. There were complaints about files being misplaced for a considerable period; of acute staff shortage and of some of the people concerned being involved in long overseas meetings and conferences. A year later, by June 1965, most of the replies from various ministries and governments were still in the hallowed language of red tape—the matter was still receiving the attention of the honorable ministers.

7. Political Uncertainties

Administrative ineffectiveness and political ineptitude only reinforced one another in hindering development. If the administrative machine had been stronger, more purposeful, united, and effective, it would have contained more of the political excesses. But its resilience did not last very long once the administrators themselves became increasingly politicized. And politics, in the context of our Nigerian discussion, was antipathetic to the kind of planning process the economy required. On its economic interpretation, it was more about how the fruits of development would be distributed among different groups; the emphasis of planning required was about how those fruits would be produced and their quantities increased.

The argument, therefore, is not whether politics is important. Political considerations are no doubt at the center of any planning process. The constitutional framework must be well designed to promote good working relations among the different social and economic institutions. Planning must also recognize the political realities of the country by guiding political energies into constructive channels through careful design and propagation of the social objectives of policy. The question is not why politics, it is what kind of politics. And this means what kind of political class. We have seen that the inept constitutional apparatus inherited from the colonial government was potentially unsuitable for the kind of political game a planned development process required. We have also seen that the character of the political class had no coherent ideological commitment and exercised little positive influence on the planning process.

The welcome disappearance of the former political powers in January 1966 thus created a new wave of optimism about the enormous potential economic success that planning could achieve. Everybody had hoped that with the politicians gone the professional economists in and out of the Civil Service could deliver what was needed for economic growth and social change. But this wild dream did not last long. First, the removal of the politicians did not mean the removal of the party apparatus from the source of political power; and the surviving party boys quickly went back in their different directions, dedicated as ever to the great masters of the game. Second, the institutions that inherited the exercise of formal political power had themselves been long converted to hardened politicians. The army, even more than the Civil Service, had little or no objective and articulated program of government to guide its exercise of political power. Apart from quickly restoring law and order and tidying up some objectionable party political practices, the army itself soon became consciously or unconsciously the tool of the old political class. Third, some of the higher echelons of the Civil Service were not disinterested parties in the new power arrangement and probably saw it in fact as an opportunity for propagating their own partisan commitments. Finally, the horizon of the citizens' economic expectations was set so unrealistically high at the time of the army take-over that it was guaranteed frustration from the beginning.

The new kind of planning required extensive corrective measures against the decision-making institutions. These measures inevitably must take time and needed other prerequisites. It was not enough for the army to be sincere. It must be manifestly sincere, honest, objective, and impartial. It must have a well-articulated program which could infuse a new sense of purpose in the citizens and guide them through the reformative process. It must have an administrative machine of such size and personnel that it would command the confidence of the people and be geared to the task of planned development. It must have an economic organizational structure that stretches decision-making powers from the middle of the hierarchy simultaneously upward toward greater centralization and downward toward greater decentralization. It should not swing the organizational pendulum completely around and impose a centralized decision-making machine without changing much of anything else.

But this was precisely what the first military government did. The famous Decree Thirty-Four, which abolished the regions and imposed a unified Civil Service, went beyond the corrective mark by miles. One could perhaps abolish institutions; it is difficult to abolish peoples and impossible to abolish sentiments arising from years of habit, merely by wishing it with a stroke of the pen. But the decree itself was only a logical sequence to the misinterpretation of the country's planning institutional problems given by the cabal of bureaucrats who now controlled the central governmental machine. According to their own reading of the problem, all that was wrong with those institutions was their lack of strong direction from the top. But there is a wide difference between simple direction and guided co-ordination. The particular form that central economic direction took under the first military regime accounted at least in part for the subsequent political holocaust.

The National Economic Council no longer existed by the very disappearance of ministers and of parliamentary government. The Joint Planning Committee, which had become unwieldy and had deteriorated to a minor reflection of the political bargaining of the different governments in the council, was allowed to die a natural death. In place of both, a smaller, more vigorous and flexible body was set up. In its theoretical conception, the National Economic Planning Advisory Group had a good chance of success if it was in fact allowed to do the job of institutional reform. By its composition, leadership, and style of operation, it had shown signs of great promise in its few months of active existence. What then went wrong? First, there was subtle conflict between the formal and informal channels of communication on economic matters. The Advisory Group provided one; the inner political group of the military regime provided another. Second, there was a parallel conflict in the Civil Service itself; and especially between the Ministry of Economic Development and the Economic Division of the Cabinet Office. There again, personalities seemed to be more important than principles. Third, as time wore on, popular confidence in the original motive of corrective government was waning; and little was done to restore political confidence in the skeptical masses. This provided an opportunity for the old political class to whip up popular emotions against the institutions which symbolized the new regime.

The return of the old political class into indirect ascendance in so short a time demonstrates one important lesson in institution-building for national development. The ultimate source of political power has always remained in the village, on the street, in the market place, and in the invisible power of social communication among small groups. The party boys learned fast and acted accordingly, but with disastrous consequences for mutual confidence. The pendulum of social organization was swinging back from latent unitarism to latent confederalism and to threatened total disintegration. And the fact that the same people who supported one yesterday have swung with the pendulum in support of the opposite today demonstrates the complete absence of a dedicated ideological conviction toward nation-building. The resulting political mess and the gradual destruction of economic opportunities indicate the bankruptcy of political pragmatism as a lasting basis of social relations.

The new experiments have not succeeded in improving relations between central and local institutions. If anything, they have poisoned such relations and damaged the development process. It needed more than a force of arms to correct institutions. With the army, many of the social ills against which people have long complained still persist and the political ills it was supposed to cure have become more cancerous. The system of patronage and bureaucratic corruption which distorts planned development still functions, though probably in a less open and shameless manner. Most of the inefficient and incompetent administrators still remain in strategic positions and the more intellectually dishonest ones probably enjoy even greater political power today. Above all, social dissatisfaction continues and has probably intensified. A political arrangement which will realize the undoubted economic potentials of the country and minimize social frictions has eluded the country's leadership for a long time. There is little prospect that the present military regime will achieve a satisfactory arrangement for successful planned development.

8. Conclusion

Aspects of the Nigerian planning organization presented above do not exhaust all considerations of the country's planning experience or its social institutions. The defects in its planning institutions do not themselves prove, and are not intended to prove, that planning has entirely failed or that much development did not occur. Since a plan consists of a set of projects and a set of public policies, weaknesses in either or in both are not tantamount to over-all failure of both. But to the extent that there were serious defects in their design and implementation due to unsatisfactory social and administrative relations, the development process was retarded.

Similarly, not all institutional relations existing in the economy have been highlighted. In particular, some would consider this paper's silence on the relations between the regional governments and local authorities a serious omission. There is no doubt that this relation exists and is historically very important, especially in the north, where the emirates constitute large administrative units and exercise greater financial autonomy. But by and large, the economic side of the relation revolves more around the question of local taxation and regional capital levies. The local authorities have not been used as a positive organ of massive planned development; and in the last two decades they have been so weakened by the regional party machine that their disappearance in most areas would not have made much difference to the over-all performance of the national economy.

Yet it is precisely in the local communities that we must begin to seek a fresh approach to institution-building for accelerating the development process. Whether or not Nigeria survives as a virile political union will depend ultimately not on the present rulers' (or, indeed, any rulers') disposition, but on the tenacity of the masses in the villages and towns. Similarly, the pace and pattern of the country's economic development will increasingly depend on how well the resources of local communities can be harnessed and guided by the upper layers of the national planning organization. The social aspirations, the potential human and physical resources, limited executive manpower, the defective system of communication, and the realities of political opinion would all suggest that planners must now focus their attention and direct their energies to the formation of local development committees, each one being a miniature unit of comprehensive economic planning in a homogeneous social area.

This writer has no doubt in his mind that this approach is not only desirable and inevitable, but that it is also feasible and practicable. He is in fact currently engaged in an experimental model of such miniature comprehensive planning unit in his own village community, and the preliminary results are quite encouraging and reassuring. The experiment has brought forcefully home to him the crucial importance of leadership in any social movement. Planning is a potent weapon for social transformation and it calls for leadership that can sustain the interest of the community, catch its imagination, command its loyalty, arrest its confidence, and guide it through the many latent frustrations of the development process.

But even this leadership, crucial as it is, is not enough. Local planning efforts are meaningful only in the context of a wider market and will succeed only with necessary supporting institutions at the top. The next logical step is therefore the creation of Area Development Authorities covering a wider geographical zone, probably approximating but not necessarily identical with the usual provincial units. These authorities would need to provide essential services such as extension work, storage, marketing, statistical intelligence, certain public utilities, and a framework of regional planning. Similarly, the Area Development Authorities would have to be related to regional or state governments with broader development functions and higher responsibility for co-ordination. At the top of the organizational pyramid would be a new conception of a federal government that is determined to operate a framework of national economic cohesion.

The underlying principle of this arrangement of a two-way planning sequence has been already reflected in the white paper published in 1966 by the federal government on the second national development plan. But unless there is a widespread extension of the kind of local experiment mentioned above, there is little hope of giving operational meaning to the general ideas of the white paper. This approach seems to me the only lasting basis for a continuous effective relation between central and local institutions in planning development.

ROBERT O. COLLINS
RICHARD GRAY
RICHARD HILL

Development Institutions in Historical Perspective: The Sudan

i. INTRODUCTORY NOTE
by Robert O. Collins

> *Robert O. Collins is Associate Professor of History and Director of the Center for the Study of Developing Nations at the University of California at Santa Barbara. He has written much about Africa, particularly about the Sudan, including* Land Beyond the Rivers *and* Problems in African History.

The Republic of the Sudan is two nations—the Northern Sudan, with its ties with the Muslim Arabic-speaking Middle East, and the Southern Sudan, with its Nilotic and Sudanic-speaking peoples who maintain their traditional religious and cultural associations with equatorial Africa. These ethnic, cultural, religious, linguistic, and social differences have produced a century of conflict between the two regions interrupted only by the *Pax Britannica* which insisted, as the primary requirement of imperial rule, that order and peace exist throughout the land. With the departure of the British imperium former animosities reappeared, animosities which even appeals to Sudanese nationalism failed to reconcile. Today, the conflict between the Northern and the Southern Sudans rages as bitterly as any time in the past, the violence only taking slightly different forms from those of a century ago.

Three fundamental social institutions have played a leading role in this conflict: the economic institutions of the Southern Sudan, the challenge of Islam in the south, and the failure of the British to develop, through the Chiefs' Courts, viable political institutions in the south.

Richard Gray describes the economic factors which contributed to the "spiral of violence" in the Southern Sudan, and the failure of the developers in our own time to create a viable economic foundation for the south, without which it will remain a poor and embittered relation in the Sudan of the future. Of all the institutions in the Northern Sudan, Islam is the oldest and the most pervasive. To the mass of Northern Sudanese it continues to give meaning to life about them. To others, however, it appears an anachronism in a secular age. Richard Hill examines the stress and strain of Islam in the Sudan today, analyzing Muslim attempts to meet, on the one hand, the secular challenge from the West and, on the other, to spread Islam southward into equatorial Africa. Finally, Robert O. Collins discusses the rise and fall of the Chiefs' Courts in the Southern Sudan from their inception by British administrators to their relegation to minor, local courts by Sudanese nationalists. To the British the Chiefs' Courts were the fundamental institution out of which national political institutions would emerge. To the Sudanese they were an autocratic instrument of local government ill suited to evolve into the democratic, national institutions they sought to create at independence.

Taken together, these three papers bring into particular focus, through the historical experience of one African state, the large questions and problems of development considered elsewhere in this volume. They particularly emphasize that it is vain to consider economic modernization apart from its roots and ramifications in the social and political life of a people.

ii. SOME OBSTACLES TO ECONOMIC DEVELOPMENT IN THE SOUTHERN SUDAN, 1839–1965

by Richard Gray

> *John Richard Gray is currently a Reader in the History Department at the School of Oriental and African Studies of London University. His publications include* The Two Nations *and* A History of the Southern Sudan.

A problem and a liability for much of the twentieth century, the southern hinterland of Khartoum had previously dominated the opening of eastern tropical Africa to the commerce and influences of the outside world. The exploration of the White Nile in 1839–1841 by Muhammad Ali, ruler of Egypt and conqueror of the Sudan, and the discovery of a navigable highway stretching one thousand miles into the unknown heart of Africa opened a series of possibilities which rapidly attracted traders, missionaries, and an imperial intervention. By the end of the 1870s, however, alternative routes, up the Congo and overland from the Indian Ocean, were being developed by Europeans, and both private enterprise and Egyptian imperial rule had already failed to lay the foundations of a peaceful, ordered economic development in the Southern Sudan. This false start, during which the early ecstatic welcome[1] was turned to hatred and sullen hostility, has crucially affected the subsequent development of the area; and although the contemporary crisis, which today threatens the progress and even the existence of a united, independent Sudan, cannot, of course, be explained solely by reference to this early economic and political failure, it is perhaps worth first examining this period more closely as it illustrates in an acute form the way in which human, social, and cultural factors have sometimes influenced development in tropical Africa.

From the start, ivory was the commodity which attracted attention. The capital expenditure involved in equipping and transporting ivory-trading expeditions effectively excluded the local Arab petty traders who still dominated the caravan trade of the Northern Sudan. At first Muhammad Ali attempted to preserve a government trading monopoly, but by 1851, as a result of European diplomatic pressure, this was abandoned, and the south was suddenly exposed to cutthroat commercial rivalry, financed and led by European, Egyptian, and Levantine traders in Khartoum. The number of boats leaving annually for the south increased from twelve in 1851 to about eighty by 1859; profits were

---

[1] Tribes along the riverbank welcomed the members of the expedition as gods, slaughtering cattle in their honor. R. Gray, *A History of the Southern Sudan, 1839–1889* (London, 1961), p. 18.

high and in these early years a few individual traders made "almost a fortune in ivory."[2]

These substantial profits, however, partly depended on gaining access to accumulated "stores" of ivory, the remains of elephants previously hunted solely for their flesh. The ivory available at the few landing places along the swamp-fringed course of the White Nile and Bahr el Jebel was rapidly exhausted, and traders depended for new sources on the emergence of local Southern middlemen prepared to search for and purchase further supplies. In many other parts of tropical Africa this challenge of long-distance commerce was met successfully, and the profits and experience of trade often helped to lay the foundations for future political and economic development. In the Southern Sudan, however, the challenge was far too sudden and intense for an effective local response, and the alien traders themselves broke through the cultural barriers to exploit short-term profits at the expense of durable development.

Isolated behind the Nuba Mountains, extensive swamps and grasslands, the peoples of the Southern Sudan were completely unprepared to meet this challenge. The great Nilotic tribes of the Dinka and Nuer were superbly adapted to their vast, forbidding environment of savannah grass periodically inundated by the flood waters of Equatoria. Their lives revolved around the cattle camp, and these proud nomadic pastoralists preserved a fierce contempt for clothing and the other inessentials offered by the outside world. South of these savannah swamps, the mixed cultivators and cattle-keepers, of whom the Bari, situated at the terminus of the navigable Bahr el Jebel, were the most accessible and hence most significant example, had before 1839 been completely excluded from any intimate, direct contact with long-distance trade. In

[2] E. de Pruyssenaere, 17.V.1856, quoted in Gray, p. 32.

this respect, the area at this date was indeed one of the most remote and untouched in the whole of tropical Africa.

The first expeditions to reach the Bari found the rain chief, Lagonu, wearing strings of beads, copper rings, and a long, wide blue cotton shirt. These marks of prestige had been obtained from a small neighboring tribe, the Pari, who had occasional contacts through the Anuak with Beni Shanqul and Ethiopian trade and, southward, through the Acholi with the developing system of interlacustrine trade of Bunyoro and Buganda. This thin trickle of goods had as yet, however, done little to modify the concept of economic self-sufficiency. In no way had it introduced a practice and experience of trading methods. Lagonu confessed that the copper was generally stolen and that friendly intercourse with the Pari was constantly interrupted by raiding for cattle and other plunder.

Yet the Bari showed a keen interest in the expedition's trade goods and, unlike the Dinka, willingly exchanged both cattle and ivory for beads. For a brief instant it seemed that they might respond to the new opportunities and develop into successful entrepreneurs. Nyigilo, brother of Lagonu, visited Khartoum in 1844 and subsequently conducted Bari trading expeditions as far as the Lotuko to the east, while ten years later he was training oxen for transport in preparation for an attempt to visit Bunyoro and the Nile sources as yet unknown to Europe. His early attempts to co-operate with European merchants and missionaries were, however, suppressed by the Egyptian officials, and he was prevented from acquiring firearms and other advantages which would alone have enabled him to overcome the competing jealousies within Bari society and emerge a powerful and effective middleman. Instead the Bari gradually became increasingly suspicious of the alien traders and missionaries, and a series of hostile incidents, including a pitched battle in 1854, led to a complete deadlock. As an ally of the outside world and as an object of the envy, Nyigilo himself became a scapegoat until, hunted by armed youths, he was eventually killed in June 1859.

All prospect of an equitable partnership, based on a balance of power with the traders limited to riverain barter, had disappeared. Henceforth, the traders decided to undertake direct expeditions into the interior and to establish permanent stations by employing numerous armed Arab servants and soldiers from the North. This decision altered the whole pattern of development. The trading frontier began to generate a plural society as the Arabs settled, obtained wives and slaves from the neighboring tribes, and established themselves as a new, ruling caste transcending the barriers of tribal society. At the same time the expansion of the ivory trade became intimately linked with the spread of violence and the slave trade. By an unscrupulous yet discriminating use of force, the traders exploited tribal jealousies and paid their tribal allies with stolen cattle and their Arab servants with captured slaves.

During the 1860s this riverain penetration linked forces in the Bahr el Ghazal with an overland slave-trading caravan route from Darfur and Kordofan. Thus reinforced, the traders struck rapidly southward across the Nile-Congo watershed into the Wele basin, while from the Bahr el Jebel caravans went southeastward through the Acholi to the Victoria Nile. It was the desire to control this expansion, to suppress its violence, and participate in its profits that led the Khedive Ismail, grandson of Muhammad Ali, to send in 1869 an expedition under Sir Samuel Baker to bring the interlacustrine area under Egyptian rule. Baker and his successor, Gordon, failed to extend the tenuous route from the navigable Bahr el Jebel and were unable to impose their rule on the lacustrine kingdoms; instead, in their relations with the Bari and

Acholi, they were forced to follow the methods of their predecessors and to rely on the influence of the traders' Arab soldiery. Near the government stations there grew up "a semi-native, semi-Arab by contact population of lads and women"[3] who worked for the soldiers, and, beyond this restricted area of biological adaptation, the tribes continued to be raided to obtain provisions, the soldiers remote from supervision continued to capture slaves, and vast areas remained unproductive and hostile. Gordon himself realized that his failure to establish a widely recognized system of "justice," legalized taxation, and ordered economic development was due to the fact that he was basically merely a spectator of a social process over which he exerted but little influence. "The roads are safe," he wrote in 1876, "and I can do nothing more, for I cannot govern not knowing the language, and even if I did, I could not expect to change the habits of the officers, etc. or of the natives. I feel it would be better for them to work out the problem of how to live together by themselves."[4]

This realization and the growth of the overland slave trade led him, when Governor-General of the Sudan from 1877 to 1879, to propose that the only solution for the south was to enforce a strict blockade of the whole area leaving the Arabs and their servants to perish through lack of supplies and reinforcements. "I am dead against any occupation of these countries. I want no ivory, I only want the people to be quiet."[5] Yet this purely negative approach, later in some respects to be so strikingly paralleled by the British during the Condominium, could hardly provide a

[3] Gordon to Waller, 29.I.1875, quoted in Gray, p. 113.

[4] Gordon to his sister, Augusta, 10.IV.1876, quoted in Gray, p. 112.

[5] Gordon to Gessi, 31.III.1879 in C. Zaghi, *Gordon, Gessi, e la riconquista del Sudan* (Florence, 1947), p. 322.

permanent solution, and in these last years of Egyptian rule his subordinates, Gessi in the Bahr el Ghazal and Emin in Equatoria, attempted to lay the foundations of a more constructive development. Between his defeat of the principal slave trader in July 1879 and his departure from the Bahr el Ghazal in September 1880, Gessi more than covered his expenses by sending ninety thousand pounds' worth of ivory to Khartoum, and he also vigorously investigated the possibilities of finding alternative and more permanent exports. Cotton was grown successfully; rubber, tamarinds, and a large supply of honey were exported to Khartoum; palm oil, rice, sugar, and timber potentialities were investigated; copper from Hofrat en Nahas supplied the needs of the province, and Gessi had plans to develop a local, modernized iron industry. The problem of transport and communications was tackled by the construction of small boats which during the season of high water at Wau were floated down to Khartoum, while the other major obstacle often encountered in the early stages of economic development in Africa—an inadequate labor supply—did not here apply. Among the small, agricultural tribes surrounding the Arab settlements a desire for cotton clothing was apparently a sufficient incentive for labor, and Gessi established eight looms worked by young African apprentices. By introducing these Southerners to a higher standard of living, Gessi hoped to reduce the stigma of inferiority when compared with their Northern neighbors, and he also opened a primary school for the sons of chiefs and local soldiers, expecting "in a few years to be able to draw the clerks from the indigenous populations."[6]

Like Emin's work in Equatoria, these efforts were mainly restricted to the immediate radius of the government stations. The far harder problem of establish-

[6] Casati to Comperio, September 1880, in Zaghi, p. 478.

ing confidence and control over the vast tribal areas of
the Dinka, Azande, and other peoples could hardly
be solved with the resources at their disposal. Outside
the narrow limits of these administrators' direct influence, the Southerners' contact with the outside
world continued to be marked by violence, the slave
trade, suspicion, and hostility. Yet within these limits
the local tribesmen were beginning to participate in
the foundations of a new way of life. Muslim material culture, dress, and ornaments were increasingly
adopted; Emin described how an Acholi chief looked
like "a thorough Dongolawi in appearance and manners, dresses exactly as they do, sits on an Anqareb
and regales his guests with coffee,"[7] and many chiefs
of this tribe, who previously had shared the Nilotic
repugnance for clothing of any kind, were beginning
to dress in long colored shirts and the tarbush. Here,
and in the attendance of the Bari chiefs at the Feast
of Id al-Saghir in 1881, were the growing points of a
new frontier of Islam; here, and in Gessi's school, were
perhaps the grounds for feeling that a future generation of Southerners might be able to face the North
on terms approaching equality. It was a feeble, tenuous assimilation to set beside the bloodshed and violence which maintained this plural society; but the
significance of this development, both then and perhaps again today, should not be underestimated.

Beyond the radius of this restricted acculturation
can be discerned the faint beginnings of another development, which also was to acquire immense significance at a much later period: the emergence of
a Southern, supratribal resistance, cemented by a bitter hostility to these alien forces. As the government
stations in the South began to experience the effects
of the successful Mahdist rising against Egyptian au-

[7] F. Stuhlmann (ed.), *Die Tagebücher von Dr. Emin Pascha*
(Hamburg, 1919), II, p. 126.

thority in the North, they suddenly found themselves exposed to renewed attacks from the Southern tribes. At first these seemed to be limited to scattered incidents among the Dinka, but Lupton, Gessi's successor in the Bahr el Ghazal, gradually became aware that the Nuer were now helping their traditional enemies the Dinka. In 1884 various Nuer and Dinka tribes, united under the leadership of a prophet called Donlutj, exterminated the garrison at Bor on the Bahr el Jebel, while the following year Emin's principal stations were attacked by a force consisting of Dinka, Aliab, Mandari, and Bari elements. Later, in the 1920's, Nuer prophets were to lead a fierce resistance to the establishment of British rule, and though the old, traditional animosities continued to divide the South, these early reactions to alien intruders foreshadowed in certain crucial respects the Southern Mutiny of 1955 and the later emergence of the Anyanya resistance.

The collapse of Egyptian rule in the South was, however, primarily the result not of this Southern antagonism, but of the Mahdist expeditions, which rapidly overran the major centers in the Bahr el Ghazal and later succeeded in evicting Emin from Equatoria.[8] Largely preoccupied with the administration and defense of their homeland, the Mahdists could spare little attention to the South; with few exceptions the tenuous beginnings of assimilation to the Northern way of life began to wither, and during the last two decades of the nineteenth century the general pattern of violence and disruption was merely intensified. Faced with this legacy, the British administrators during the early years of Condominium rule naturally felt that the overriding, primary need of the area was for a cautious, gradual policy of pacification, for a slow expansion of confidence and security. It is hardly sur-

[8] R. O. Collins, *The Southern Sudan, 1883–1898* (New Haven, 1962).

prising that this process in some areas took two decades; even if greater resources and force had been available, it is at least arguable that at this stage any attempt at more rapid development might well have proved self-defeating. It is also perhaps understandable that in this early period of the Condominium contact between North and South was restricted by the British, but gradually this protective isolation was intensified rather than diminished, until in 1930 it was embodied as a leading principle of a separate Southern policy. Paternalistic benevolence, so essential and successful in the early stages of pacification, fossilized, and the eradication of Arab influence was in places carried to ludicrous lengths.[9] The entrepreneurial links between North and South were severed, and, save for a few Greek and Syrian traders, the impetus of private, small-scale economic development was effectively excluded. The impact of this policy was all the more disastrous as public investment and government expenditure in the South were restricted to a minimum: British interests were satisfied by the bare maintenance of law and order, economic development was concentrated in the Genzira cotton-growing plan in the North, and the South during the years of depression was run on a shoestring.

It was not until the end of World War II that a plan for Southern development was eventually formulated. As a first step, and as a large-scale experiment, it was decided to build up a self-contained industrial complex in the remote Zande area near the Congo

[9] M. Abdel Rahim, "The Development of British Policy in the Southern Sudan, 1899–1947," *Middle Eastern Studies,* II (3), 1966. R. O. Collins, "The Sudan Link to the North," typescript. R. Hill, "Government and Christian Missions in the Anglo-Egyptian Sudan, 1899–1914," *Middle Eastern Studies,* I (2), 1965, examines one aspect of the origins of the Southern policy.

frontier, over 300 miles from the river port of Juba. At a time when Gezira cotton was still exported for processing, it was proposed to establish a cotton growing and manufacturing industry among the Azande, complete with ginnery, spinning and weaving mills, powered by locally produced electricity from charcoal. Besides clothing the Azande the industry would provide finance to cover the few imports considered indispensable for the area. Other crops—sugar, oil palms, coffee, and jute—were to be added, and the basic concept of the plan was self-sufficiency: a multiple development within what would continue to be largely a closed circuit, designed, wrote Dr. Tothill, the author of the plan, to assist "the Social Emergence of Indigenous Races in Remote Regions." As Dr. Reining has shown, however, the basic concept was quickly modified in favor of commercial considerations. For the first years of the plan, solvency was achieved by exporting large quantities of the compulsorily produced cotton; Zande enthusiasm and co-operation turned into resentment; cotton production slumped disastrously, and the industrial complex at Nzara became "an enormous white elephant" bringing merely "inconvenience and distress" to the Azande.[10] Thus, ironically, the one major effort by the British to develop the Southern Sudan ended by alienating the Southerners, and the popular feeling against chiefs and administrators found expression in the Nzara riots of July 1955, which in turn contributed to the tragic mutiny of the following August and, hence, to the present conflict.

In retrospect few people would deny that British policy, however altruistically conceived, constituted a major obstacle to economic development in the South during the first half of the twentieth century. Tothill's

[10] C. C. Reining, *The Zande Scheme* (Evanston, 1966), pp. 210, 227.

scheme was designed to solve the problem of the South's backwardness and remoteness; but it was also, of course, even if this was not explicitly stated, the child of the Southern policy of protective isolation. A railway, such as that later constructed by the Abboud regime from El Obeid to Wau, would have provided a simpler and more effective approach to the problem of isolation, had the political and social implications of so close a link proved acceptable. Reining even reports how "a particularly cynical Zande" observed that the introduction of the mango tree from the Congo, which subsequently seeded itself and provided a valuable source of food, "had been the most important contribution of the Europeans to Zande welfare."[11] Such a view overlooks, of course, the immense achievement of having introduced for the first time into the area a wide-ranging framework of law and order, within which an increasing use of money was beginning to widen the opportunities of the subsistence economies. It overlooks also the foundations of education, very largely the work of Christian missions, and the subsequent emergence of a small educated elite whose horizons transcended those of the local ethnic group. Nevertheless, the fact remains that when the British in 1947 suddenly reversed their Southern policy, working for integration with the North in view of their imminent withdrawal from the Sudan, they left the South still tragically unprepared to meet the North on anything approaching terms of equality, and during the Condominium they had done little to reduce the feelings of scorn and contempt, on the one side, and of suspicion and hostility, on the other, that the nineteenth-century contact had engendered.

[11] Reining, p. 72. Further criticisms of British neglect are voiced in a by no means anti-British source, S. Santandrea, *A Tribal History of the Western Bahr al-Ghazal* (Bologna, 1964), pp. 319–28.

It would, therefore, be wrong, especially for an Englishman, to minimize the grave responsibility incurred by Britain in leaving so divided an inheritance to the independent Sudan. But it would seem equally false to ignore the mistakes of the North which have contributed so considerably to the contemporary crisis, with the result that the fundamental framework for development has been widely damaged and destroyed. As in the case of the European ivory traders and the British administrators of the Zande scheme, the crucial failing seems to have been an inability to foresee and understand Southern reactions, and an insensitivity to the consequences of a policy of inflexible compulsion in a situation where two cultures are in conflict. Such an approach was manifest in the decision of the Sudanization Committee to replace British administrators in the South with Northerners, leaving only a handful of junior posts for the less qualified Southerners; for this decision, more than any other action, convinced Southerners in 1955 that they were merely exchanging one colonial rule for another. During the early years of parliamentary rule after independence, insensitivity was shown also in the disregard for the Southern demand for a federal type of constitution, which could have given Southerners a voice in their own affairs while leaving the Sudan a united entity. Southern grievances, including the well-founded belief that, while the North was embarking on rapid educational and economic development, the South was being left to stagnate,[12] could find no outlet under the military regime which came into power in November 1958. The country, therefore, drifted to civil war, with Southern leaders and students forced into exile and armed Southern resistance being organized by the Anyanya, led by some of the 1955 mutineers. The

[12] J. Oduho and W. Deng, *The Problem of the Southern Sudan* (London), 1963.

overthrow of the military regime in October 1964, partly as a consequence of Northern dissatisfaction with the war in the South, brought a new wave of hope to Southerners. With the collapse of the Round Table Conference in April 1965, however, followed by the exclusion of the Southern Front from the central government and the massacres at Juba, Wau, and other centers in the South in June and July 1965, which led to a further flood of refugees,[13] the disillusionment of the South has come perilously close to destroying all foundations for a possible reconciliation.

[13] Estimates released by the United Nations High Commissioner for Refugees in November 1966 show 45,000 in Uganda, 30,000 in the Congo, and 25,000 in the Central African Republic. These figures omit Ethiopia (estimated by one source at 50,000), and they relate only to those refugees officially recognized and cared for by the U.N. Commission. Thousands of others, however, have crossed the frontiers, settling either among kinsmen or isolated by themselves. A careful observer's personal count in May 1966 gave around 100,000 in Uganda alone, and *The Vigilant,* a newspaper run by Southerners in Khartoum, states that well over half a million Southerners are refugees.

iii. SUDANESE ISLAM IN A DEVELOPING AFRICA
by Richard Hill

Richard Leslie Hill was in the Sudan Civil Service from 1927 to 1949. He has been Visiting Lecturer at the University of California at Santa Barbara. His publications include Egypt in the Sudan *and* Slatin Pasha.

Introductory Note

Because the Sudan came late into the consciousness of a Europe undergoing a long education in understanding Islam, the Islam of the Sudanese has on the whole been correctly interpreted in American and European literature (though it was savaged by war correspondents during the fighting between the Anglo-Egyptian forces and the Mahdists between 1883 and 1898, but from chauvinism and ignorance rather than malice). Christian missionary writings of that day showed only too clearly that ignorance of Islam prevailed in the West outside the small circle of scholars, though the quality of literature about Islam has greatly improved over the years.

The most persistent detractors of Sudanese Islam, who are blissfully unaware that they are detractors at all, are still found among the playwrights and the journalists. Sir Laurence Olivier, convincingly playing the Mahdi in the film *Khartoum,* in one incident rivals the crudity of A. E. W. Mason's novel, *The Four Feathers*, published in 1904, by pulling a severed human arm from a basin. A prominent British journalist writes of the present head of the Mahdist community as 'the present Mahdi.' But these are trifles which wound individuals but do no great harm.

When students from the West begin to observe Islam in one of its homelands, they are frequently baffled by the failure of educated Muslims to assume intellectual attitudes which are expected of them. The relative unimportance in Islam of belief in the spiritual verities may be noticed. Muslims would find it most unusual for a Muslim of the Sudan to abandon the community of Islam merely because he had lost belief in the supernatural elements of his religion. Muslims and Christians also place different values on the usefulness of learning about religions other than their own. The great interest shown by Christian and Judaic scholars of the nineteenth century and today in the history and institutions of Islam, the inclusion of Islam as a subject in the religious studies programs of our secondary schools, for instance, has no counterpart in the Sudan, where such matters are left to the *'ulamā*. In America Christian theology is considered everyone's business, and people in California, who have never heard of Arius, or for that matter Athanasius, discuss Bishop Pike with the greatest zest.

The modern spirit of ecumenism seems to have extended the boundaries of Christian good will to the other great faiths. The most recent substantial description of Sudanese Islam is J. S. Trimmingham's *Islam in the Sudan*, published in 1949; so rapid has been the advance in Christian thinking since it was published that, were Professor Trimmingham to rewrite his survey for publication in 1969, he would probably revise his text in several places to reflect the changing Christian outlook on Islam on the Nile.

Lest, however, the reader be tempted into a cloud-cuckoo land of universal religious brotherhood, let him remember that, although Islam gives theological recognition to both Christianity and Judaism (though not in a form acceptable to either), Christianity and Judaism continue to withhold formal theological recognition from Islam.

The Character of Islam in the Sudan and its Relations with other Religions

About the only generalization that may safely be made about Sudanese Islam is that it is straightforward, robust, pietistic and nonintellectual in character. Islam was introduced into the Sudan by nomad Arabs in the early Middle Ages. It received a more disciplined expression from learned men who entered the Sudan, mostly from the Hijaz, from the sixteenth to the early nineteenth centuries. From 1820, the year of the first penetration by the Turco-Egyptians, until today, with the interlude of the Mahdist theocracy from 1885 to 1898, the greater influence has come from al-Azhar University in Cairo. But the Azharites in the Sudan produced no Shaykh Muḥammad 'Abduh, no *salafiyyah,* no intellectual movement at all to ruffle the surface of those deep waters.

In approaching Sudanese Islam we recognize a many-sided institution inclusive of many schools ranging from worldliness through Mahdism to the austere position of the Muslim Brothers. But in spite of this rich diversity, there is unanimity on one point: Muslims discuss Islam only within the framework of Islamic apologetics. It is essential to remember how difficult fundamental self-criticism is for fundamentalists of any sort, let alone for those devoted professionally to any one religion.

There is still a popularly accepted mythology of Sudanese Mahdism which has room for miracles and portents. Some of the phenomena of this kind were recorded in a manuscript history of the movement by a Yemenese scholar, 'Abd al-Raḥmān Ḥusayn al-Jabrī, who recounted that he was converted in his youth to belief in the Mahdi after reading a copy of the Mahdi's order of prayer. On the other hand, traditional inhibitions in relation to the arts of painting, sculpture, and photography have been long superseded in the Sudan or rather never had an occasion to develop, for there has been almost no artistic tradition in the Northern Sudan, even though the Mahdi found it necessary to warn the faithful of the snares of representational art. Nowadays the film flourishes and the live theater is struggling for serious recognition.

How does the average Muslim in the Sudan regard his two neighbor religions, Christianity and Judaism? The writer does not know, and he doubts the value of any investigation based on an "average Muslim." Student friends in Khartoum seemed to give little thought to either. If drawn into discussion they would talk in terms of "Western imperialism" and "Zionist imperialism." The theological content of either faith had no interest for them. But in order to balance this attitude it is only fair to add that these students were in the department of history, not of philosophy. Would the young philosophers have thought differently?

Or would their elders? No Sudanese scholar in contemporary Sudanese Islam exists to trace through history the progressive unfolding of the Muslim understanding of Christianity, the growing awareness among Muslim savants of a sense of Christian values. The only anthology of Christian documents edited by a Muslim that I have seen was a propagandist exposé of Christian error. There is no immediate likelihood of a Muslim counterpart to N. A. Daniel's *Islam and the West: The Making of an Image* (Edinburgh, 1960) being published by a Sudanese.

This indifference to the tenets of other religions has been due partly to government action. As Christian missionary propaganda is not permitted distribution in the Muslim North, the Muslims do not have an opportunity to read and weigh it. The only missionary sheets known to me were being distributed in Omdurman by members of the heretical Aḥmadiyyah community, though Muslim friends say that they have seen missionary literature issued by a Protestant body in Egypt, but directed not against Islam, but against other Christian bodies. It is not Christian missionary literature that riles Muslim readers in the Northern Sudan. And when during a night of fighting in Khartoum in December 1964 between Negroes and Arabs an Arab mob set fire to property of the United Presbyterian Church of America, who have a mission in the Upper Nile province, mass hysteria, not Christian propaganda, seems to have been the cause. Not long before this a similar mob had burned the editorial offices of one of the few independent Khartoum newspapers, *al-Rayy al-'āmm,* whose Muslim editor is widely respected for his objectivity.

What in other places might be mistaken for specifically religious fanaticism may simply be the survival of the frenzy which unaccountably seizes some people at rare intervals and is not confined to urban Sudanese Muslims. Collective anger can take vicious and violent forms, as we know from the history of Christendom. We must consider here the very recent advent of toleration among Christians, and the presence in the Sudan of Christian bodies, both Western and Oriental, which are quite intolerant of the faith of Muslims living next door to them. General Wingate, an early governor general, was quick to notice the fraternity of mutual misrepresentation between Shaykh 'Alī Yūsuf of Cairo and Winnington Ingram, Anglican bishop of London.

The case of Shawqī Muḥammad 'Alī in late 1965 is an example of this collective frenzy. This young man was a student in the Higher Training Institute for Teachers at Omdurman. In the course of a discussion in public he appears to have lost his temper and attacked the religion of Islam from the Communist viewpoint. He attacked Islam as Christianity is so often attacked in the West, where nobody takes any notice. But not in Omdurman. The junior apostate's words soon got around and were probably embroidered in the process. A mob collected and promptly, in a fit of exaltation, burned down the local offices of the Communist Party, which had nothing to do with the young man's temper. The incident gave the Sudanese parliament justification, contested in the courts, for outlawing the Communist Party. The boy received a sentence of six months' imprisonment. In vain the accused asserted that all the prosecution witnesses were Muslim Brothers; his Institute expelled him. Altogether, for the student of Sudanese Islam, this was an illuminating affair. Though the sentence was generally regarded as just, the local Communists must have regretted the failure of the young convert to have availed himself of the historic resort of the persecuted to *taqiyyah,* dissimulation, or the more common-sense expedient of keeping his mouth shut.

The Imām al-Hādī al-Mahdī, head of the Mahdist community in the Sudan, supports the idea of an Islamic constitution for the Sudan, a logical stand for the great-grandson of the original Mahdi, whose life's work was dedicated to the establishment of a theocracy. The Imām al-Hādī, who has been traditionally educated, has his roots in the old Muslim apologetic and from time to time speaks his mind in a way which would have caused his father, the Imām 'Abd al-Rahmān al-Mahdī, a diplomat of the highest order, to wince. He is reported in January 1967 to have said that his followers, the *Anṣār,* would impose an Islamic constitution by force if the Constituent Assembly failed to pass the measure. He afterward denied having said so. (On three other occasions he has been credited with statements which he has later denied.) But in this instance, though his denial would, of course, be accepted even by some of his political opponents, he is in no way bound to accept the imposition of an Islamic state by a mere show of hands.

The Imām al-Hādī, the patron of the Umma party, announced in January 1967 that he would be a candidate whenever a presidential election would be held. The Imām has been in conflict with his nephew, Ṣādiq al-Mahdī, formerly prime minister in a coalition government with Ismāʿīl al-Azharī's National Unionist party. But too much should not be made of this conflict between uncle and nephew; it is a conflict of emphasis rather than of fundamentals. Uncle's view of the modern world was gained through a traditional Muslim education informed by piety; Nephew sees the same world through the chastening filter of a Western education. Uncle sees only black and white; Nephew observes also the pinks and the grays.

The Islamic position of Ismāʿīl al-Azharī, president of the Supreme Council, is interesting. In his younger days he won much religious support by reason of his family connections, for he comes of a saintly and scholarly family. But he is also a great nationalist leader and is not today regarded as having particularly close affiliations with any religious leader or Islamic brotherhood. His recent assumption of the office of titular head of the Islamic University of Omdurman marks him a Muslim without frills, certainly no sectary.

As for the non-Muslim faiths in the overwhelmingly Sunnite Muslim Northern Sudan, all that need be said is that they are concentrated in the towns, mainly in Khartoum, and that they give no trouble to the Muslim government. Except for the restrictions imposed on the *ahl al-dhimmah* during the Mahdist regime, compulsory ghetto life has been unknown in the Sudan. The various Orthodox and Uniate churches cater to the Greek and Levantine population. Those Christian bodies having daughter churches in the

Southern Sudan such as the Roman Catholic, the
Episcopalian, and the United Presbyterian Church of
North America, have been living under a certain stress
since the collapse of civil government in the South.

The Muslim Brothers

The active presence of the Muslim Brothers in the
Sudan poses a number of embarrassing problems for
the government. The Brothers are a small body, an
elite, a pressure group, with an exceptionally intelligent leadership. Though the Islamic Charter Front is
the political affiliation favored by the Brothers, the
Front contains many who are not formally members
of the *Ikhwan al-Muslimūn*. The secretary-general of
the Front, Ḥasan al-Turābī, is a former member of the
faculty of the University of Khartoum and a doctor
of the Sorbonne.

For the official Islamic hierarchy it is embarrassing
to have this *imperium in imperio* continually watching
and sometimes criticizing; it is as though Ibn Ḥanbal
were continually watching Abū Ḥanīfa and tripping
him up on points of Islamic law and practice. The
very presence of the Brothers leading demonstrations
in the streets of the Sudan roughens the smooth conduct of Sudanese-United Arab Republic relations. For
the Cairo government has had a long and bitter fight
with the Brothers—a fight to the death; the monarchy
killed Ḥasan al-Bannā, the republic killed al-Quṭb and
let al-Hudhaybī rot in prison. The United Arab Republic is surrounded by states which shelter the
Brothers. It is a difficult problem in inter-Arab relations which Arab solidarity against Israel masks but
does not remove.

The Islamic Charter front gains from the temporary
understanding with the Sudanese Mahdist community,
but in the event of a Sudan-wide acceptance of the
Muslim Brothers' standpoint, the prestige of the

imāmate of the Mahdi would diminish, as would the prestige of the heads of other religious fraternities. As the National Unionist party freed itself from the Mīrghanist fraternity influence, so in the same way the Muslim Brothers may seek to detach the more fellow-traveling section of the Umma party from any connection with the Mahdist movement. At the moment of writing Mahdism is a convenient rather than an essential ally.

The following is a responsible statement of the Brothers' position: In a report of a symposium held at the University of Khartoum in October 1966, Muḥammad Ṣāliḥ, a lecturer in the university and a member of the Islamic Charter front, said that they were commanded by their religion to carry out God's wishes, one of which was to preach Islam and to guarantee that in those areas where Islam holds sway the life and government of the people is ordered according to the tenets of Islam. It was therefore their duty to try to convince everyone to accept Islam. This was an ideology based not on racialism like that of Jamāl 'Abd al-Nāṣir, whose Arab nationalism raises serious racial problems. Sayyid Muḥammad Ṣāliḥ said that their own scramble for Africa was a peaceful one and not like the earlier scramble by the Western imperialists.

The appeal of the Brothers is to the earnest, particularly to the educated earnest, the university student, the junior officer in the fighting forces, who yearns to be a good Muslim but sees nothing but discouragement in all around him. These are the young men who ask questions, to which the Brothers can provide the answer. Here at last is a movement with a point of view which is intellectually acceptable, a movement which can attract not only one's intellect but also one's burning loyalty. The call of the Muslim Brothers comes all the clearer when economic depression is added to political chaos. The Muslim Brothers have set up an organization which has introduced the Western-educated Muslim to a conception of Islam which he can nevertheless accept without reservation. To some who feel very deeply, there is scarcely an alternative.

Nevertheless, the Brothers do not neglect the multitude, which is not at all moved by intellectual or even by rational considerations. What mob ever is so moved? In August 1966 the Islamic Charter Front organized a procession of about one thousand people to protest the killing of three members of the Muslim Brotherhood convicted of a plot to assassinate President Jamāl 'Abd al-Nāṣir. Shaykh 'Aṭīyah led the mourning prayer and Dr. Ḥasan al-Turābī eulogized Sayyid al-Quṭb and his friends. No attempt was made to examine the proceedings of the trial. There was no need, for in the view of the Muslim Brothers these good Muslims had been condemned by a secular court, repulsive to Islamic justice and controlled by a government which, by its actions, had long ceased to be Islamic.

There has understandably been some local reaction. Some Khartoum newspapers, cold to the Muslim Brothers, have pointed out the trail of trouble, violence, and intolerance which the Brothers had left in the United Arab Republic, where some of its leaders were caught red-handed in an attempt to kill the president; in Syria, where they added one more to the many elements of political instability; in Pakistan, where, with the Wahhābīs, they coerced the government into imposing censorship on foreign literature, and in Ethiopia and Chad, where they have been accused of giving help to militant Muslim minorities.

The Muslim Brothers make no impression at all on the easygoing members of the Islamic majority who have accommodated their Islam comfortably to the frontier conditions of the Sudan, who squirm at the very thought of personal striving for the Faith, who both drink and smoke, attend the Friday prayers when there is an interesting preacher, and perform a minimum of personal prayers. To these, including a large section of the ruling institution, the Brothers are a disturbing nuisance.

Suppose the principles of the Muslim Brothers were to become accepted by a majority of the Sudanese ruling group and an Islamic constitution were established. Would it be a façade of an Islamic constitution in which non-Muslims would be permitted effective equal citizenship with Muslims, or would it be one which harked back to the classical conception of the Christian and the Jew holding inferior citizenship and of the heathen holding no citizenship at all? Or will the Muslim government of the future simply expel all non-Muslims who are unconvertible, as the Christians of Spain expelled the Jews?

The Development of Islamic Education

Islamic education in the Sudan has a continuous history since the sixteenth century of the Christian era. The basis of schooling was the teacher of Islam, the *faqīh,* and his *khalwah,* both a school and a community of disciples. The *khalwah,* in its teaching aspect, has survived to this day but is disappearing in the face of a rapidly expanding state educational system and by the emergence of a more comprehensive Islamic education.

From 1899 to 1956 Sudanese education was controlled by a non-Muslim government. The British-dominated Condominium government has been much accused of starving Islamic education. In one sense the charge was freely admitted: the Condominium never made a priority of education except at the lowest and the most utilitarian level. The small, poor, and admittedly philistine department of education conceived that its first duty was to give the rudiments of elementary education to a generation largely illiterate even in Arabic and, where literate, literate only up to the low level of the _khalwahs,_ and wholly ignorant of the outer world.

Legally the Condominium was the political emanation of a Muslim Khedive of Egypt and a Christian Queen who was also considered Queen of India, which included Muslim India. It was a trickily anomalous situation for a government politically dominated by Christians to rule a community of devout Muslims, but the anomaly was robbed of political danger by Lord Cromer's assurance to the Muslim notables of Omdurman in 1898 that Christian missionary proselytizing would be excluded from the Northern Sudan.

Cromer gave this assurance because, when the foundation of Gordon College in Khartoum in 1900 introduced into the Sudan the elements of a Western-type education, there were Sudanese *'ulamā* who firmly believed that the object of the founders was the undermining of Islam. And even today Dr. Kāmil al-Bāqir, vice-chancellor of the new Islamic University of Omdurman, points out that there is still much support in the Sudan for the view that the existing Western-oriented educational system is foreign if not hostile to Islamic culture, as well as foreign to Sudanese national aspirations and social values.

On the religious plane the Anglo-Egyptian conquest signaled the triumph of Egyptian-centered, Azharite Islam with the tacit approval of the Islamic brotherhoods, notably the Khatmiyyah, then the most influential organized anti-Mahdist group in the Sudan. The administration of Islamic law was placed in the hands of a hierarchy of Egyptian judges headed by an Egyptian *qāḍī al-quḍāt.* Only the mufti of the Sudan was a Sudanese.

By Azharite Islam, all I mean is a central expression of Sunnite Islam by the best-known school of

Islamic learning. Graduates of al-Azhar, some Egyptian, some Sudanese, have worked in the Sudan since the earliest days of the Funj sultanate, and since 1820, the year of the first Turco-Egyptian penetration, the link with al-Azhar has been strengthened except during the years of the Mahdist theocracy. Today the link tends to weaken as al-Azhar becomes embroiled in the reformist policies of the government of the United Arab Republic.

The board of *'ulamā* of the Sudan was re-created, after the Mahdist theocracy, by an act of the Condominium government in 1899 when Shaykh Aḥmad Muḥammad al-Badawī Nuqud was made its first president. The governor general used the board of *'ulamā* as a consultative committee on Muslim affairs. Part of the *'ulamā* formed themselves into an informal teaching body and began instructing students who, on completing the course, staffed the minor *sharī'a* bench. It was not until 1912 that an organized, formal institute of the Islamic sciences, a *ma'had al-'ilmī,* was created. For the first time in the history of the Sudan, "modern subjects," i.e., arithmetic, history, and elementary Arabic literature, were introduced. The Condominium government had no carefully thought-out Pan-African Muslim policy. It did not think of Islam in terms of Africa but as a potentially powerful force in the Sudan which might be rendered politically dangerous either by resurgent Mahdism or by Egyptian nationalist influence working upon Sudanese religious scruples. The Condominium introduced Western-type civil and criminal law and restricted the *sharī'a* to the realm of private status. The restriction is still in force, though its validity may be contested by those who would reintroduce an Islamic state into the Sudan.

The *ma'had al-'ilmī* provided a course in three stages; elementary, secondary and higher, with the central mosque at Omdurman as its teaching center and with classes held in circles corresponding to the *riwwāq* of al-Azhar. The *ma'had al-'ilmī* became the recognized center of Islamic learning in the Sudan. The higher stage of students claimed to be on a level roughly the same, if not higher, than the senior class in the government college in Khartoum, Gordon Memorial College. The claim is attractive but the teaching was traditional, the entrance restrictions few, government recognition of its graduates grudgingly given and those of its graduates who entered the legal department of the government miserably paid in comparison with expatriate judges of the Islamic law from al-Azhar.

It was not until 1948 that the Sudan Government formed a committee called the higher council of the *ma'had al-'ilmī* with the Grand Qadi as its chairman. This committee reformed the syllabuses, strengthened the modern subjects taught, bettered the pay of the teachers, and at last got the government to provide a special building for the institute.

Private regional Islamic institutions (there were fifty-four in 1954) struggled on to provide for the thirst for education of pupils unable to enter the state schools. The problems constituted by these regional schools caused the government in 1955 to create a department of religious affairs, which was charged with the mission of supervising and reforming the regional institutes and upgrading the Omdurman institute to the status of a university with the object of narrowing the gap between Islamic and secular educational standards and a degree of public esteem. It was intended that the higher stage of the upgraded institute would produce graduates of well-rounded education but specializing in Islamic law or in Arabic language and literature.

Finally, in 1960, the council of ministers confirmed and amplified the decision of 1955, increased the

amount of Arabic and religion in the curricula of the
state schools, thus reversing what a distinguished
Muslim critic stigmatized as the shame of the Condominium, of separating religious from secular education and of making the former less financially rewarding than the latter.

Until quite recently the academic standards of Islamic education were low. The graduates of the
ma'had al-'ilmī, the judges and Islamic notables of
the future, had no need to master an elaborate apologetic discipline for their life's work, which would be
spent among a simple, believing, unquestioning, loyal
Muslim community of peasants and pastoralists. But
it had its drawbacks. The provision of adequate Sudanese teachers in Islamic education has been a continuing difficulty. The secular world moved on; the
training of religious teachers stood still. It was becoming more and more difficult to find teaching
shaykhs who knew anything about the modern world
and hence were fitted to teach Islam in a changed atmosphere of questioning. It is a perennial problem
and it is not of course confined to Islam; Judaism and
Christianity have wrestled with the same problem.

The Sudan Government must bear some part of the
responsibility for this. As we have seen, the founders
of the Condominium, in self-protection, shielded the
Sudanese *'ulamā* from the verbal onslaughts of Christian zealots, and the *'ulamā* have not hitherto had any
need to develop an apologetic relevant to the intellectual atmosphere of the ever-questioning, unsure
modern world. Sudanese *'ālims* have preached and
taught as far afield as Indonesia and Nigeria, but their
intellectual equipment limited them to dialogue with
simple Muslims or with simple pagans. Sudanese Islam
has no Muslim Kenneth Cragg, no C. S. Lewis to explain Islam to the educated of the West. The intellectual Christian counterpart of al-Sayyid al-Hādī al-

Mahdī, judging from his public utterances, is neither of these, but Peter the Hermit.

The Role of Sudanese Islam in Africa

The foundation in 1966 of the Islamic University of Omdurman was an important event in the history of Islam in Africa. The choice of the site of the new foundation was historically apt. Omdurman was a mere village until it became in 1884 the capital of the Mahdi's realm and ever since has been regarded nostalgically by the Sudanese as the very heart-city of Sudanese Muslim culture.

The new university has already issued an official guide (*dalīl*) though it has not yet issued its syllabuses. There are at present three faculties: Islamic and civil law, an admittedly imperfect translation of sharī'a wa qānūn, arts, and a women's college. The total enrollment for the academic year 1966–67 is 425, of whom 213 are attached to the faculty of law, 196 to the faculty of arts, and 16 to the women's college.

The Islamic university is alive to its future role in Africa. It plans to attract the faithful from the countries to the west and south and to act as a religious and intellectual focus for them. In order to encourage students from foreign Muslim communities, particularly in Africa, but by no means confined to Africa, the university has this year offered fifty-two scholarships to students abroad. The institution has come under criticism from those who contend that, like the Islamic Institute of Higher Studies at Karachi it has been created by a latitudinarian government to bring the wild men of Islam, including the Mahdist backwoodsmen, into intellectual subjection to the civil power by a subtle introduction of doses of the secular world through an intellectualized Islam reinforced by "modern subjects." Others contend that government interest springs from a desire to produce broadly edu-

cated leaders of Muslim public opinion in order to reduce the possibility of a setback to the cultural development of the Sudan.

There is also felt to be a need in the Muslim Sudan
for a postsecondary college education for girls whose
parents stand in the traditional ways and wish to see
their daughters educated in a sheltered religious atmosphere away from what they would regard as the
dangerous hurly-burly of the secular, egalitarian education offered at the existing University of Khartoum.
Such a girls' college is necessarily restricted at first to
the arts and there is a widespread belief, obsolescent
in the West but strong in the Sudan, that the arts are
a more womanly object of study than the sciences.

When a questioner asked Dr. Kāmil al-Bāqir, the
vice-chancellor, what he includes under the heading
of Islamic education, he replied that the curriculum
which he envisaged consisted of many subjects having
direct and indirect bearing upon Islamic culture.
Arabic language and literature already play an important part of this culture, and with literature go logic
and philosophy. In future Islamic art and architecture
may be added. The addition and expansion of "modern subjects," he continued, was a plain necessity.
Ultimately the university hopes to add faculties of
science and of medicine when funds allow. Africans
trained only in the Islamic traditional disciplines in
the stricter sense found it difficult to obtain relevant
and adequately paid work when they returned to their
homes, particularly if they lived in states in which
Muslims were in a minority and did not participate
actively in the public services. The African role of the
Islamic University of Omdurman has been thrust upon
it by the march of events in the United Arab Republic.
As the result of the policy of the Cairo government
to bring the 'ulamā and students of al-Azhar under
some measure of its control, that formerly autono-
mous Islamic university is now only a few stages away

from the status of a branch of the Ministry of Education.

In the Sudan, on the contrary, there has been no disharmony between the Sudan Government and the Islamic university over essentials, though there have been administrative disharmonies over courses and programs. There is a legal tradition inherent in the administration of the *sharī'a* that the *qāḍī* may take direction from the Muslim state; the university governing body has not up to the present had any need to accept direction in matters of fundamental policy, a situation quite different from what it has been at al-Azhar. To several faithful in the Sudan to whom the writer broached the question it is apparent, rightly or wrongly, that the venerable al-Azhar is in secular chains but that the Islamic University of Omdurman is free. The contrast may not be lost on the rest of Muslim Africa.

This is not a criticism of United Arab Republican religious policy. It would be wrong to write that the Cairo government minimizes the value of support from the Muslim communities in the rest of Africa. And to belittle Egypt's great cultural work for Islam in a hundred fields would be silly. It would also be wrong to misinterpret that government's deliberate forcing of "reform" in the face of ineffectual *'ulamā*. An "unreformed" Muslim university of world stature situated in the capital city might have become a bastion of opposition to the regime. If foreign students are to return from al-Azhar to their homes with a respect for the institutions of the United Arab Republic and the Egyptian social and technological revolution, it is necessary that they should receive an introduction to "modern" education in order to understand them. Without such indoctrination the traditionally minded foreign students in a reformed al-Azhar would return to their native lands certainly confused and possibly hostile.

For the very concept of the secular state, in which all people dwelling within the same geographical boundaries are equal and co-operative neighbors, who partake of equal rights and duties of citizenship (including equality of opportunity in the armed forces and the civil service), irrespective of differences of race or religion or opinion or way of life, is under fire almost everywhere, though politicians habitually mask the criticism by their irrelevant party-political patter. The one-tribe state, the one-religion state, the one-color state, the all-thinking-alike state—are these not much more intelligible forms of political association for many people than the exotic product of eighteenth-century Western European political philosophy, which over a large part of the world has failed to work?

The concept of Islam can militate against the concept of the secular state in this sense. The border tensions between the Sudan and the Chad Republic in 1965 and between the Sudan and Ethiopia in 1967 may be interpreted as a regional symptom of this lack of confidence in the secular state, when the urge of *ijtihād,* to go to the assistance of coreligionists beyond your own borders, becomes stronger than the desire to live at peace with the *ahl al-dhimmah* and the *kuffār* next door. In July 1967 the Nigerian Federal commander-in-chief had reason to remind his Muslim troops engaged against the secessionists of Biafra that they were not fighting a *jihād.* A Northern Sudanese Muslim soldier in garrison in the non-Muslim South must, if he thinks at all on the matter, be caught up in the same dilemma: to whom should he give his first loyalty?

Secular government was first imposed on the Sudan by the Anglo-Egyptian Condominium in 1899, on the ashes of a Muslim theocracy which had itself succeeded a frontier form of Ottoman rule. The Sudanese have no long practice of working a government such as this. If the present Sudanese parliament decides to

abolish the existing secular state framework and to re-
establish an Islamic state, it will be resisted by many,
but it will at least be no novelty for the Sudan.

iv. AUTOCRACY AND DEMOCRACY
IN THE SOUTHERN SUDAN:
THE RISE AND FALL OF
THE CHIEFS' COURTS
by Robert O. Collins

The long period of pacification in the Southern
Sudan clearly conditioned the form of imperial rule
which, in turn, shaped the evolution of African society.
The immediate task of the Condominium government was to consolidate its authority, not expand it,
and many British officials realized that this could be
most easily and inexpensively accomplished by enlisting the traditional chiefs and headmen on the side of
the government. Kitchener implied as much in 1899,
when he laid down the general line of policy to be followed by British administrators in the Sudan:

Mudirs and Inspectors should learn to know personally
all principal men of the district and show them, by
friendly dealings and the interest taken in their individual concerns, that our object is to increase their prosperity. It is to the individual action of British officers,
working independently but with a common purpose, on
the individual natives whose confidence they have gained
that we must look for the moral and industrial regeneration of the Sudan.[1]

[1] *Annual Report on the Administration of the Sudan. 1899,*
p. 55.

What was more natural than to enlist in the task of governing the "principal men" of the district who were the accepted leaders of the community. To enroll the tribal authorities in the task of government was a practical response, arising not from any preconceived plan or political theory about ruling subject peoples but a pragmatic solution to the problem of controlling a vast land with insufficient troops and a limited number of British administrative officers. Not only would instructions from the government reach the people through the authorities they had traditionally accepted, but the enforcement could be made according to the customary laws of the tribe. Reliance on local institutions precluded the need for a centralized, costly bureaucracy and gave recognition to the tribal leaders without which they would remain a constant danger to the government. Once associated with the administration, they could hardly conspire against it with any unanimity, for to divide those leaders willing to act for the government from those who remained implacably hostile was, of course, to rule them both. To rule indirectly in the Southern Sudan was practical, conservative, and inexpensive, and as early as 1911 the official administrative policy of the Bahr al-Ghazal was "to rule the country through the medium of the tribal chiefs and sultans."[2] All the inspectors in the many districts would have agreed with H. W. Channer's statement from Tambura that "the policy of the Government here as throughout the country is to support the sultans and chiefs in their dealings with their own subjects—allowing them to administer according to their tribal customs as far as possible."[3]

Despite Channer's pretentious pronouncement, and many others like it, the actions of British administra-

[2] *The Bahr al-Ghazal Province Handbook, 1911*, p. 37.

[3] "Report on Tambura District, December 1910," by H. W. Channer, Mongalla, I/5/32.

tors in the Southern Sudan did not in practice conform
to this policy. During the first decade of British rule
the administrative officers were actually more concerned to limit the power of tribal chiefs than to support it. The British had come to the Upper Nile to
conquer, to secure, and to control, and this required
that African leaders give up their independent powers.
Moreover, British ideas of humanity and justice insisted upon limiting many practices which the chiefs
employed to retain power. Thus, administrative demands of the conquerors not only undermined traditional prerogatives but reduced the chief to a servant of
the government rather than the leader of his people.
The authority of the chief was diminished to that which
the administration, through ignorance or opportunism,
permitted him to keep, not by virtue of his position
among his people but at the convenience of the government. Those who refused to co-operate were broken.
Those who abused their position were sacked. Their
successors were chosen by the government to carry out
the government's will, and their selection frequently
did not correspond to custom or tradition. Consequently, their influence and prestige decreased and
their power was circumscribed by the intervention of
the administration. The conquest of this vast land and
the imposition upon it of an alien administration were
simply inimical to a policy of ruling indirectly.

The institutional, if not personal, authority of the
chief was most dramatically diminished by his outright
dismissal. His successor was usually a fellow tribes-
man whose primary qualification to rule was subservi-
ence to the government and willingness to co-operate
with it. Many such appointees were hacks without respect or influence among the people beyond that which
the presence of government forces could inspire. Such
a man was Chief Oku of Yambio District, who was
arbitrarily appointed in 1905 even though he was a
Zande and not from the ruling Avungara class. At the

time Oku protested and "openly stated that his following was so small that he could not maintain his position if the troops were withdrawn." Within a few months poor Oku was "continually running away and leaving his people in the lurch"—clearly not helping the cause of ruling indirectly.[4]

Occasionally, however, an appointed chief possessed sufficient administrative talent to enable him to manage his people effectively in the eyes of the British inspector even though his position would have been untenable without government support. Such was the case in the neighboring district of Maridi, where in 1906 Yango, a Zande, was made a paramount chief. Like Oku, Yango was not a member of the Avungara and "owed his present power to Government," but, unlike Oku, he ruled his region to the satisfaction of a succession of British inspectors.[5] Yango remained convinced, however, that the Avungara would murder him for his presumption to rule, and he later moved his village near Maridi in order to be close to the protection of a government post and farther away from his principal antagonist, his former Avungara chief, Mangi. The inspector, L. D. Spencer, approved Yango's move, for by encouraging Yango and securing his safety, he could divide the two chiefs and so better control them. "I have always regarded the difference between the two Sultans as advantageous to Government, as Yango would give early information here (Maridi) of any projected rising on Mangi's part," while he and his people "would still form a screen between Maridi and Mangi, as they do now."[6]

The deposition and appointment of chiefs were not

[4] Lieutenant Colonel A. Sutherland to Civil Secretary, December 20, 1905, Palace Papers, III/3/19.

[5] Sudan Intelligence Report (SIR), No. 151, App. B, February 1907.

[6] SIR, No. 162, App. E, January 1908.

confined to the Zande country. In the western Bahr al-Ghazal Chief Murad of the Kresh was dismissed "owing to his disobedience to government orders and his treacherous conduct towards the Inspector of Raga District."[7] Muhammad Sughayar, who had no claim to the position except the confidence of the inspector, E. H. Ross, was appointed in his place. Twenty years later the district officer at Raga commented that "it appears to have been the policy of the D.C. here in the early days to break down any tribal organization that ever existed—with the result that *real* chiefs do not now exist."[8] At the same time another experienced inspector in the Eastern District of the Bahr al-Ghazal blamed his predecessor for destroying any sense of tribal unity in the region by the recurrent dismissal of Dinka headmen. In Shilluk territory the situation was much the same. Within a few months after the occupation of Fashoda, H. W. Jackson was supporting Kur Nyidhok (Abd al-Fadil) for Reth of the Shilluk against two competitors. Jackson's candidate, not surprisingly, prevailed but still "required a bit of a tight hand and firm dealing with before he is of any use."[9] Evidently, British tutelage of Kur was not a success or perhaps his perpetual state of intoxication rendered him unfit for instruction in British administration. He was deposed in 1903 on the charge of unjust and oppressive rule. Kur was quickly replaced by a government nominee, Fadiet, and although the Shilluk went through the motions of a traditional election, he was regarded as a tool of the government.[10]

[7] SIR, No. 165, April 1908.

[8] D.C. Western District to Governor, Bahr al-Ghazal Province, March 4, 1930, Bahr al-Ghazal I/1/2.

[9] H. W. Jackson to Wingate, January 1899, Wingate Papers, Sudan Archive, Durham University, 269/1.

[10] F. X. Geyer, *Durch Sand, Sumpf und Wald* (Freiburg, 1914), p. 61.

Until after the World War I chiefs were dismissed and appointed in every part of the Southern Sudan controlled by British administrators with a confident casualness that soon made the event hardly worthy of mention in official reports, or if recorded, done so with a disarming, offhand manner more characteristic of the sacking of a personal servant than a community leader. "There have been a few changes of sheikhs, the only one worthy of notice being the reinstatement of Fiki instead of Bima, who has disobeyed orders."[11] The reasons for such depositions ranged from incompetence to insubordination to personality clashes with British inspectors. Invariably their successors were men primarily committed to the government and only secondarily to their people and who, as appointed, government chiefs, frequently had to endure uncomfortable, ambiguous positions. Often such a chief lapsed into menial servility, not realizing that "however much the government must insist on obedience, he is regarded as and expected to show himself, a big man amongst his own people."[12] It was difficult, however, for one to be a "big man" among his own people when his final claim to leadership rested on the judgment of the British inspector and ultimately on British arms.

If we too often interfere the people not only give us little thanks for it, but they cease to look to the Sheikh for their redress or to obey him. They play him and the government off the one against the other and consequently the Sheikh has no effective power, finding himself in an impossible position and is tempted to make a catspaw of the government.[13]

[11] SIR, No. 165, April 1908.
[12] SIR, No. 192, July 1910.
[13] Memorandum on General Administrative Policy, 1924, Civil Secretary (Civ. Sec.), I/9/30.

160   *Nations by Design*

World War I produced a profound change in British attitudes and assumptions toward subject peoples. The Olympian belief in the superiority of Western civilization had been eroded away on the battlefields of Europe; British self-confidence, which had built and ruled a vast empire, was beseiged by doubt. The war itself, the Fourteen Points, and the Mandates undermined the moral justification for imperial rule. Christianity, commerce, and civilization were no longer good enough, and even the duties and responsibilities of the White Man's Burden were now expressed in terms of trusteeship and tutelage. In the past, trusteeship had always been implied and frequently appealed to as an integral part of the imperial mission, but the generalities of the term precluded specific application and its termination consigned to some far-off future time. Now, however, when former apologies for empire appeared shabby, trusteeship took on new meaning. No longer did it mean simply protection of subject peoples, but the training of the inhabitants of tropical dependencies for self-government and eventually independence.

In club and residency British officials were generally agreed that they must now begin to train primitive peoples "to stand on their own feet." But how? Certainly, "it is wiser not to leave the matter to chance, but to see where we are going and act accordingly. We must have a definite policy . . . before the irresponsible body of half-educated officials, students, and town riff-raff takes control of the public mind."[14] The Report of the Milner Commission to Egypt and the Sudan in 1920 proposed just such a definite policy, involving the devolution of authority to the traditional rulers under British supervision. "Decentralization and employment, wherever possible, of native agencies" should be undertaken, and the Governor General of

[14] C. P. Browne, Governor, Berber, in Proceedings of Governors' Meeting, 1920, Civ. Sec. I/9/30.

the Sudan urged all British administrative officials to "foster tribal organization wherever it exists" and to submit detailed proposals on how to do it.[15] Thus, in the Sudan and elsewhere in British Africa officials sought to apply the policy of devolution of authority by encouraging and supporting those indigenous leaders they had ignored in the past. By entrusting power and authority "to the natural leaders of the people whom we must support and influence as occasion requires . . . the country will be parcelled out into nicely balanced compartments, protective glands against the septic germs which will inevitably be passed on from the Khartoum of the future." Only then will the Sudan be made "safe for autocracy."[16]

The revival of the authority of indigenous leaders was readily accepted by British officials in the Southern Sudan. Several had deplored the cavalier treatment of the indigenous authorities in the past, while others had, on their own initiative, sought to use headmen and chiefs to relieve the district commissioners of unbearable burdens of administration. Now urged by senior officials in London and Khartoum, the district officers began to seek ways and means to transfer and then to institutionalize the power and position of the native authorities in their own districts. Without exception they sought to accomplish this objective by supporting, and in some instances creating, the judicial functions of the local leaders, either traditional or appointive, by instituting a chiefs' court in which that authority could be expressed and even develop wider powers.

[15] Memorandum on General Administrative Policy and Governor General to all Governors, April 14, 1920, Civ. Sec. I/9/30.

[16] Minute by Sir John Maffey, Governor General, January 1, 1927, Civ. Sec. I/9/33.

Justice was the logical and most convenient function of authority for the British rulers to institutionalize. Unlike executive or legislative powers all societies in the Southern Sudan, even those with segmentary lineages, possessed means to redress wrongs. Indeed, the most burdensome task of the British officials was the adjudication of disputes. Thus, the prospect of turning over the endless cases involving adultery and cattle to those authorities accustomed in the past to dealing with them was a tempting incentive for British administrative officers to institutionalize indigenous judicial procedure. Moreover, the British officers were keenly aware of their own history and traditions in which the British constitution evolved from the Witenagemot and the Curia Regis. Senior officials in Khartoum might suggest the introduction of advisory councils or town committees, but local officers argued that this required a scale of literacy which was unknown in the Southern Sudan.[17] Chiefs' courts appeared the best instrument to implement the policy of devolution, the object of which was to strengthen the indigenous authorities. British officials began at once to introduce courts where they did not exist, develop those which had survived the British intervention, and institutionalize them all.

The officials first sought to institutionalize the judicial powers exercised at that time by individual chiefs. Such authorities were few and concentrated in areas where chiefship was traditional. The Bari, for instance, possessed courts of ancient lineage, and the Reth of the Shilluk had never completely surrendered his judicial functions to the British. In Zandeland the Avungara chiefs continued to adjudicate disputes despite the limitations imposed upon their authority. Elsewhere in the Southern Sudan, however, courts had to

---

[17] E. D. Bally, Governor, Bahr al-Ghazal, June 5, 1920, Civ. Sec. I/9/30.

be created by British officials from the informal and scattered materials of the past—headmen, custom, and authority. To accomplish this object, courts were created in which the local authorities sat as a panel of judges, employing local custom to settle disputes. The judges were appointed by the British district commissioner, who continued to act as an appeal court and to try criminal cases under the *Sudan Penal Code.* The introduction of a court required, however, certain regular and uniform procedures which tended to alter customary law and its application.

Some of the first courts were established in Opari District, Mongalla Province, on the pattern of the more well-developed courts in Uganda. The court, or *lukiko,* as it was called after the Uganda model, sat once a month and could impose a maximum fine of a year's imprisonment. No fee was charged, but an appeal to the district commissioner cost five piastres. Each court had a clerk who wrote up the case in English, and the docket enabled the British officials to supervise the decisions and operations without actual attendance.[18] Similar courts were soon established in the Bahr al-Ghazal, particularly among the Azande, whose Avungara chiefs showed an aptitude and enthusiasm for judicial work. By 1923 the Dinka at Rumbek were induced to have "Sittings" of an informal character to determine cattle disputes although the institution of more formal courts evolved slowly.

The courts were not meant, however, simply to enhance the power of the indigenous authorities or to relieve the district commissioner of unwanted burdens. Once the chief had been given powers, British officials hoped to awaken tribal awareness which could then rally about the chief. Soon the court was regarded as an instrument to encourage "tribal consciousness . . .

[18] R. H. Walsh to V. R. Woodland, Governor, Mongalla, May 31, 1920, Civ. Sec. I/9/30.

by the drumming to council by the chieftain of his dependants or the flying of a tribal flag over the court
house and the appointment of court police and court
clerks. Thus the establishment of a native judiciary
and the regeneration of the tribal soul are seen to be
mutually dependent and their growths intertwine."[19]

The courts proved popular. In 1923 the Latuka District courts settled 1500 cases alone, and even the
Dinka cattle "Sittings" got through so much business
that the police force was reduced and the district commissioner relieved of an enormous burden of litigation. Everywhere the courts seemed to be a dramatic
success, and the more optimistic officials predicted not
only the awakening of "tribal consciousness" but the
growth of "a national ideal, and interest in national
development, and a career for the literate members
of the community in local clerkships and municipal
enterprises."[20]

When symbols of authority are either deficient or inadequate, and where no tribal institution is capable of
modification to that end, the tribal consciousness has to
be encouraged by alien means, such as a tribal flag or
chief's police, council halls and court houses. The patriarch sitting under the village fig tree dispensing tribal
justice, the chieftain drumming his dependants to council
in the shade of the tamarind, the augur fulminating
under the shadow of his ancestral arch—in each of these
is the seed of development and the embryo of destiny.
But rocks, tamarinds, and figs are not unique, they are so
common having none but a local significance; they can
never become universal, never symbolized and for regeneration a symbol is required first and foremost. For

[19] Unsigned Memorandum on Administrative Policy, August
25, 1929, Civ. Sec. I/49/130.
[20] "Note on Administration in the Southern Sudan," J. H.
Driberg, May 25, 1924, Civ. Sec. I/9/31.

this reason, paradoxically, a council hall or court house is built before the council is mentally ready for it; it takes the place of the patriarch's and chieftain's trees and while carrying with it the old associations it adds to these and superinduces a spirit of communal homogeneity, a tribal consciousness. It is the symbol of authority the emblem to which the whole tribe or clan may look for leadership, justice, and continuity.[21]

Unhappily the ignition of tribal consciousness and the development of a national ideal never evolved out of the chiefs' courts. Increasingly, their operation came into conflict with the purpose of their foundation, and the more acute among British administrators realized that the policy of devolution contained inherent contradictions. To many Southern Sudanese the chiefs' court did not appear to embody the patriarch sitting under the fig tree dispensing tribal justice. To them the introduction of formal courts lodged in government court houses, applying a uniform code of criminal procedure and carefully watched by the district commissioner was more European than African in concept, method, and jurisdiction. "To the native mind," to quote from a Yei district diary, "our chiefs' courts are regarded rather as Government than Native courts."[22] Moreover, in some areas indigenous courts continued to function in competition with the official chiefs' courts until suppressed by the authorities. For instance in the Central District of the Equatoria Province "investigations have elicited the existence of indigenous chiefs' courts generally under the big rain chiefs assisted by tribal elders. It also appears that there is a tendency to have two chiefs, the rain chief and the government chief who is generally a relative of the former and whose *raison d'être* is to relieve him of the

[21] *Ibid.*
[22] Yei District Diary, April 1931, Civ. Sec. I/39/104.

growing burden of secular affairs."[23] Nor was this
attitude confined simply to the court as an institution.
The Africans were well aware that the British demands
for uniform court procedure, as well as more humane
penalties, seriously modified their customary law invariably in favor of Western legal concepts. Not only
did the Africans recognize that such modifications
were not along lines of their own choosing, but their
attitude toward the government frequently resulted in
unconsciously undermining the tribal law itself. In one
very complex case involving a mission girl the customary law was overruled in the missionaries' favor. The
reasoning of the chiefs was that the district commissioner and the government were friends of the mission
and that therefore the district commissioner would
wish them to rule for the missionaries in spite of the
contravention of tribal law.[24] Cases of this nature
were by no means unusual and played an important
role in diminishing the effectiveness and respect in the
eyes of the Africans for their customary law and tribal
traditions.

Although the inauguration of formal chiefs' courts
may have enhanced the prestige of the chief, it did not
necessarily strengthen his position of authority. The
demands which the administration of justice placed
upon the chiefs were considerable. No longer was justice merely a matter of dispensing decisions within the
context of tribal law from beneath a large tree. They
now involved the keeping of records, fees, transcripts
of cases in the best traditions of the English law courts.
Many chiefs had neither the ability nor the competence
to contend with court records or financial statements
and were consequently sacked and replaced by indi-

[23] Central District Intelligence Report, April 1931, Civ. Sec.
I/39/104.
[24] C. N. Wilson, D. C. Latuka, to Governor, Mongalla, September 16, 1929, Civ. Sec. I/39/42.

viduals who, the district commissioner hoped, could carry on the work more effectively. During this period the district records contain many statements on the hazardous occupation of chief:

> Chief Quoich Kuma has been making efforts at rein-statement, but they are typical and will avail him nothing.

> Chief Akoavungura has been removed from the list of chiefs courts for laziness in his work, but has been retained as regent.

> Chief Tagi, who was dismissed recently for incompetence, has shown signs of intellectual activity, and has been reinstated on probation.

> There is reason to hope that the people of the imbecile Chief Ngare will ask to be put under Chief Nginda.[25]

Indeed the principal problem of the administration was to find a sufficient number of able chiefs who could fill the role of servant to the government. V. H. Fergusson, the famous Fergie Bey, district commissioner in the Eastern District of the Bahr al-Ghazal, wrote in 1927:

> Our most difficult task at the present moment is to find suitable chiefs with sufficient tribal authority to control those under them and at the same time being capable of appreciating the Government's methods to such an extent as to be able to act as teachers of the people.[26]

Fergie Bey had a particularly difficult task in attempting to implement chiefs' courts among the Nuer and the Dinka of the Eastern District. To these tribes

[25] Iambio and Rumbek District Intelligence Reports, November 16–December 31, 1921, Civ. Sec. I/13/43.
[26] "Report by Fergusson Bey on the Eastern District," June 1927, Civ. Sec. I/13/43.

the institution of a single chiefs' court to decide all
cases in which the tribe was involved was indeed a
novelty, for neither the Nuers nor certain Dinka tribes
had ever possessed, as an indigenous institution, a
chiefs' court until one was imposed by the government. Under these conditions the attempt to apply the
principles of devolution to tribal authorities turned
from the sublime to the ridiculous. In March 1927
the governor of the Bahr al-Ghazal admitted failure
when attempting to apply chiefs' courts to the Nuer:

> Cattle cases are only heard by the cattle chief, land cases
> by the land chief, and so on . . . unfortunately, when
> we first started administering this province, this an-
> cient system was not known and it has only recently
> been realized. In our ignorance we presumed that a
> chief was a dispenser of justice in every case and was
> generally paramount in the tribe. Undoubtedly in many
> instances a kujur or witchdoctor had usurped this para-
> mount right and the old system had fallen into disuse.
> Through lack of knowledge and inexperience we failed
> to grasp this point, and jumping over this stage, we
> appointed chiefs to whom we looked as the responsible
> head. This being so, it can readily be understood that
> many cases of failure of a chief to hear cases and
> of the loser to accept the decision was due to the chief
> knowing that he could not deal with the case and to the
> parties to the action not recognizing his authority in the
> particular class of case. Hence much trouble arose which
> at times developed into the chief and his people being
> erroneously regarded as contumacious of government
> control.[27]

Thus throughout much of the Southern Sudan the
chiefs' court was regarded by Africans and admitted

[27] Governor, Bahr al-Ghazal to Civil Secretary, March 21,
1927, Civ. Sec. I/10/34.

by many district officers as fundamentally a European innovation, utilizing only to a degree, and in some cases not at all, an indigenous institution. The use of a paid government servant, for the chief was in effect just that, dispensing justice within an imposed alien framework of judicial procedure could hardly be regarded as the revitalization of tribal custom and tradition. Without constant care and attention by the district commissioner the chiefs' court would have flourished in only a few areas of the Southern Sudan, and his continual intervention was a ready reminder of the alien, nonindigenous character of the court, no matter what its espoused purpose may have been. The Legal Secretary of the Sudan Government, Nigel Davidson, clearly saw that this dependence on the district commissioner contradicted the very principle the courts were to preserve.

It (the system of chiefs' courts) does not lead anywhere in the development of devolution. It may enhance to some slight extent the prestige of the chief, but it is so entirely dependent on the D.C. that it can add very little to their authority or sense of responsibility. So far from relieving the D.C. of work or responsibility it must add very considerably to both. So far from guiding native custom gradually in a higher direction it stereotypes what is a very low standard of morality and is largely concerned in enforcing that portion of customary law which is the most debased.[28]

The basically alien procedure of the chiefs' courts should not, however, obscure their overwhelming success as judicial institutions. Grafted to African circumstances and nurtured by the district commissioner, the chiefs' courts functioned effectively in many districts

[28] "Notes on Chiefs' Courts, Yei," May 7, 1929, by Nigel Davidson, Legal Secretary, Civ. Sec. I/13/42.

even where the indigenous judicial powers of the chiefs had been minuscule. Although regarded as a government institution chiefs' courts multiplied rapidly throughout the southern provinces, adjudicating by tribal custom a host of civil cases, mostly of a domestic nature, which before had frustrated the solomonic wisdom of the district commissioners. Not only did the Africans receive better justice, but they clearly preferred it to that of British officials. The courts at once increased the powers of the chief to rule outside the court by enhancing his prestige even though he was regarded as a "government man." For the first time in over half a century the precipitous decline of the chief as a tribal leader was checked, while among those Nilotic peoples who had never recognized a permanent leader the new institution partially satisfied the needs of a changing society in which the more traditional forms of minimal government were becoming inadequate. The new chief was thus transformed from a symbol of declining authority to a position of predominance, for whether the chief and his court were created without precedent or were simply a revitalized form of an ancient tribal institution, the British acknowledged the participation of the Southern Sudanese chiefs as a part of imperial rule and consequently had to support them. Moreover as the locus of the court was the chief, the centrifugal tendencies of the more decentralized societies in the Southern Sudan were counteracted. The African was now encouraged to take a part in the regulating of his own society, thereby evolving greater interest in affairs which directly and personally affected him. The government appeared less alien, and there was less reason to feel politically restless or hopelessly indifferent.

British officials were, of course, enthusiastic over the introduction of Africans into the administration. Not only did the district commissioner in the southern provinces welcome the relief from petty judicial business, but in a more positive spirit hoped to broaden the powers of chiefs' courts to take on administrative as well as judicial functions. Even more than the British administrators in the field, officials in Khartoum and Whitehall regarded the chiefs' courts as the basis for the continuing evolution of native administration. They were deeply imbued with the principle of entrusting local administration to traditional authorities, known generally as "indirect rule," which among colonial officials had passed "through three stages, first of a useful administrative device, then that of a political doctrine, and finally that of a religious dogma."[29] Like British officials in Nigeria, Tanganyika, and Uganda, those in the Sudan soon revered the principles of indirect rule with a mystical awe. Ignoring the fact that the institution of chiefs' courts in the Southern Sudan was in many areas an alien instrument while elsewhere it was but tenuously connected with traditional institutions, the Sudan Government set out to bring uniformity to the multiplicity of courts whose diverse regulations and dissimilar powers created concern among those British officials who sought to control them.

As early as 1924 the Civil Secretary of the Sudan Government, Sir Harold MacMichael, raised the hope that a "greater degree of coordination as between the practice in different districts of the same province and in the several provinces appears to be desirable."[30] He suggested to the legal secretary that perhaps a short permissive ordinance might regularize the different practices followed in the many courts. Once again the contradiction between policy and practice was exposed. If the courts were to awaken tribal conscious-

[29] Lord Hailey, "Some Problems Dealt with in an African Survey," *International Affairs,* March/April, 1939, p. 202.

[30] Minutes of Southern Governors' Meeting, 1924, Civ. Sec. I/9/31.

ness, as many hoped, any attempt to standardize the wide range of court procedures would discourage that development. It would be a further imposition of yet another alien device on a structure whose indigenous character had already been compromised by the inclusion of non-African regulations and procedures. There was wide disagreement about the necessity for a legal basis for the chiefs' courts. The district commissioner from those districts where the courts had functioned longest not only supported an ordinance but wanted to give the chiefs greater authority by permitting them to inflict more severe penalties. Those officials from districts, usually in the Nilotic regions, where the courts were still an innovation and the judges inexperienced opposed any regulation which might restrict their evolution and confine experimentation. At the annual meeting of the Southern governors in 1925 they agreed that the chiefs' courts were "still in a very experimental and primitive stage and as there is a considerable divergence in the way they are conducted, due mainly to different local conditions," no special legislation was required. Of course, without enabling legislation the courts had no legal basis, being dependent for their existence and jurisdiction on the whim of the district commissioner.

Prodded by the civil secretary, the governors continued to debate the need to regularize the chiefs' courts, and in 1926 they seriously considered but failed to adopt the Court of Elders Ordinance, which had been designed for use in the Northern Sudan. For the next three years widespread, thorough discussions and exchanges took place among British officials in the South and with senior officials in Khartoum. As the courts proliferated and the chiefs gained experience in rudimentary judicial procedure, the pressure by the Southern governors for standardization increased, on the one hand, while on the other the authorities at Khartoum became concerned that the courts had no legal sanction. Finally, in December 1929, at a conference of the governors, representatives of the civil secretary and the legal secretary, a draft Chiefs' Court Ordinance was drawn up to sanction these courts and, "where necessary to control all these varieties of courts," while giving constitutional recognition to the execution of the courts' decisions.[31]

To draft a suitable ordinance providing flexibility, on the one hand, and standardization, on the other, at first defied even the talents of the legal secretary. For another year draft and counterdraft, suggestion and countersuggestion were shuttled back and forth between Khartoum and the Southern Sudan until the Chiefs' Court Ordinance was finally adopted in 1931, but it was not until the summer of 1932 that the appropriate warrants were drafted to invest the courts with legal sanction. The last requirement of institutionalization, legal recognition, had been achieved.

Like most institutions once established, the system of chiefs' courts became more refined and more complex. The original courts (called "B" courts) were given increasing responsibility by being allowed to assign greater penalties—up to two years' imprisonment, twenty-five-piastre fine, and twenty lashes—while below the "B" courts a large number of "A" courts were founded which could grant only minor sentences—up to three months' imprisonment, two-piastre fine, and ten lashes. Thus, the "B" courts rapidly became courts of appeal and were also used as a consultative body by the district commissioner. Some hoped the "B" courts would form the embryo of future advisory councils, just as the "A" courts tended to supplement vil-

[31] Explanatory Note—Chiefs' Courts Ordinance—Civ. Sec. I/13/42. At that time the Bahr al-Ghazal had forty-six courts which tried 5522 cases in 1929. Mongalla possessed sixteen courts, trying 3363 cases, and Upper Nile Province had forty-three courts with 2500 cases.

lage councils. In this way a judicial institution would be transformed first into elementary councils giving advice and ultimately into an instrument of local government with legislative and executive powers. Most officials predicted that the municipal council would be the first institution to emerge from the chiefs' court.

Such a development of the "B" courts, however, would require larger territorial units, which in turn would require transcending tribal distinctions when the purpose of devolution was to encourage the growth of tribal consciousness. True, the tribe in Britain was a transitory unit, and "it does not necessarily follow that we are forbidden to cut it out of the evolutionary process."[32] Nevertheless, the means and ends of chiefs' courts appeared antagonistic and presented contradictions which were only resolved when the intervention of Sudanese nationalism terminated the evolution of the courts.

British administrators were not unaware of the dangers inherent in the institutionalization of the chiefs' court. Throughout the decade before World War I increasing criticism of indirect rule and its institutions provoked passionate defenses, on the one hand, and re-examination on the other. The practitioners of indirect rule vehemently denied the charge that the chiefs' courts were designed to "make the natives stay put."[33] They readily admitted that they had introduced autocratic institutions into societies that had hitherto been characterized by a strong grass-roots democracy, but the chiefs' court was but a transitional stage to a wider application of representative government. The introduction of the courts created a paradox between the theory and practice of indirect rule, but the purpose was not to create static institutions.

[32] "The Future of Native Administration in Mongalla," Civ. Sec. I/39/105.
[33] *Ibid.*

"There must be and should be a change. The plea of the advocates of Indirect Rule is that as far as possible that change should be evolutionary and not arbitrary."[34] And so evolution it was to be, and the district commissioners set about to develop the institution which they had created with the exhortations of the governor general spurring them on.

The humanitarian aspect of our administration, it seems to me, is to facilitate an evolution of native organs to assist primitive folk to meet—profitably to them—radical changes of their circumstances that we as pioneers of European civilization are bound to effect. Indirect Rule —not the best or the wisest of them—seemed at times to ignore this ultimate objective and to aim at a stationary condition. This is . . . a negation of our trusteeship as properly understood. We must be builders, not mere caretakers."[35]

And so they began to build. The chiefs' courts throughout the Southern Sudan were amalgamated into larger units and with greater powers. In 1936, for instance, thirteen "A" courts in four districts were replaced by four courts with permission to mete out greater penalties.[36] Among the Dinka and the Nuer such development proceeded more slowly than in the non-Nilotic regions. The Azande in the west and the peoples east of the Nile took most readily to native administration. The lesser courts functioned smoothly, appeals being taken to the central courts which in Zandeland began to exercise nonjudicial functions, including registration and collection of poll tax and numerous minor administrative matters.

[34] *Ibid.*

[35] Governor General to Governor Mongalla, March 23, 1935, Civ. Sec. I/39/105.

[36] Governor, Equatoria, to Civil Secretary, February 20, 1936, Civ. Sec. I/39/105.

Then suddenly the halcyon days of quiet, conservative development of the courts came to an end. The evolution of this institution as a means of ever-increasing control in local and provincial affairs by the Southern Sudanese was brought to a rude halt during World War II. In those difficult and turbulent years new British administrators appeared and remained only a short time. The experience, knowledge, and commitment to develop the courts from a judicial to an executive and legislative function departed with the British officials, and the courts became during World War II what the critics of indirect rule had feared native administration would become in the Depression—preservers of the status quo and an autocratic institution in an age of democracy.

The end of the war brought no change in the role of the chiefs' courts. There were no pleas for "back to normalcy," and few were the British officials who naïvely anticipated to take up the evolutionary process of the courts where they had left off in 1939. The gradual development of the courts into wider institutions of government could not stand against the rising tide of Sudanese nationalism. British administrators in the South soon found themselves confronted by new institutions—Advisory Councils for the Northern Sudan, followed by the demand for a Legislative Council for the whole of the Sudan which would ultimately develop into a parliament. Certainly, participation in a court where the principal concerns were adultery and cattle seemed inadequate preparation to deal with the larger questions of nation-building being considered by the advisory and legislative bodies at Khartoum. Moreover, the position of the chief was now challenged for the first time by a new class of mission-educated civil servants who could claim a position of authority only by appealing to a democratic process just as the chief sought to justify his authority by appeals to autocracy—and, as the Governor General of the Sudan had observed twenty years before, the dice were loaded in favor of the former.

Although the South was largely represented by chiefs at the Juba Conference of 1947, which had been called to determine the future of the Southern Sudan, their influence was soon overwhelmed by the demands by the elite, both North and South, for democracy. British officials desperately sought to fashion provincial councils in the South as an intermediary instrument of local government between the courts and the legislative council in Khartoum. They failed. On the one hand, the obstacles against establishing provincial councils were very great. "Language alone prevents it," lamented one district commissioner, and the governor of the Upper Nile Province commented that the only experience with government by the Dinka— "sitting under a tree smoking a pipe and dealing with their interminable cases by Tribal Law"—made them ill suited to discuss larger questions.[37] On the other hand, the purpose of the councils compromised their implementation. From the beginning they were regarded by many officials not so much the next step in the evolution of the chiefs' court from local judicial institution to a provincial advisory one, but to provide a conservative mechanism for the indirect election of representatives to the central legislative council. Such an objective could hardly stand against the appeals by Sudanese nationalists for democracy. If the councils had been in operation, they might have been used to elect such representatives. To create them, however, for that purpose rendered them unnecessary. The elections of 1952 appeared, to the Sudanese elite, to confirm that opinion.

Thus the chiefs' courts had failed to accomplish

[37] "Notes on Proposed Southern Conference," June 1947 and Governor, Upper Nile Province to Civil Secretary, October 19, 1948, Bahr al-Ghazal, I/1/2.

their wider objective. They strengthened the authority of the chiefs, where they were present, and created new and autocratic authorities where they had not previously existed. They provided a useful judicial institution to settle local litigation and many developed sufficiently to take on minor executive functions and administrative duties. In some districts the courts did awake tribal consciousness and rally tribal unity, but although this may have been regarded as a wholesome and progressive development in the interwar years, it was looked upon as a source of reaction in the years after World War II. The courts never evolved beyond that, however. They never provided a national ideal and in fact proved an obstacle to national development. They never provided a career for the African elite beyond that of clerkships, and in fact alienated this class and turned them toward more radical, democratic means of participation in the political process. To them the chiefs' courts were the bastion of local loyalties, not the citadel of nationhood. As an institution, the courts have never resolved this conflict, and today remain a purely local judicial institution.

ROBERT R. GRIFFETH
MARTIN A. KLEIN
G. WESLEY JOHNSON
CHEIKH TIDIANE SY

Development Institutions in Historical Perspective: Senegal

i. INTRODUCTORY NOTE
by Robert R. Griffeth

Robert R. Griffeth is an assistant professor in African history at the University of California at Los Angeles. He has just returned from a year in West Africa, where he was working on a research project.

The central event of modern Senegalese history was undoubtedly the conquest of its peoples by France during the latter half of the nineteenth century. So overwhelmingly important has this event loomed in the eyes of those who have sought to understand institution-building processes there that the history of Senegal has frequently been presented from a somewhat two-dimensional perspective. The essence of this perspective is that the conditions of life in Senegal were so drastically altered by the imposition of alien authority that the preconquest institutions encompassing the political, social, and economic life of her peoples were made hopelessly outmoded and came into the twentieth century ill equipped for the realities of a modern world.[1] Such institutions are frequently labeled as "traditional," belonging to an African era irrevocably concluded by outside conquest. The corollary of this view is that all which followed the conquest is best understood by examining the processes whereby "traditional" institutions are subjected to the pressures of "modernization" which force them either to accommodate and adapt or to wither away.

Notwithstanding the more subtle views of those who see institutional and structural change as an extremely complex process where traditional institutions are modernized at differential rates of change, this general perspective still passes too quickly by a significant dimension of historical understanding.[2] In the case of Senegal, this might be called the internal, or African, dimension,

[1] From the self-justificatory literature produced by the conquerors themselves such as Paul Gafferel's *Le Sénégal et le Soudan Français* (Paris, 1892), down to and including contemporary works of synthesis such as E. Séré de Rivières, *Sénégal-Dakar* (Paris, 1953) and H. Deschamps, *Le Sénégal et la Gambie* (Paris, 1965), the focus of attention has remained on the attempts of France to "modernize" her colony, even after independence was achieved. Perhaps it is this practical, utilitarian view that obscures the relevance of the lines of historical analysis suggested in these papers.

[2] C. S. Whitaker's brilliant critical analysis of the theoretical literature on the concept of political change, "A Dysrythmic Process of Political Change," *World Politics* (Vol. XIX, 2, January 1967, pp. 190–217) demonstrates the perils of employing dichotomous models such as the "traditional-modern" one. Indeed, Whitaker's careful analysis of Northern Nigeria in the 1950s using the notion of a dysrythmic process of change might be well suited to a study of Senegalese institutions over a much longer time span.

a perspective which predicates processes of institution-building that conform more to the logic of an internally situated dynamic than to the pressures of external demand to accommodate and adapt.

From this internal point of view it does not always make good historical sense to speak of institutional and structural change as a process primarily involving transformations from traditional African forms to modern, Western ones. For the historian, there is sometimes an unhappy quality of predestination about change measured in these terms which masks other levels of understanding. In a similar vein, the complementary notion of conflict and harmonization is too commonly restricted to this apparently overriding issue of development *as* modernization. This neatly balanced dialectical concept often applies with equal force to an understanding of the dynamics of development processes on the internal level.[3]

In the historical study of Senegalese institutions, if these criticisms are valid, one may detect parallel lines of development in key areas of political, social, intellectual, and economic life. The use of the term parallel in reference to spheres of development does not, of course, mean that those spheres operate independently. On the other hand, only with the assistance of such an analytical device is it possible to trace change from the historical point of view; for it allows a look at aspects of cultural dynamics that antedate and carry beyond the central events of alien conquest.

The tendency towards modernization—a direct outgrowth of alien influence following conquest—is best represented by the growth of urban centers in Senegal after the 1850s. The communes as they evolved into urban entities acted as the catalysts molding change and directing it into modern channels. In the long view of Senegalese history, the role of the cities will surely rank far

[3] In particular, see Whitaker's critique, *ibid.* pp. 199–202.

above the relatively brief interlude of outside political control as the key ingredient in the complex processes of modern institution-building. As nearly everywhere, both in Africa and the rest of the world, the conditions and opportunities of city life in Senegal provided the most favorable milieu for the rapid growth of new and radically restructured institutions.[4] The new cast given to chiefship, on the other hand, did not have such a pronounced effect until well into the colonial period.[5]

From the perspective of internally fostered change, however, a fundamental transformation of Senegalese life was inspired by a development that owes little—apart from a tendency to accelerate that development—to alien pressures. That development might be called, in general terms, the Islamicization of Senegal. The steady growth of Muslim brotherhoods which transcend ethnic cleavages and the rise of a pervasive maraboutic power which exercises deep influence in large sectors of Senegalese political, social, intellectual, and economic life are consequences of events that antedate the French conquest by more than four generations.[6] Many authors have been tempted to see this outburst of Islamic activity primarily in terms of reaction and conservative accommodation to the overwhelming power of the alien intruder.[7] While there is certainly truth in this view, it

[4] See G. Wesley Johnson's paper, below.

[5] See Martin A. Klein's paper, below.

[6] On the Islamicization theme, see Robert R. Griffeth and Tidiane Sy's papers.

[7] Since the Futa Toro region of the Senegal Valley was a seedbed of reforming Islamic ideology which served to inspire Muslim groups throughout West Africa; and since many of these groups proved in the event to be the most vigorous resisters to European encroachment in the latter part of the nineteenth century, Islam is frequently equated with either reaction or ultraconservative accommodation. On the first of these themes, resistance, see J. D. Hargreaves, *West Africa: The Former French States* (Englewood Cliffs, N.J., 1967), pp. 49–58,

nonetheless overlooks the vigorous features of Islamic development that have been recanting the framework of Senegalese life over a period of nearly two hundred years.

The following set of four papers is an attempt to follow out and interpret these two parallel themes in Senegalese history by focusing primarily upon the development of political institutions. Chronologically, the starting point should be 1776. Robert Griffeth argues in the first paper that Islamic reform appeared in that year as a substantive political force presaged by the Tokolor overthrow of the pagan Denianke dynasty in the Futa Toro. From that point forward, the dual processes of harmonization and conflict in Senegalese institution-building invariably centered upon the rapid spread of an Islamic ideology which sought to challenge and supplant patterns of vested local interest with an all-embracing, rigorous new pattern of Muslim rule. The leaders of this revolutionary movement in the nineteenth century and their heirs become the main agents of internally based institutional change on into the twentieth century.

Not until the 1850s and later did the leaders of this Islamic revolution come against a challenge that effectively limited and redirected the avenues of change. But with the military initiatives of Faidherbe in the 1850s and 1860s and the full-blown pattern of French conquest in the '80s and '90s, new conditions appeared in the actual and effective presence of alien rulers throughout the land. One consequence was that the "traditional" pagan chiefs of Senegal who had resisted or made grudging compromises with Muslim chiefs were now faced with an altered set of prospects. Out of this three-cornered conflict—between French authority, aggressive Muslim leaders, and pagan chiefs—emerged new patterns

92–96; on the second theme, conservative accommodation, see J. C. Froelich, *Les musulmans d'Afrique noire* (Paris, 1962), pp. 101–13.

of political authority. These new patterns owed as much
to forces which had been set in motion prior to the conquest as they did to the designs of the French conquerors. Thus Martin Klein takes the narrative on by
outlining this evolution in the role of chief from mid-
century to 1914.

The historical outline of the development of Senegalese political institutions in the twentieth century is drawn
out with reference to the parallel set of themes in the
papers by G. Wesley Johnson and Cheikh Tidiane Sy.
Mr. Johnson traces the growth of modern political institutions, particularly in reference to elite group structure and party formation since 1914. Mr. Sy examines a
contemporary expression of Islamic institution-building in
the absolutely crucial development of the leading Muslim brotherhoods in Senegal.

Taken separately, these four contributions illuminate
particular aspects of political institution-building in various parts of Senegal at differing time periods. Taken
together, it is hoped that the four papers will shed some
light on the nature of the underlying processes which
have been gradually transforming Senegalese modes of
political life over nearly two centuries.

ii. THE ISLAMIC THEME IN SENEGALESE
INSTITUTION-BUILDING:
THE NINETEENTH CENTURY
by Robert R. Griffeth

The spread of Islamic ideas and institutions into and
beyond Senegal is a basic theme of its historical evolution. Over a thousand years ago, various inhabitants
of the Senegal River Valley were among the first sub-

Saharan Africans to embrace the creed and practices of that vigorous world religion, a heritage which has never since been lost. Throughout the intervening centuries the political and dynastic history of Senegal has experienced many changes in which non-Muslim kings and chiefs exerted their supremacy for varying periods of time over the adherents of Islam. But the absorption of new and reforming ideas, particularly from the stimulus of events in Northwest Africa, ultimately led to a political and social revolution which produced sweeping consequences for Senegal beginning in the year 1776.[1]

The agents of this Islamic revolution were the *torodbe* (clerical) class of the Tokolor peoples who inhabit the middle section of the Senegal Valley. Under the leadership of a talented *torodbe* cleric named Sulaiman Bal, the pagan rulers of the region (the Fulbe Denyanke dynasty) were overthrown. In place of the Denyanke, whose power was based upon their status as a warrior class (*tyeddo*), a Muslim state was created in which the elective principle of kingship was instituted. Chiefs of the various regions of Futa Toro swore allegiance to one of their number called the *almami*. The first *almami*, 'Abd al-Qadir, sought to embody both political and religious rule in one person whose authority was derived from the divine law of Islam. This attempt was only partially successful, for the elective system left open wide areas of power to local chiefs.[2] On the other hand, the new system did provide an extremely effective means of spreading Islamic influence to neighboring peoples, since the re-

[1] All accounts which attempt to fix a date for the beginning of the *jihad* in Futa Toro draw upon the oral compilation of Siré Abbas Soh, *Chroniques de Fouta Sénégalais,* edited by H. Gagen et M. Delafosse (Paris, 1913).

[2] P. Marty, *L'Islam en Mauritanie et au Sénégal* (Paris, 1915–16), pp. 275–76.

ligious authority of the *almami* was unimpaired by local disputes and continued to grow.

The underlying causes of this revolution were certainly drawn as much from social and economic discontents as they were from any sense of religious grievance. However, it should be emphasized that the new reforming wave ushered in by Sulaiman Bal and Bal and 'Abd al-Qadir did much more than merely replace a class of hated oppressors. This *jihad* laid the foundations for a new social, political, and economic order. This war waged in the name of the Prophet established important directions of change and institutions of such durable qualities that they have left imprints visible in Senegal to this day.

These new directions were expressed in three major ways. The first was to elevate the importance of holy men, the teachers (*marabouts*), who were the vanguard agents of reforming Islamic ideology. In the nineteenth century the role played by marabouts in introducing to Senegal ideas current in other parts of the Muslim world—particularly the concept of the religious fraternity—provided a framework in which reform could be institutionalized.[3]

The second expression of a new direction in Senegal is associated with the rise of certain marabouts who were at the same time capable military leaders. This distinction was crucially important, for, most of the societies of the Western Sudan had long known and sheltered Koranic teachers in their midst—both pagan as well as Muslim communities. But an affective chal-

---

[3] P. Marty, *Études sur l'Islam au Sénégal* (Paris, 1917), two volumes. In spite of his many errors of fact, frequently coupled to what often appears as an anti-Muslim bias, Marty's studies of Islam in the various parts of the old *A.O.F.* represent an incredibly rich collection of data. These two volumes contain much on the activities of maraboutic families, teachers, and the content of what was taught by them.

lenge to the old order of society depended upon leaders who could attend to the practical details of enforcing a new order. Following 'Abd al-Qadir, the figure whose name is most directly associated with militant Islam in Senegal is al-hajj 'Umar Tal, a *torodbe* of the Futa Toro. Although 'Umar was forestalled by the French from making any territorial acquisitions in Senegal during his career of state-building (late 1840s to 1864), the example of what he accomplished in the mid-Niger region proved to be extremely attractive to a number of Senegalese leaders who preached the sorts of reform that inspired the *tijaniyya* movement of Umar.[4] Among these leaders the names of Maba (in the Gambia, Sine, and Saloum region), Lat Dior (in Cayor Province), Abdul Bubakar (in the Futa Toro), and Mamadu Lamine (in the Guidimakha region of the upper Senegal valley) stand out. These names have become known in contemporary textbooks primarily because all were prime figures in military movement that resisted French expansion. Of perhaps greater importance, however, Umar and these four among those who took up his cause were instrumental in spreading social and political institutions based upon the rule of Islamic law (the *shari'a*) and in propagating the *tijaniyya* order with its radical doctrines of social equality of believers.[5]

A third direction of lasting importance derived from the ways in which French officials came to interpret the activities, and successes, of maraboutic leadership. From an attitude of great hostility fostered by the inhabitants of the tiny colonial settlements against the

[4] J. Abun Nasr, *The Tijaniyya: A Sufi Order in the Modern World* (London, 1965).

[5] *Ibid.* Despite the fact the Umar introduced a principle of succession based upon devolving authority on family members, there was a very distinct strain of egalitarianism in this brotherhood that represented a radical departure from the usual patterns of social hierarchization.

Muslim chiefs who ruled the river valley in the 1850s there developed, especially in the period of Faidherbe's governorships (1854–61, 1862–64), a rather more positive attitude toward Islamic institutions. Thus from the earlier period which was characterized by more or less paranoic fears about Muslim fanaticism against "whites" colonial officialdom came to appreciate that Muslim chiefs, working through Islamic institutions of law, might be their greatest allies in stabilizing French rule over the colony.[6]

The cumulative effect of these three new directions was to set the pattern for a significant change in the social and political order of Senegal as the lands which comprised that unit were brought into the twentieth century as a unitary entity. To reiterate the point of emphasis here, this pattern—based upon Islamicization of many of the diverse ethnic groups which formed the population of the colony—was both initiated and carried through by reform-minded Africans. It was not, as some have hinted,[7] merely the means of accommodation—or harmonization—with the harsh facts of alien rule. Perhaps the most significant test of this interpretation is that it was ultimately the alien ruler (and later on, the Western ruling elite) who came to recognize the strength of this new social order even when that recognition flew in the face of such grandiose schemes as the policy of cultural assimilation.

[6] The anti-Muslim view is found in F. Carrère and P. Holle, *De la Sénégambie Française* (Paris, 1885), p. 135. The more positive outlook is expressed by Faidherbe himself in his *Le Sénégal; la France dans l'Afrique occidentale* (Paris, 1889). (See also Klein's paper, below).

[7] J. C. Froelich, *Les Musulmans d'Afrique Noire* (Paris, 1962), pp. 101–12. A somewhat more balanced view may be found in S. J. Trimingham's *A History of Islam in West Africa* (Oxford, 1962), pp. 232–33, although Trimingham, too, sees the success of contemporary Islam primarily in terms of value accommodation to European rule.

There are many levels on which this process can be studied, going from the psychological (reorientation of life values that acceptance of a universalist religion requires)[8] to the demographic (altered land distribution and use patterns under the system of maraboutic control).[9] For purposes of illustration in this paper, however, a brief look at the processes of change during the time of militant maraboutic leadership in the nineteenth century should suffice.

The central problem faced by the militant reformers was to overcome resistance on the part of local chiefs who jealously guarded their prerogatives of rule. This was true regardless of the religious adherence professed by a particular chief. So forceful was the challenge that sweeping reform, particularly the introduction of the *shari'a*, promised that Muslim and pagan chief alike sought to negate the activities of revolutionary preachers in their midst. This accounts for the anomalies of the electoral system instituted in the Futa Toro at the time of the original *jihad* where 'Abd al-Qadir was forced to dilute his reformist ambitions by guaranteeing to the strongest rulers of the region a large measure of local autonomy. Similarly, when al-hajj 'Umar began to preach reform along *tijani* lines in the middle valley, his most serious opponents were at first these very chiefs who constituted the body of electors for the *almami*-ship.

When the French began interior expansion in earnest, they were thus confronted by a situation in which local chiefs were locked in a desperate struggle with the militant marabouts. In so far as their conquest of

[8] See relevant portions of S. J. Trimingham, *Islam in West Africa* (Oxford, 1961), for a wide-ranging analysis on this level.

[9] A good recent example of this approach may be seen in J. L. Boutillier, et al., *La Moyenne Vallée du Sénégal* (Paris, 1962).

Senegal was affected, the French employed either local chiefs or, occasionally, *jihad* leaders—whichever
best suited the aims of territorial aggrandizement in a
particular instance. But it must be emphasized that
this practical use of "divide-and-rule" tactics by the
French only interrupted and sometimes deflected tendencies that were in progress long before their arrival
on the scene. The conquest accelerated in some cases
and impeded in others this fundamental process of
Islamicization: but it neither created nor sanctified
that process throughout the three generations of imperial control.

A second noteworthy feature of this revolutionary impetus is to be found in the wide appeal it possessed. The fact that *jihad* leaders were also the leaders of movements to resist the French has obscured
the point that other reasons, beyond these involved
in the attempts to forestall alien control by Europeans,
led men to take up the banner of reformist Islam.
While al-hajj 'Umar was unable to establish his control over the Futa Toro, partly owing to local resistance and partly owing to the simultaneous arrival
there of French military columns, the central core of
his army was formed of recruits from that very region.
During this period the appeal to these Tokolor who
joined forces with 'Umar was as much the positive one
which his new order promised as it was the negative
one of resistance.

And so it may have been with later leaders. Certainly the vigor of Maba's movement in the Gambia
area and Lat Dior's in Cayor had attractions that
went beyond the purely negative ones associated with
resistance to the French; for if this were not so, how
then would they have been able to attract the rather
sizable followings they mustered in face of the continuing resentments expressed by the local chiefs? The
same is true regarding the success of Abdul Bubakar

in the Futa Toro and Mamadu Lamine in the upper Senegal region. A common thread woven through all these movements is that they represent an internal social upheaval in which the promise of a new social order is the principal motivating influence. The later, startling successes of preaching (as opposed to militant) *marabouts*[10] in reordering the institutions of Senegalese life seem not to be so startling if this interpretation is correct.

A final point which has some relevance for the theme of harmonization also concerns the breadth of this appeal to Islamic reform. It is that the appeal cut very deeply across the lines of ethnic cleavage. Whereas 'Umar and Abdul Bubakar were both Tokolor whose followings were made up largely of their fellow countrymen, much of Maba's retinue came from Mande groups, Lat Dior's army was Wolof, and Mamadu Lamine drew upon the Seninke peoples of his home region. A major study which details the personal connections among these leaders has not been attempted. In the absence of such a study, the prevailing interpretations have focused upon the common ground that all were movements that were basically engaged in resistance to the French.[11] And from that common ground the next logical step was to demonstrate that they were thus something akin to "protonationalist" movements each consisting largely of cohesive, homo-

[10] This subject, the rapid spread of movements such as the Muridiyya, led by Ahmed Bamba, have received more attention from scholars than similar topics in the earlier period. Perhaps this accounts for the view expressed in them that conversion to Islam was sudden, resulting largely from the conditions created by colonial conquest (for example see Trimingham, *A History of Islam in West Africa*, p. 227).

[11] A very able exposition of this theme may be found in J. D. Hargreave's recent survey, *West Africa: The former French states* (Englewood Cliffs, N.J., 1967), pp. 97–112.

geneous ethnic followings.[12] Such interpretations over-look the higher level of common ground—participation in acts that promoted wide-scale social and political change—that is also relevant to an understanding of them.

The major contention of this paper is, therefore, that a three-dimensional understanding of the processes of institution-building in Senegal must take into account the lines of internally fostered social change—principally those which have molded the Islamic institutions of so many Senegalese—if contemporary development plans are to possess depth of meaning.

iii. THE EVOLUTION OF THE "CHEFFERIE" IN SENEGAL
by Martin A. Klein

> *Martin A. Klein is Professor of History at the University of California at Berkeley. He is the author of numerous papers on Senegal and Senegambia.*

The history of African political institutions during the colonial period is a subject for which extensive documentation is available. In spite of this, most descriptions of the transformation of these institu-

---

[12] An interesting example of this view, though not directed to Senegal, is included in J. Suret-Canale's, *Afrique noire,* Vol. I (Paris, 1962), pp. 201–10.

tions rely more heavily on the works of colonial political theorists than on an examination of processes of change in particular societies. We read of "direct rule" and "indirect rule" without any clear picture of the distribution of power or authority at given periods of time. In fact, most administrators were rather pragmatic. They had to be in order to survive. This paper will examine the interaction between administrators and the societies they ruled in Senegal.[1]

Until the appointment of Major L. L. C. Faidherbe as governor of Senegal in 1854, France's domain consisted of two island communities and a series of trading posts for which France paid tribute to African rulers, and in most cases, a generous export tax.[2] In several military campaigns, Faidherbe freed France from financial obligations to African rulers, asserted French military supremacy, and forced the concession of low tariffs. A number of new forts were created, but at most of these French rule was asserted only within cannon range of the post. Only in areas near St. Louis and Dakar did France take political control. In these areas, a head tax was established and chiefs were appointed, generally from those traditional chiefs who had sided with the French in order to free themselves from the domination of traditional enemies or overlords, Faidherbe had been impressed with the experience of the *bureaux arabes* in Algeria and was convinced that a small group of alien officers could control an African population by confirming and manipulating traditional chiefs. Faidherbe's thinking differed from

[1] For a more detailed description of the problems raised in this paper, see Martin Klein, *Islam and Imperialism in Senegal: Sine-Saloum 1847–1914* (Stanford, 1967), and "Chiefship in Sine-Saloum 1887–1914" in Victor Turner (ed.) *Societal Aspects of Colonialism* (Stanford, forthcoming).

[2] The best introduction to Senegalese history is Hubert Deschamps, *Le Sénégal et la Gambie* (Paris, 1964).

that of Lord Frederick Lugard primarily in that he sought to preserve traditional chiefs without perpetuating the façade of the traditional state. This remained a basic difference between French and British policy.

In 1862, legislation announced by Governor Jauréguibery regulated the income due to the chief from the peasant and provided for the chief to turn a percentage of all criminal penalties over to the administration. It is probable that this was never effectively enforced. In some villages refractory to French authority, taxes were not regularly collected for over twenty years. In others, taxes were seen largely as tribute and chiefs collaborated with both the French and their enemies. French authority sat lightly on these limited areas and they accepted it largely because it involved protection from traditional enemies. Outside this small area, France's relationship with Senegalese states was what D. A. Low has called "sway." French power was a key point of reference in all conflicts and those who sought power kept the French informed of their intentions and their friendship.[3]

From 1879 on, the French gradually extended their control over the rest of what is now Senegal. By 1891, this task was largely completed. During this same period, the colonial administration passed from military to civilian control and professional administrators replaced military officers. These early civilian administrators tended to be republicans and were more influenced by the ideal of political and cultural assimilation than their military predecessors had been. Many of them blithely assumed that they could transform African societies into carbon copies of a French ideal. In none was this goal more unrealistically expressed than the first civilian governor, René Servatius:

[3] D. A. Low, "Lion Rampant," *Journal of Commonwealth Political Studies*, II (1964), pp. 235–52.

The goal of France in Senegal is manifest in the spirit of the republican government which presides over its destinies . . . she should lead to her all nearby peoples, not by force of arms, but by the natural attraction which free institutions exercise on all men. In other words, we must lead the barbarous peoples of Senegal, without violence, successively to the status of subjects and then of French citizens. The day when we will have constituted the peoples of Senegambia into municipal institutions, the day when each village will have become a *commune de plein exercice,* in that day, France will have finished her work.[4]

For Servatius, it was essential for Africans to become subjects before they could become citizens. To do this, of course, it was necessary to attack the decision-making machinery of traditional society. Ironically, for those officials who were genuinely assimilationist, the day when Africans would participate on a large scale in French or French type political institutions could only be brought about by a period of enlightened despotism. The effect, however, was simply to maximize the arbitrary power of the administrator.

From an early date, the idealistic notions of men like Servatius were consigned to textbooks on colonial theory. The colonial regime found itself involved with political pressures both in France and in the colonies that limited its freedom of action. First there were the humanitarian forces on the French Left. In 1880, Victor Schoelcher, the aging *doyen* of the French abolitionists, gave a speech in the French Senate, in which he charged that the slave trade was being conducted under the French flag.[5] Within a year,

[4] Report addressed to Minister of the Navy, March 8, 1883, *Situation Politique,* Archives of the Republic of Senegal.

[5] Victor Schoelcher, *L'Esclavage au Sénégal en 1880* (Paris, 1880).

French courts in Africa began freeing slaves in areas under French administration. This led to the massive migration of slave-owning Fulbe pastoralists from the *cercle* of St. Louis and forced the administration to disannex this area and place it under a protectorate. Until 1920, most of Senegal was at least in theory ruled under a series of protectorate treaties.[6]

Second, the funds available to administer the newly acquired empire were limited. French rural interests did not care whether France had an empire.[7] They did object to paying for one and consistently opposed colonial appropriations in the French Chamber of Deputies. The Grand Conseil of Senegal, representing the Four Communes, was also loath to finance the administration's projects and insisted on using funds at its command for its own interests.

Third, the administration was under pressure from commercial houses to facilitate the expansion of the peanut trade. Thus, the administration had to develop the economy and restrict institutions offensive to European humanitarians, but it had limited forces at its command. The first administrator in a district was often aided only by a clerk and interpreter. At best, he had a small force of Africans, most of them, like himself, strangers to the district. Though often scornful of the chiefs, the early administrators were completely dependent on them, and in some cases, the chiefs completely controlled access to the administrator. In Nioro, for example, the chief actually had the co-operation of *tirailleurs* in preventing peasants from seeing the

[6] André Devaulx, *Les Protectorats de la France en Afrique* (Paris, 1903). Unfortunately, though Devaulx offers extensive information on the use of protectorates, he says very little about the practical issues involved in different areas.

[7] Hubert Deschamps, *Méthodes et doctrines coloniales de la France* (Paris, 1953), pp. 150–54.

administrator without his approval. One French official described the dilemma of the administrator on tour:

> He is almost always accompanied by local chiefs escorted by a troop of horsemen and foot soldiers who naturally live on the country. A good guard is kept around him; only those who have the consent of the chief can approach him. Those who would do without this formality will pay dearly for their audacity. . . . The chiefs and their entourages even profit from his presence to inflict, on the least pretext, fines and penalties which are often considerable; thus they ruin populations they are charged with administering. All that is done, of course, in the name of the Europeans, who become, as a result, an object of terror in the minds of the Negroes.[8]

The imposition of the head tax was the most important factor in the confirmation of this dependence on the chief. The colonial administration was very unhappy about the Conseil General's reluctance to finance administration projects, and thus was forced to seek funds outside the control of the Conseil. In 1891, Governor Henri Lamothe decreed the establishment of a head tax and of a special budget in protectorate areas. The creation of a head tax made the French dependent on those chiefs who could collect it. In many areas, the tax was resisted. The administration, which had earlier tried to restrict the use of force by chiefs, was now forced to give them free rein. "Let the Bour undertake whatever repression he may judge useful," one governor wrote an administrator, "but do not go with him."[9]

[8] Farques, Director of Political Affairs, report on boundary commission, February 2, 1896, Archives of the Republic of Senegal, 1 F 19.

[9] Penciled note on letter, Administrator Sine Saloum to Director of Political Affairs, June 24, 1892, ARS, unclassified.

The head tax was followed by several other tax reforms. In Sine and Saloum, the export tax was replaced by a patent paid by traders directly to the Bour. A tax on migrant farmers, traditionally exploited by the warriors (*tyeddo*), was taken over by the administrator's office and revenues went directly to the Bour. These financial reforms had two important effects on the structure of the traditional state.

First, they freed the chief from dependence on his entourage. Made up largely of slaves known as *tyeddo*, these entourages had a will of their own and were frequently able to control both the choice of rulers and their conduct of office. Now these forces became completely dependent on the chiefs. The French were able to reduce the size of these bands, though a small force of retainers remained the basis of the chief's power up to independence.

Second, the position of the chief within his own society was stabilized. The traditional state involved a rather wide distribution of power and frequent internal conflicts. It was conflict and the possibility of conflict that forced all rulers to keep their political fences mended. French rule focused power in the hands of one chief and made the relationship with the administrator more important than the chief's relationship to key social groups in his own society.[10] Politics increasingly became the quest for the administrator's favor and depended primarily on the ability of the chief to control his access to information.

In other respects, changes made during the first phase of French rule were minimal. The French pressed the African states to eliminate certain customs they considered barbarous, for example, an ordeal which involved passing a hot blade over the tongue of

[10] Robert Cornevin, "L'évolution des chefferies dans l'Afrique Noire Française," *Penant*, Nos. 686–88 (1961), pp. 235–50, 379–88, 539–56. See especially p. 236.

the accused. It was believed that if he were guilty, the blade would stick. Judicial proceedings, however, remained in the hands of the chiefs. The French approach to the slave trade was to force the chiefs to sign a treaty providing for an end to the trade and liberation of slaves who were mistreated. This operated in favor of the chiefs since the chief freed slaves being mistreated or being moved in the trade. The same chief gave these "freed" slaves land and they often remained dependent on him.

In the second phase, which began in 1898 in Sine-Saloum, chiefs were placed on salaries, the administrator established his control over judicial proceedings, and the canton system was imposed. The cantons were conceived, like French *départements,* as neat logical units with approximately the same size and population. In practice, most administrators proved rather pragmatic and found it desirable to respect traditional political and ethnic ties. In 1909, the pragmatism of the local administrator found its echo in Governor General William Ponty's *politique des races,* which proclaimed both that canton lines should respect the autonomy of each ethnic group where possible and that chiefs should be chosen from the dominant ethnic or religious group:

> In principle, it can only be an advantage to us to choose a native chief in a family from the tribe he represents; we have no right in effect, to sacrifice the future of one tribe to another; each people should preserve its autonomy in relation to its neighbor. . . . In addition, in permitting each tribe to evolve within its own particular mentality, in preserving as much as possible the particularism of the tribe, we favor the birth of individual effort within each group totally free of the political or religious influence of the neighboring group.[11]

[11] Cornevin, pp. 246–47. Most Senegalese kingdoms contained smaller units, some with hereditary ruling families, some

The cantons were originally grouped in provinces, which were generally traditional kingdoms, or half a kingdom. The canton chiefs, most of whom were holders of important hereditary titles, gradually became more important than the provincial chiefs. In part, this was because the administrator was looking over the shoulder of the *grand chef;* in part, because of the hostility of many administrators to those chiefs whose position was rooted in tradition; in part, because the canton chief was the man who collected and who distributed. In 1907, Lieutenant Governor Camille Guy even proposed phasing out the last seven "grand chefs."[12]

Ponty's policy of respecting traditional groupings and traditional elites was confirmed by several later governors general. Martial Merlin suggested in 1920 that

under chiefs appointed by the king. These smaller units often were the basis of the canton. In areas conquered by the Moslems, the canton was often similar in size or extent to the area controlled by one of the marabout chiefs.

[12] Guy had a reputation as a liberal and an assimilationist. The proposed changes of 1907 were outlined in a long memo in which he outlined his criticisms of the major chiefs:

Although they receive high salaries, most of them cannot meet their needs because of their many retainers. . . . Demands for money in addition to the tax, fines inflicted illegally in the name of the administrator, demands for animals as gifts during the census, demands for double payment of the tax. . . . In effect, living off their *administrés,* costing a high price, they create an insurmountable barrier between the natives and the European administration. The natives do not know us and because of fears of inevitable reprisals, they never complain, even when they are plundered, and since the administrator receives his information only from the *Chef Supérieur,* he knows nothing of the glaring abuses and misappropriations committed by canton and village chiefs and he can only suspect the real needs and desires of the taxpayer. Lieutenant Governor to Governor General, June 1, 1907, Archives of the Republic of Senegal, 13 G 71.

"where there still exist native organisms capable of functioning well, we should re-enforce them in order to take from them all possible advantages."[13] And in 1932, Jules Brévié reiterated that chiefs should be chosen from traditional chiefly families.[14]

French policy served to increase the power of the chief within his own society at the very time when his authority was being sapped from within, and in fact, the two processes were mutually reinforcing. The most important single factor in the weakening of chiefly authority was a social revolution which was only half completed at the time of the conquest. Rooted in centuries of antagonism between warrior and peasant, a series of violent revolutions broke out in Senegambia in the 1850s and 1860s.[15] The revolutionary forces were channeled by a series of charismatic Moslem leaders, of whom, the best known is Al Hajj Umar Tall. By 1880, most of Senegal was dominated by leaders allied to the Moslem revolution, and it was the members of what one French governor called "a tijani league" who resisted French expansion most vigorously. As a result, in many areas, France conquered in alliance with traditional elites, and in some, detested rulers were reimposed on populations that were committed to a new elite.

In areas where Moslem chiefs were recognized, these chiefs often proved very effective, but in collecting taxes and recruits for France, they lost some of their own standing. In other areas, chiefs who had long resisted became Moslems, in some cases with the hope of conciliating antagonistic Moslem populations. In doing so, they deprived the traditional state of its reli-

[13] Cornevin, p. 249.

[14] Cornevin, *Penant*, No. 687, p. 381.

[15] Martin A. Klein, "The Moslem Revolution in 19th Century Senegambia," *Boston University Papers on Africa*, Vol. III, forthcoming.

gious sanctions, replacing these only with the support of the alien conqueror. One result of this was that in the generation after the French conquest, the new maraboutic elites established a position of predominance in Senegal. The most influential were a series of men who did not take political power, in particular, Al Hajj Malik Sy, Amadou Bamba, and Al Hajj Abdoulaye Niasse. Beneath each of these men was a network of humbler marabouts who took over in the villages many of the social and political functions once exercised by the chiefs.

Without intending to do so, the French aided the replacement of chief by marabout by changing the chief's role in his own society. He was given unpopular tasks (tax collection and recruitment) at the same time he was deprived of much of his traditional role. Gilbert Grunitzky describes the situation clearly:

> The competence of the chief is henceforth assigned legal limits while previously, everything that affected the life of the group was the concern of the chief. . . . He was both spiritual and temporal authority, he symbolized the unity of the group, but he became only an intermediary between the administration and the local population.[16]

Grunitzky goes on to point out two other factors. First, the chief lost authority to the degree that he was chosen by the French. Second, the chief no longer played the same economic role. In traditional society, the chief distributed much of the wealth. With the extension of a market economy, the chief's revenues increasingly became merely the reward for a small group, while the marabouts both adapted to the changing economic situation and took over functions earlier exercised by the chiefs. Marabouts were responsible for developing new

[16] Gilbert Grunitzky, "Evolution de la chefferie tradition-elle," unpublished memoire, Ecole Nationale de la France d'Outre-Mer.

lands and extending peanut cultivation. As a result, they controlled the marketing of much of the peanut crop and distributed a substantial part of the profits.

A comparison between Sine and Saloum makes clearer the relationship between Islamicization and the demystification of traditional chiefship. Saloum was a Serer state with a large Wolof and Tokolor population. During the religious wars, almost all of the Wolof areas slipped into the Moslem camp, but the French conquest restored these areas briefly to the control of the Bour Saloum. The conversion of Bour Saloum Guédel M'Bodj was probably motivated by a desire to reconcile his very refractory Moslem subjects, but the effect was to weaken the Bourship itself. After 1900, the Bours were all weak figures with relatively little power. The Serer areas of Saloum were about 10 per cent Moslem in 1891, almost half Moslem by World War I.

Sine was solidly Serer and had resisted Islam. As a result, the Bour remained the focus of traditional life and kept the loyalty of the mass of peasantry. In 1898, France tried to divide Sine into two provinces, but only the legitimate Bour was able to collect taxes effectively. As a result, Sine remained a meaningful unit and a form of indirect rule evolved. Bour Sine Coumba N'Doffène Diouf was the most highly paid chief in Sine-Saloum and the Resident for Sine was placed in the commercial center, Fatick, rather than in Diakhao, the Bour's capital. Both Coumba N'Doffène and his successor, Mahecor Diouf, were well aware of the sources of their power, and though subjected to the blandishments of the Moslem brotherhoods, particularly the Mourides, they kept Sine heavily pagan until after World War II.

In Sine the kingdom remained the effective unit of administration, while in Saloum, it was the canton. This does not mean, however, that in Saloum the French succeeded in imposing chiefs external to the societies being ruled. They tried in a number of cases, but generally with little luck. The chief who had hereditary rights to rule was more likely to be accepted. He generally had his band of retainers and therefore had less need to impose himself by force. Ponty's *politique des races* recognized this and the number of ex-*tirailleurs* who became chiefs as a reward for service decreased with time. The imposed chiefs seem to have been most successful in two kinds of areas. The first were stateless areas where an outsider who could command force was often more effective at imposing himself than local leaders. The second was the area of direct administration, the major trading towns where the community being governed was essentially a new one with few traditions.

By World War I, the political institutions of much of western Senegal had moved into a third phase, that in which the chief had become a professional bureaucrat trained in French schools. From the first, the French pressured chiefs to send their sons to French schools. After completing their education, these men were given minor bureaucratic posts until chiefships became open. By World War I, an increasing number of cantons were under the direction of literate chiefs who had worked as clerks or who had served in the army.

In effect, the traditional state had been incorporated into the French bureaucratic state. This does not mean that the state ceased to exist or that the chiefs became faceless expressions of the administrator's will. The chief's position in relation to his people was determined by his hereditary rights and the chief's authority was made effective through a band of retainers who were either relatives or dependents. The chief's freedom of action was strongly limited by the French administration. He could not levy his own taxes, though he frequently received "gifts" or had his fields worked for him. He had no control over basic policy, but he was very powerful. The French administration acted on the basis of information provided by the chief and acted through the chief. The chief's power was greatest in guaranteeing his own prerogatives. Robert Delavignette recognized the relationship between the traditional and the modern in the chief's authority when he wrote:

> We are caught up on certain necessary contradictions; on the one hand, we feel strongly that it is indispensable that we leave unchanged the traditional nature of the *chef de canton's* authority and take advantage of the feudal spirit which persists; on the other hand, we are led by the force of the same colonization to bend him to our administrative mentality.[17]

The French success in bureaucratizing the chiefs limited their influence, which, in turn, induced the French to improve their relationship with the marabouts. During World War I, France needed both the assurance that its African domain would remain quiet and that it would provide needed troops. France had been hostile to many of the marabouts and some of the more militant among them had carefully avoided contact with French authority. During the war, however, even Amadou Bamba was persuaded to advise his disciples to enlist in French ranks. After the war, co-operation between the French and the Moslem brotherhoods improved and the Mourides provided most of the agricultural colonies that opened up new areas near the railroad lines to peanut cultivation.

The *grands marabouts* never, however, became involved in administration. Their influence was sought and they were often carefully cultivated, but they remained outside and parallel to the administrative hierarchy. The tendency within this hierarchy remained the extension of the autocratic power of both chief

[17] Robert Delavignette, *Service africain* (Paris, 1946).

and administrator and the breakdown of the capacity of subject communities to act independently in their own interest. This was particularly true in economic questions and has had important deleterious effects on subsequent development policy. In the early years, the only group organized to limit this autocratic power was the commercial houses. Increasingly, after 1900, two other factors operated to limit administrative autocracy and to differentiate Senegal from other, less fortunate French colonies. This was the development of a large literate population and of a politically self-conscious African community within the Four Communes.

Literacy was important in that it involved a community that could address claims to superior authority. After 1900 a class of professional letter writers emerged in Senegal capable of addressing letters in the proper terms to the proper authorities. The administrators were very disturbed by the presence of this group, but many of them were citizens and thus immune from the administrator's arbitrary authority. At the same time, the development of African politics within the Four Communes meant that people from the protectorate had increasing access to political representatives that the colonial administration could not ignore.

One result of the early and effective bureaucratization of chiefship is that chiefly power has not been a central issue in contemporary politics. With the extension of electoral politics to rural Senegal after 1946, it was the *grands marabouts* who swung large blocs of votes. In Guinea and Mali, where the chiefs played a major role in conservative political parties, the radical victors felt it desirable to "abolish" chiefship.[18] Senegal merely reformed it and in reforming it completed the process begun seventy years earlier. The reforms

---

[18] Jean Suret-Canale, "La fin de la chefferie en Guinée," *Journal of African History*, VII (1966), pp. 459–93.

were simple. First, all chiefs were to serve outside the area in which their family had traditional rights. Thus, though almost all chiefs are still from chiefly families, their authority comes from the state rather than from their inherited rights. Second, older and more conservative chiefs were retired. Third, each chief was assigned three paid and uniformed guards who took over tasks traditionally performed by the chief's personal retainers. The evidence of the success of this transformation came after Mamadou Dia's unsuccessful attempt to take power in 1962. While Dia's supporters were purged from large parts of the government, the cadres of the *chefferie* were largely untouched even though most had been placed in their posts by Minister of the Interior Valdiodio N'Diaye, Dia's most important ally. The *chefferie* did not represent a threat to the new regime.

Obviously, we must now ask the relation of this to a symposium on development. I think that there are several elements that are important. The bureaucratization of the chiefs means that authority in rural Senegal is wielded by men who are capable of understanding and carrying out development policies. Barriers to development are more likely to come from the diffusion of power in the Union Progressiste Sénégalais and from the *grands marabouts*. The success of the marabouts is due in part to the fact that they are a modernizing group that has successfully adapted to change. This makes them all the more effective as a conservative force and puts them in a position both to influence development policy and to effect its implementation. Thus, the transformation of the *chefferie* has created a somewhat ambiguous situation in which the chiefs have become an effective instrument of state policy, while their position in traditional society has been taken over by a group that can limit the alternatives available to development planners if it wishes.

iv. THE DEVELOPMENT OF LOCAL POLITICAL INSTITUTIONS IN URBAN SENEGAL
by G. Wesley Johnson

George Wesley Johnson is Assistant Professor of History at Stanford University. Among his numerous publications are Political History of Senegal: 1900–1940 *and* Africans in the French Army 1914–1918 (*with Michael Crowder*).

Introduction

The growth of local political institutions in Senegal is bound up with French colonial policy, French administrative needs, and the historic character of coastal urban settlements such as St. Louis and Gorée. The fact that an African colony received political institutions so early is a reflection of the larger French colonial system and a desire to have a uniform look about the empire. It also reflects the fact that a number of interested Frenchmen, Creoles, and Africans wished to have a say in local urban affairs, especially in political and economic questions. At the same time, certain administrative needs were satisfied by providing local government so that local appointed (later elected) officials could cope with municipal problems rather than employing military officials (later the civil bureaucracy).

Consequently the French colony of Senegal was the

scene of political activity during almost two centuries preceding independence. Unlike most modern African nations, Senegal's coastal towns developed local institutions which allowed participation of Africans in local government long before the important political activity which burst after World War II. On the eve of that conflict in 1939, Senegal could boast of municipal government which traced its origins to the 1760s, of a Colonial Council which dated from the 1840s, and of a deputy in the French parliament, first elected in 1848. The object of this paper is to discuss the evolution of these three primary local institutions-municipalities, deputy, and General Council—within the framework of conflict and harmonization. Two distinct periods of conflict can be perceived in the development process. First, the attempt by French, Creole, and African interests to have local government established. Second, the question of which political elite group was to control local government after it was established.

I. The Establishment of Local Political Institutions

a) *Municipal Government*

The fame of the so-called Four Communes of Senegal (St. Louis, Gorée, Rufisque, and Dakar) sprang principally from the fact that by 1890 they were governed in the same fashion as comparable cities in metropolitan France. Their citizens, of whom 90 per cent were African, were under the same organizing and regulating laws that Frenchmen in metropolitan cities enjoyed, which meant they did not have the same initiative in some affairs that English and American towns possessed. Nevertheless, a great deal of local participation in government was afforded citizens interested in municipal politics. Some powers were reserved to the central administration (in Senegal to the colonial government rather than to the prefect, as in France), which reflected the centralizing tendency in France which has persisted unbroken from Louis XIV through Napoleon. The municipal government in the communes consisted of a Municipal Council, elected by eligible citizens of the city, and a mayor and his assistants, chosen from members of the council. They in turn appointed a goodly number of clerical, service, and janitorial positions for the diverse functions of the local city hall.

Gorée was probably the first Senegalese town to have its own mayor. Because of few extant sources no definite point in time can be fixed; nevertheless, the work of former Governor of Senegal Léonce Jore indicates that sometime before 1763 the Senegal Company in Gorée appointed a Catholic African named Kiaka to act as mayor of the local populace, to replace one Kiémé, who had previously held the post. Again mention is made in 1778 of a mulatto mayor of Gorée, and when the British again occupied the island during the first part of the nineteenth century, local government continued in the hands of an indigenous mayor and municipal council.[1]

It is probable that St. Louis had a mayor from the mid-eighteenth century also, but the earliest authenticated reference is that of 1778, when the wealthy Catholic Creole merchant Jean Thevenot served as mayor. (In this paper Creole refers to a Senegalese of mixed European and African ancestry). He was succeeded the next year by Charles Pierre Cornier, another Creole who presided over St. Louis's municipal life during the decade of the French Revolution. Cornier was also instrumental in helping draw up the *cahier de doléance* of St. Louis citizens, which requested that the French Assembly establish on a permanent basis

[1] Léonce Jore, "Les etablissements français sur la côte occidentale d'Afrique de 1758 à 1809," *Revue française d'histoire d'outre-mer*, LI, p. 257.

the local municipal organization which had grown up informally in the two communes. Governor Blanchot favored this plan, for he thought that an indigenous mayor and council served as an effective intermediary between the colonial administration and the indigenous Africans in the towns, and that in time of emergency they could provide military aid and the backing of the local populace for the governor.[2] The Assembly, however, failed to approve this request.

Senegal was cut off from France during the era of the Revolution and the Napoleonic Wars. Few Frenchmen came to the colony for almost three decades and local inhabitants, mainly Creole and African, became used to the idea of conducting their municipal affairs with *de facto* mayor and councils. This ad hoc tradition of local government continued (even during the British occupation) until the French reoccupied Senegal again in 1816. But this tradition of local initiative in municipal affairs was never fully understood in Paris, for Governor Roger, a Bourbon appointee of the early 1820s, was shocked that the citizens of St. Louis should have their own mayor and claim that they had always elected him. Roger stopped elections and appointed a new mayor in an effort to show that local government sprang from the king's emissary and not the people; however, in a dispatch to the Minister of Marine he admitted the usefulness of a local mayor in dealing with the mob and that he had prudently appointed the man who probably would have won in an election.[3]

Down to 1870 the municipal institutions of St. Louis and Gorée continued to exist as manifesta-

[2] Commandant of Senegal to Minister of Marine, November 12, 1823, Archives de la France Outre-Mer, FOM, Senegal VII-8.

[3] Lafon de Fongaufier to Minister of Marine, February 12, 1872, FOM, Senegal 51.

tions of local interest in self-government but without any basis within the colonial governmental framework of the colony. The birth of the Third Republic of France and a wave of liberality for colonial government during the decade of the 1870s changed this. In 1872, after petitions had been sent to Paris for several years, signed mostly by Africans, the Minister of Marine decided to ask the French Chamber to create St. Louis and Gorée *communes de plein exercice*. Senegal's deputy in the French parliament, Lafon de Fongaufier, supported the petitions and the Africans' right to vote and hold office. He wrote to the minister:

> You don't really know Senegal if you don't understand the contributions made by the African Muslims for generations in Saint-Louis and Goree . . . They pay the same taxes as the French, for they are happy and proud of their French status which they have acquired by their devotion. . . . It is not the merchants themselves who go trading up the river, but rather the natives from Saint-Louis and Goree to whom the largest houses of Marseille and Bordeaux don't hesitate to consign hundreds of thousands of francs' worth of merchandise.[4]

The minister was impressed and agreed to have the president of the republic sign the enabling decree. Meanwhile, a campaign to discredit the African petitioners was unleashed by new French merchants and conservative colonial officials, but this did not cause the Africans to lose heart. They wrote Lafon de Fongaufier that if necessary they would send a delegation of notables "to visit Monsieur Thiers in person at his residence at Versailles" and give the National Assembly another petition. Such a visit was not neces-

---

[4] See Minute, FOM, Senegal VII-7; also Georges Hardy, *La mise en valeur du Sénégal* (Paris: Larose, 1921), p. 231.

sary, however, for Thiers signed the decree on August 10, 1872, which established in French administrative law what had existed in practice for more than a century—municipal institutions (mayor, assistants, municipal council). In 1882 the town of Rufisque was organized and given the same municipal statute, and in 1887, Dakar was split off from Gorée and became the fourth commune. After a series of conflicts with central administration officials—colonial governors from the Old Regimes, Revolution, Napoleonic era, Bourbon Restoration, July Monarchy, Second Republic, and Second Empire—the local inhabitants finally won their desire to have legalized their own local government, for which they had applied to the First Republic. It took the Third Republic's ideal of assimilation to put into practice their wishes.

b) *Representation in Paris: the Deputy*

From a historical point of view, the second institution which developed in Senegal was a representative of the colony in France. This was advocated as early as 1791 by the Frenchman Dominique Lamiral, who had helped Mayor Charles Cornier draft the *cahiers de deléances* in 1789. Lamiral was appointed to carry the *cahiers* to France and he stayed on there for several years, hoping to be named Deputy from Senegal to the National Assembly. This never occurred, but Lamiral nevertheless acted like a deputy and lobbied for the welfare of the colony; he was able to win free trade for local merchants in 1791, which ended the Senegal Company's monopoly.

The idea of a deputy in Paris was revived in 1837, when the Governor of Senegal wrote Paris that local Frenchmen, Creoles, and Africans had requested a deputy to represent the colony in Paris on the advisory Conseil des Délégués des Colonies. This was not approved until a few years later when the Ordinance of 1840, a fundamental colonial organizing law, was promulgated. This provided for a delegate to Paris from Senegal, but only in an advisory capacity. It set a precedent which affected the leaders of the Revolution of 1848 in France, who called for an elected deputy from Senegal to sit in the new parliament. In the first regular public election in Senegal (of which about 90 per cent of the voters were Africans) the Creole Durand Valantin, *de facto* Mayor of St. Louis, was elected to the post in Paris. In a liberal gesture, the Minister of Marine had ruled that all indigenous peoples in Senegal who could show a residence of at least five years in the two communes would be eligible to vote. These ministerial instructions, formulated in the midst of revolution, became the cornerstone of African political liberties in years to come.[5]

In the elections of October 30, 1848, Valantin triumphed over Victor Schoelcher, the great French abolitionist, who had visited the colony a few months before the revolution started, and who consequently had been nominated. Elections were held again on August 12, 1849, and Valantin was elected to another term, this time defeating Masson and Petiton, local Frenchmen in the colony. Valantin's victory was explicable because the great majority of voters were African or Creoles; only several hundred Frenchmen were in the colony at this time.[6]

Valantin retired in 1851 to devote his energies to his business and serving as Mayor of St. Louis. His first assistant in the municipality, John Sleight, was elected deputy but was soon disqualified because he held a lucrative contract to supply the French army in Senegal with millet (not allowable for such a public official); furthermore, he was suspect to many St.

[5] Minister of Marine to Commissar of the Republic in Senegal, May 10, 1848, FOM, Senegal VII-44.

[6] See the *procès-verbaux* for election of October 30, 1848, and of election of August 12, 1849, FOM, Senegal VII-44.

Louis citizens because he had been born in Bathurst, Gambia, of an English father and African mother. Before Sleight could be replaced, Louis Napoleon signed the decree of February 2, 1852, which abolished all colonial representation in Paris. For the next twenty years, the urban Senegalese were without a deputy in France.

In 1871, after the Franco-Prussian War had begun and brought the Third Republic to the fore, France's new republicans once again sent out a call to Senegal for a deputy.[7] This time a Frenchman was elected, Lafon de Fongaufier, who had seen service in Senegal with the French navy. The inhabitants of the new towns of Dakar and Rufisque were also allowed to vote which brought the total number of registered voters to 4277.[8] The post of deputy was suppressed in 1876 but reappeared in 1879, when another Frenchman, Alfred Gasconi, was elected deputy.[9] For the next sixty years, until Vichy suppressed Senegal's deputy in 1940, Senegal was represented continuously in Paris by its deputy elected in the Four Communes and surrounding urban areas. After World War II the colony was given two deputies in the National Assembly, the franchise gradually was extended to the rural areas, and its example was taken as a model by France in establishing deputies in its other African colonies. When Senegal became independent, it had enjoyed official representation in the metropole since 1848.

c) *Local Assembly: the General Council*

Senegal's third institution of local government was

[7] Decree of February 1, 1871.

[8] *Moniteur du Sénégal,* April 4, 1871.

[9] Once again citizens of the Four Communes had petitioned the ministry, demanding that their local representative to Paris be reinstated. President Jules Grévy on April 8, 1879, signed the decree which gave victory to the local forces over those conservative elements in the colonial administration who feared the influence a deputy might create complications in Paris.

a kind of territorial assembly known as the General Council from 1840 to 1848 and from 1879 to 1920; as the Colonial Council from 1921 to 1939; and as General Council and Territorial Assembly from 1944 until independence. The General Council was originally modeled after the Conseil Général (which is an assembly in each French *département*); however, the Senegalese assembly had far greater powers and influence than its metropolitan counterpart.

Senegal's urban citizens first served on an embryonic colonial council in 1822, when the governor appointed one *habitant* and one *notable* (probably one Creole and one assimilated African) to sit on the Conseil du Gouvernement, a private council which advised the governor on local matters. This arrangement continued until September 7, 1840, when a royal ordinance of Louis Philippe gave Senegal an entirely new legal framework and established a General Council, as in other French colonies. The Governor of Senegal was to draw up a list of forty to sixty leading citizens of St. Louis, who in assembly were to elect members of the council. It was composed of ten members, eight from the ranks of wholesale businessmen, two from small entrepreneurs. Frenchmen, Creoles, or Africans were eligible. It was to meet annually to give the governor opinions on budgetary matters, economic policy, and administrative needs. Members were to serve for five-year terms.[10] Gorée, which was considered separately from St. Louis and the Senegal River area, was also given a similar type of council, the Conseil d'Arrondissement.

Both of these original Senegalese councils were not subject to popular election and therefore were a reflection of the governor's views on drawing up a list of "safe" notables and on the notables electing from their midst council members who would safeguard

[10] Analysis of Ordinance of 1840, FOM, Senegal VII-9.

their vested interests. By the time the Revolution of 1848 occurred, the councils lapsed into obscurity under the new regime. Briefly, at the outset of the Second Empire, attempts were made to set up Chambers of Commerce in St. Louis and Gorée, but these failed. Conciliar government had to wait until the uneasy years of 1869, 1870, and 1871 could spur the local citizens to petition the ministry for the creation of a new council. These requests brought, however, the creation of municipal councils after 1872 and a General Council was deferred until a later time.

Finally, in 1879, in response to regular petitions from concerned citizens for over a decade, the ministry decided to give Senegal a permanent General Council. The decree of February 4, 1879, created a council composed of sixteen members to be elected by popular suffrage in the Four Communes, from the same lists used for deputy and municipal elections. Frenchmen, Creoles, and Africans were eligible to vote and to stand for election. St. Louis predominated at the outset, having the right to elect ten councilors; Gorée was authorized six. The creation of Dakar and Rufisque as *communes de plein exercice* in the following decade altered this composition.

Many members of municipal councils also served as General Council members; nothing prohibited duplicate service. But only inhabitants of the communes were eligible to stand for election, so the interior of the colony (known as the protectorate) did not have representatives on the General Council. This dichotomy was given legal status from 1892 to 1920, when the budget of the protectorate was controlled exclusively by the governor and the urban areas budget was subject to the council's approval. After 1920 the situation reverted to the original arrangement when the protectorate was abolished and the entire colony came under the jurisdiction of the newly created Colonial Council. So as to give representation to interests of

the interior nonurban areas, tradition and warrant
chiefs were appointed by the governor to serve on the
Colonial Council. Thus during the interwar years of
1921-39, the French administration, noted for its reliance on direct administrative rule, revived a form of
limited indirect rule by having chiefs sit in the council.
Some were subservient to the colonial administration,
on whom they were financially independent; others
leagued with the elected urban members to oppose the
governor and administration.

Generally speaking, the General Council's powers
were limited but broad enough to make it more than
a simple debating society on local questions. In summary, its powers were 1) to give opinions on a range
of questions to the administration when called upon;
2) to legislate on about a dozen topics; 3) to deliberate and debate on a number of items; 4) to approve
part of the colonial budget.[11]

First, the council was empowered to give opinions
on topics requested by the governor—for example, the
creation of new *communes-mixtes,* problems of local
administration, visitors to the colony, and so forth. A
fixed list did not mean the council was necessarily
muzzled. For other topics it wanted to discuss, it was
free to do so by *voeux* (resolutions) which were often
extremely important from a moral and political standpoint, listened to in St. Louis, Dakar, and Paris. By
this means the council had direct access to public opinion because all of its sessions were printed for public
perusal in either local newspapers or in book form at
the end of the year.

Second, the council was able to *statuer,* or legislate,
on a number of topics including disposition of public
property, gifts to the colony, classification of roads,

[11] Raymond Leslie Buell, *The Native Problem in Africa*
(New York: Macmillan Co., 1928), I, pp. 969-74. The analysis
which immediately follows is based partly on Buell's research.

contributions of the colonial budget to public works projects, and other matters of this nature. Theoretically, after 1895 these decisions could be vetoed by the Governor General of French West Africa within two months, but in practice this seldom occurred.

Third, the council could deliberate certain matters of colonial government such as the tax rate and how it was to be assessed and collected in the urban areas. This gave the urban citizens of the colony a qualified but realistic measure of control over the governor and local administration, especially when this was compounded with the tax-assessing powers of the municipal councils. It could debate questions of taxes on public works, the administration of certain market centers, fares charged by ferries at river crossings, and the alienation and acquisition of property for public use.

Fourth, the area of greatest council control and hence the cause of frequent controversy with the administration was the budget. Here the council had no power of initiation, since the budget was prepared by the governor and submitted to the council for approval or rejection. There were two categories of expenditure in the budget—mandatory and optional expenses. The mandatory expenditures (payment of state debts, expenses of the governor, funds for departmental services, etc.) were not within the province of the council; the governor retained complete control over the fundamental services necessary to make the administration function in the colony. These mandatory expenses could not be stopped by the council, but all other categories, called optional expenses, were fair game. Most new construction projects, many governmental services, and most nonessential public services were so classified. If the governor requested too much for a new budget, more than the anticipated revenue would pay for, the council members could simply reject the budget until the governor modified it to their liking.

It was quite apparent that ultimate control of much of this quasi-legislative process stayed with the governor, but within this framework of the council, local politics was able to bring enormous pressure to bear on the administration. Qualified observers who saw the council in action were impressed with its political capabilities. Buell, who visited Senegal in the mid-1920s, wrote:

> The members of the Colonial Council of Senegal have more power than the unofficial members of any other consultative assembly in Africa, including the Legislative Councils found in British territory. They can block the imposition of new taxes and withhold about half the expenditures of the government.[12]

The conflict of the local inhabitants of urban Senegal with the colonial administration—their desire to have local political institutions for their own governance—was finally resolved in favor of the local inhabitants by 1880. By that time, the three basic local governmental institutions in which Africans could participate as electors and candidates were permanently established in terms of French administrative law. They would stand as the primary means of political expression for the next eighty years (excepting the Vichy interlude) and serve as training institutions for eventual independent governance.

Several reasons can be given for the success of the local inhabitants in pressing their case for local government. First, the example of other French colonies in the West Indies, India, and the Indian Ocean. Second, the liberal political climate engendered by the First, Second, and Third Republics, during which the respective institutions received their greatest fillip. Third, the ideal of assimilation, which was articulated

12 Buell, *op. cit.*, I, p. 979.

during the French Revolution and which continued to
have a real influence on colonial officials in Senegal to
the close of the nineteenth century, and which reached
its high point in Paris during the decade of the 1870s.
Fourth, and perhaps most important, the freedom allowed local inhabitants to petition the metropole—
whether in 1789 with the *cahiers,* in the 1830s for a
General Council, in the 1870s for municipal organization, or again in 1879 for a resuscitation of the General
Council. These and other reasons worked against the
natural tendency of the colonial government—dominated largely by military men until the late nineteenth
century—to control all aspects of the local scene.

II. The Question of Control over the Local Political Institutions

Senegalese urban political history until 1920 was
characterized by one dominant issue: who shall control the local institutions?

Frenchman, Creole, and African had co-operated in
winning them for the colony, but this alliance soon
gave way to a three-cornered contest for political supremacy on the local scene. The Creoles had furnished
political leadership from the earliest times and had
provided the continuity of interest and purpose lacking
among the French during the interludes of the French
Revolution, Napoleonic Wars, and the British occupation. The Creoles were intimately linked to the assimilated and nonassimilated Africans in the communes,
for whom they exercised a tutorial function. Frenchmen were rarely permanent settlers in the colony, but
served usually in business enterprises long enough to
make a fortune in order to return to France. Only
after the Third Republic started French expansion in
tropical Africa did greater numbers of Frenchmen with
interests in local politics invade the colony.

These three political elite groups were remarkably

self-defining in their ethnic, religious, legal, and socio-economic composition. Each group was committed to a policy which reflected the particular political goals and ambitions characteristic of its members. Each group was conscious of its social and political differences and separateness from the two other groups. And, in fact, each group was predominantly of one color or racial composition. However, there was no formal color bar in the Four Communes, and French, Creole, and Africans lived in the same neighborhoods and same buildings. (Senegal's urban centers grew up as multiracial communities and have continued as such until the present day.)

First, the French elite. There never was any question that Frenchmen would have voting and civil rights under local political institutions. They were a small community, divided into several categories: government officials, civil servants, wholesale businessmen and their agents, small businessmen, clerks, and *petits colons*. Administrative personnel were legally forbidden to participate in campaigning and elections but could vote. In practice, however, this restriction was openly flaunted by numerous functionaries who became involved in local politics. The French elite was in a privileged position in the colony, because they held the primary levers of economic and political control.

Second, the Creoles, who were extremely conscious of their status since it was based primarily on race. Because they professed Christianity and were highly assimilated by education, taste, and style of life to the French, they were associated with the French elite group from the days of 1789, when Cornier and Lamiral joined forces to draft the *cahiers*. The Creoles had dominated municipal politics from the beginning and sought to control the General Council as well. They were a small community, based primarily in St. Louis and Gorée, with only a token representation in the newer communities of Dakar and Rufisque. There had never been any attempt to deprive the Creoles of their civil or political rights because they were living testimonies to the virtue of the policy of assimilation.

Third, the African elite. The policy of assimilation in Senegal was primarily responsible for the extension of metropolitan political institutions and rights to France's first African colony. This institutional transfer was complicated by the composition of the electorate, however, because from 1848 on Africans were in the majority in all elections. Because they were content to be led by French and Creole politicians, there were few problems until about 1900; but when in the first part of the twentieth century a political awakening occurred, then the composition of the electorate became a matter of concern for all in Senegal.

The policy of assimilation was also responsible for the creation of a precisely defined African political elite. When politics first began in St. Louis and Gorée in the eighteenth century, urban African dwellers took an interest in who would become mayor and councilors. This interest grew in the years that followed, especially after 1848, when the electoral voting instructions of the Minister of Marine authorized all urban Africans with five years' residence to vote for the colony's deputy. From then until 1915, courts, decrees, and orders hammered away at defining who among the African urban class would be eligible to have electoral rights for the municipal, council, and parliamentary elections. In this process a definite African political elite, definable in terms of law, was created in the Four Communes. Its members were drawn from the urban African class but did not by any means include all the municipal inhabitants. Thousands of African city residents who came from the interior, from other French colonies, from Gambia, Portuguese Guinea, and the Cape Verde Islands were assimilated to urban life, urban values, and became members of the urban work force. But they did not become members of the political elite, which was eventually reserved by the Blaise Diagne laws of 1915 and 1916 to those who had been born in the communes, could show long residence there, or who were the descendants of such Africans. They became known as *originaires,* and after the Diagne laws went into effect, they became full-fledged French citizens yet with the option of keeping their personal statute for matters of family, marriage, and inheritance. The *originaires* were the only Africans who could participate in the local political institutions until after World War II, when the suffrage was broadened and politics was changed from an elite to a mass base.

The conflict among these three urban elites can be summarized as follows: 1) From the inception of local politics in the eighteenth century to the beginning of the Third Republic, local institutions were dominated by Creole leadership. French participants tended to lose interest or to leave the colony; African participants were usually not oriented toward political leadership and did not aspire to become candidates. When the General Council was created in 1840, it became a preserve of Frenchmen and Creoles, which indicated that Africans might be excluded from future political considerations. But the freeing of the slaves in 1848 and the guarantee by the Minister of Marine of African voting rights kept the Africans in politics.

2) During the second period, from about 1870 to 1914, there was conflict between the French and Creole forces for mastery of local politics. This was caused by the growing number of Frenchmen active in new businesses in the colony after the rise of the New Imperialism. After the three local institutions were permanently established by law during the decade of the 1870s, French and Creoles battled for control of the municipalities, council, and deputyship as well as for control of the majority of the African electorate. This

rivalry finally resulted in an uneasy alliance, the French-Creole entente, designed to divide the spoils of local government: the General Council was dominated by the Creoles, the municipalities were shared, and the deputy was French. The entente rested on the tacit assumption that the majority of Africans would remain content to be voters and not candidates. The few Africans who were elected to office tended to be "yes" men and followers, serving at the pleasure of the French and Creole local political bosses. This was the era of rotten borough politics in Senegal, when elections and electors could be bought by the highest bidder. By 1902, however, the French-Creole entente was threatened by dynamic Creole advances: François Carpot, a Creole lawyer, was elected deputy to Paris and the Creole Justin Devès began his ruthless drive to power, which eventually made him Mayor of St. Louis, President of the General Council, and king-maker in local politics.[13]

Of great significance from 1900 on was the African awakening—a period of unrest, dissatisfaction, and frustration which came over the urban African community, and which caused African elite members to take an active interest in local politics. More educated Africans were on the scene—men able to cope with the French and Creoles on their own terms and to do battle in local politics. The number of Africans elected to the General Council and municipal councils increased slowly but significantly after 1900. As a counterpoint to this increased activity was the attack of the French colonial administration on African political rights. A series of court cases and administrative decisions sought to reduce African political participation at the precise moment the African political *crise de conscience* was taking place. In fact, they helped stimulate each other—greater African interest made the

[13] Both Carpot and Devès were educated in France.

French administrators worry about African designs, and French attacks determined the African elite to move quickly to defend its political rights. The African dilemma was exacerbated however by the fact that the Africans were divided into a number of factions and there was no unified program or purpose for resisting the efforts of the conservative French administrators, with the tacit approval of the French and Creole politicians, to diminish (if not eliminate) the number of African electors.

3) The conflict between the administration and Africans on the one hand, and the French-Creole combination and the Africans on the other hand, was finally resolved by the elections of 1914 and 1919, the most important in Senegal's political history. Blaise Diagne, a Senegalese serving in the French colonial customs corps, won election in the hotly contested 1914 election as Senegal's first African deputy to Paris. He demonstrated that an African could aspire to high office and win an election; he united the African factions and forged a political group which within five years' time almost completely eliminated Frenchmen and Creoles from local politics.

Diagne first clarified the status of the urban Africans in the 1915 and 1916 Diagne laws, which he induced the Chamber of Deputies to pass in the heat of wartime. The *originaires'* status was guaranteed by fiat of the French parliament; this ended the question of whether or not Blaise Diagne was entitled to sit in the Chamber (it had been charged by his local French and Creole opponents that he was not a citizen and therefore not eligible to hold office). It also opened the door for all other urban Africans to participate as candidates in local politics.

Hence, in 1919, Diagne led his Republican-Socialist Party to a resounding victory at the polls. Diagne was re-elected deputy, his candidates took over all four municipal governments, and the General Council was taken away from the Creoles. Only a handful of French and Creoles were left in office, and these were politicians who had seen the handwriting on the wall—that the future belonged to the Africans—and who had joined the Diagne forces. Diagne's victory meant that by 1920, 95 per cent of local elective offices in Senegal were in African hands. The French-Creole entente was absolutely liquidated from local politics.

In conclusion, the Africans had won the right by 1920 to take charge of Senegal's local political institutions and to help develop them for immediate and future African needs. Their example during the interwar period would serve as a model for other French-speaking Africans for the postwar world.

v. RURAL MODERNIZATION IN SENEGAL
by Cheikh Tidiane Sy

Cheikh Tidiane Sy is Professor of Sociology and Director of Studies at the National School of Applied Economics at the University of Dakar; among other publications, he has written The Evolution of Agrarian Structures in Senegal.

Introduction

Economists have only recently begun to accept the idea that, beyond the enlargement of the market economy, development in general is conditioned by the response of the social system. The contemporary social system reacts automatically to the introduction of new techniques, for it is impossible for the economic, administrative, and political power centers to ignore their effect without running the risk of appearing insignificant.

But the notion of material progress by itself is not sufficient. One must restore all its human and moral content, in other words, its social meaning. In other words, as was said by Jacques Berque, true decolonization will occur only with modernization of this long-neglected "traditional" sector.[1] Major and fundamental forms and values bequeathed by history must adjust to "modernity" or risk repudiation. How can we help them to make this great leap?

Adaptation, readaptation, these are the key words which are used to describe the process by which the model to which we aspire shapes itself or is shaped. Viewed as a phenomenon of modernization, this process presents us with an ambiguity.[2] For, wherever adaptation or readaptation of historic structures, or those bequeathed by colonialism, confronts us in the context of the readjustments of those techniques which brought the developed countries their glory, it seems that we find ourselves questioning the social structure of the developing society and the values it holds. Therefore, if modernization not only is to be viewed as merely the injection of new techniques, but has as its ultimate goal the establishment of a harmonious society, it cannot be realized without upheaval. Far from providing an equilibrium of the social forces in conflict, modernization, in terms of its effect upon civilization, is not simply constrained by the willingness of the people to comply with its demands; indeed, it is subject to an entire series of conflicts, not to say

[1] J. Berque, "Quelques aspects d'une sociologie de la décolonisation," *Cahiers de Sociologie,* No. 1 (Rabat, 1965), p. 8.

[2] Not all Africans regard this concept as "Europeanization."

contradictions. In the face of these difficulties, if modernization is not supported by the society itself, it is simply an insidious process of alienation. This is the inevitable result if the modernization process does not play "the key-board of commands and symbols which manifest to a given society its own person and allows it to control, up to a point, its future."[3]

Thus, we must establish the premises for an "idcological definition" of modernization (or if we prefer, of development), but such a definition must nevertheless be based on reality. In Senegal this has been, it seems to me, the basis of modernization. If, however, what has been termed "socialist construction" does in fact unite the masses, the level of commitment of its actors within the mass is not always the same. Ideology speaks the future, and it is impossible to build a world where man will be able to develop fully his own existence without turning his back on traditions of the past.

I should like, therefore, to consider development as a historical movement, with the demands of humanization and universality which history makes. This is far from an idealistic concept of history. I simply believe that a dialectic of history cannot be established if, grasping a reality, one does not synthesize its disparate elements to recapture, by giving them new meaning, a new perspective.

Senegalese development has offered an opportunity, over the last few years, to study a country propelled by a doctrine of rural modernization. As we shall see, this doctrine can be clearly stated even though it gives rise to certain contradictions in that it is characterized by the efforts of certain traditional and modern notables to maintain personal stability, quite contrary to the evolution dictated by the option to modernize. These contradictions are apparent at the three different levels at which rural modernization is pursued:

[3] J. Berque, *op. cit.*, p. 10.

those of rural animation, co-operative structuralism, and agrarian reform, the three instruments of the socialization and democratization of the rural people of Senegal.

Senegalese Society before Independence

At the eve of Senegalese independence, a sociological analysis of the country would have revealed, generally, all the characteristics of a society dominated by financial imperialism, built around these main pillars:

A. *In the urban areas,* social categories were differentiated according to the link they had with financial imperialism: *colonial administrators* of European origin; Levantines linked directly with commercial capital and, therefore, agents of imperialism; a *small autochthonous bureaucracy,* employed by the colonial machinery, but in a large measure linked with the movement of national liberation; a *nascent industrial* proletariat, chiefly made up of men from the peasantry, precarious wage earners, who could lose their jobs without even a day's notice, whose position *vis-à-vis* the process of liberation from colonial domination was ambiguous.

B. *In the rural areas,* two groups existed, whose close interdependence gave rise to a relative "stratification": One, the *large mass of illiterate peasants* (80 per cent of the population). Overexploited by the prevailing socioeconomic system, the peasant masses constituted, without a doubt, the real proletariat of the nation. Second, a *few traditional or religious chiefs,* to whom the colonial machinery and its administrative needs offered a status by associating them, along with a few professional politicians, to a "comprador" bourgeoisie.

What is of supreme importance is that most of these social differences, born in a rural milieu, favored the rise of the Moslem brotherhoods. Indeed, the marabouts, who have commanded and "animated" the new religious movements, have reconstructed the entire traditional political order. By building new villages and by channeling the economic activities of their followers (*taâlibé*) the marabouts took on all of the ancient attributes of the traditional chiefs, and indeed, those of the kings. *Primus inter pares,* they became the civil and religious chiefs. The sacred character of their leadership (*Baraka*) turned the maraboutic block into the real repository of power in the rural milieu.

The most striking example of this social syncretism, which characterizes Islam in West Africa, is *Ahmadou Bamba's mouridism* (Islamic sect of northern Senegal). Although the ancient traditional social framework had disintegrated as the result of the colonial intrusion, the ancient social and political functions vested in the king or his representatives were recovered by the marabouts who intended not only to reign but to rule as well. The decisive importance in politics of the maraboutic "class" was the economic pressure which it exercised for a long time in the country. The expansion of their religious community led to a quasi-occupation of the largest part of available land, which their followers cultivated without wages, of their own choice.[4]

Our major analytical problem, however, is that we do not find antagonistic classes in the rural milieu, or at least, if classes do exist in fact, class antagonisms have not yet clearly appeared. Why is this? There are large producers (marabouts) who have at their disposal a servile body of manpower (*taâlibés*). The distinction between these two groups is hardly to be equated with the differentiation between capital and labor. A state of conflict, which in Marxian terms

---

[4] For more details on this question see, Sy, "Traditionalisme mouride et modernisation rurale au Sénégal," University of Paris, 1965.

results from the separating of capital and labor in a class-differentiated society, does not yet exist. What we find instead is a system of "collective social security" resulting from the combination of capital and labor.

The large maraboutic landholdings are far from being their absolute property, and consequently the Senegalese marabouts do not display the characteristics one expects of capitalist landlords. Conversely, we do not find their "adepts" showing evidence of the revolutionary virus. We are dealing, as Porteres wrote, with agrarian communities where servility is a state which in the last analysis is freely accepted by the "adepts." The social tension which theoretically should exist has failed to evolve for two reasons: (1) the civilization in which these phenomena take place remains agrotraditional and (2) the maraboutic elite has not yet become a rural "bourgeoisie."

On the economic level, two factors are important: the economic dependence of the country, and the peasants' uneasiness, which is its logical consequence. The country depends on the cultivating of a single crop, peanuts, which represents 86 per cent of Senegal's export. The peasant is uneasy because he is caught by the inexorable requirements of the single-crop economy and has difficulty acquiring the basic necessities of life: he is the victim of a system of exchange entirely beyond his control.

Politically, one of the consequences of colonial occupation has been, as mentioned earlier, the dislocation of ancient political systems. However, political "evolution" did not bring about a new social organization. Social values which reflected the homogeneity and stability of the Senegalese political systems did not disappear with colonization, especially in the rural areas. There, the colonial administrative machinery found it necessary and expedient to utilize the principle of "indirect rule." Even here, however, one must take note of the deviation, or, more specifically, the diverting of certain functions, as the result of contact with the colonial economy. Centered on production and looking toward external markets, the criteria of the colonial economy were the "values" of the capitalistic economy: production and a cash economy. These completed, politically, the disintegration of traditional societies. Wherever the new hierarchy was established on the bases of acceptance of and devotion to the colonial system, confidence and honor disappeared. The hierarchic, traditional influences, wherever maintained, had to serve the colonial administration. Governor W. Ponty clearly expressed this concept of using traditional powers to maintain colonial power: "According to my instructions we must continue, as before, to lavish exterior marks of honor and consideration on them, to fulfill obligations which we may have contracted with them, to use their services by making them auxiliaries of our administration, but in doing so to busy ourselves with attenuating their power over the people."[5]

If the stunning blow of civilization has brought about a certain "evolution," it is only in the sense of a destruction of the traditional political structures, on the one hand, and in the use of certain traditional chiefs to secure its authority, on the other. The administrative machinery which is set up has incontestably given birth to a small urban bourgeoisie. Such are, in the main, the "changes" introduced by the colonial system.

Administrative Institutions Born with Independence

The colonial state, for the needs of its metropolitan economy, had set up structures of domination which enabled it to interfere on any level of the country. From the point of view of social evolution, the producer

[5] *Circulaire du Gouverneur W. Ponty,* August 1913.

was in fact only enslaved by the commercial capital owned by the colonial companies (S.C.O.A., N.D.S.-O.C.D., C.F.A.O., etc.). These commercial enterprises, ill adapted to the social context in which they operated, were so centralized and restrictive that it was impossible for the masses to assume economic and political responsibilities.

The new state which appeared with independence was to some extent bound to the movement of national liberation and was an instrument of a new political economy. The state had to remove these structures of colonial domination so as not to appear to be an appendage of the old metropolitan power. This is what explains the administrative and economic reforms of 1960:

Reforms of the administrative institutions inherited from the colonial system.

A. *The Regional Institution:*

The country was divided into the seven regions corresponding to seven zones, each quite distinct from the other—(Caf-Vert, Thies, Siné-Saloum, Fleuve, Sénégal Oriental, Diowebel, and Casamance). The fundamental criterion of this reform was the economic and mostly sociological homogeneity of the people who inhabited each. The regions reacted favorably to this administrative decentralization and there now exists a closer bond between the administrators and the administered.

B. *Departmental Institutions:*

In 1862, the French established the administrative organization of the Senegalese territory because of the territorial expansion of the colony. The entire colonial strategy centered on administrative machinery organized in Dakar—an elite "circle" of colonial administrators—to achieve direct administration of the people. This policy resulted chiefly in the emigration of rural Senegalese to the coast, where, in the ports, administrative organization operated chiefly in exploitation of the colonial economy. The distribution of land made by the colonial government between 1862 and 1924 was based on no rational criterion except that of maintaining the peasants in the peanut production system. The colonial elite characterized the entire administrative structure of the machinery of colonial domination. Furthermore, as Surret-Canal points out very aptly: "The civil administration retained the marks of military despotism—the exterior form and the vocabulary of 'command,' uniforms, and the requirement of the military salute."[6]

Not only the colonial administrator but his centralized system of government had to go when Senegal achieved independence. In their place, departments were created. This was not merely a matter of reaction, but a rational approach to decolonization, like the creation of the seven regions, which sought to maximize local action and responsibilities. It gave reality and depth to the policy of administrative decentralization, which, as a result, is one of the political foundations of the new Senegalese state.

C. *The District Chieftainships*

It is well known that everywhere in Africa during the colonial period the traditional chieftainships were used as indispensable wheels in the execution of tasks exacted from the people by the machinery of colonial domination. The district chief was appointed by colonial authorities as an "agent of the indigenous administration." The institution of chieftainship, rather than reflecting the will and aspirations of the people, as formerly, was now rather a tool of the government

[6] J. Surret-Canale, *Afrique noire* (Paris, Social Publications, 1964), Vol. II, p. 95.

altogether in the hands of the colonial state. Feared
for the power he derived from the colonial administration, the district chief contributed considerably, at his
level of action, to colonial exploitation, his various
tasks characterized by demands and abuse commensurate with the oppressive nature of the colonial regime
and what it required of its "agents of indigenous administration."[7] The district chieftainship therefore had
to be suppressed when the time for reform came.
The new Senegalese state substituted an institution
whose character was purely administrative, the district, which aimed at decentralization, as did the reforms mentioned earlier. Its role was to give the new
state, on the administrative level, the means of renew-
ing a dialogue between the country and its leaders,
which two long periods of colonization had broken
off.

What must, of course, not be lost in this process of
reform, this transition to regional and local units of
administration, is what the centralized and authoritarian type of institution was able to produce with the
economic means and the authority over the masses
which were available to it—marked economic growth.
On the one hand the internal logic of the results in a
colonial style (let us think of forced labor), and, on
the other hand, that it would not give birth to development, that is to say, both the largest and most conspicuous participation of the basic collectivities, and
disappearance of exploitation of man by man, through
the individual accumulation of rare factors of production.

In choosing its methods of development, Senegal
thus has established a new kind of relationship between the people and the state. In doing so, it pointed
out what is perhaps the fundamental problem of development: the structural aspect. In other words, de-

[7] *Ibid.*

velopment is not merely a problem of popularization or of the introduction of new techniques. Neither can be accomplished outside the sociopolitical structure through which mobilization must be achieved.

Mobilization Structures

If we accept the idea that development cannot result from the sole effort of the state, or quasi-state institutions, without participation of the masses, it is obviously necessary to create structures which are able to bring about the total mobilization of the nation. In Senegal, the party political bureau and the government closely and constantly related at the highest level, in setting national objectives. At a lower level, the National Planning Commission permits different categories of professionals to initiate and carry on a dialogue about the objectives to be pursued by the plan.

On the regional level, where the Party elects the Regional Assembly, the Regional Development Committee discusses and chooses regional objectives by synthesizing departmental or local projects, thus arriving at an authentic expression of the will of the basic communities. These various institutions have permitted the change-over from an administration imposing its *a priori* will to an administration able both to receive impulse and to give impulse to the people. However, between the role of the Party, on the one hand, and the roles of administrative institutions, on the other, a problem arises, primarily political. The Party, of course, is a "class" which has succeeded "politically," while the cadres of the administrative institutions constitute an elite, who are technically in the process of succeeding. As a result, politicians and administrators do not always speak the same language. This may bring about, within the institutions, a sort of "nervous paralysis" which does not exactly facilitate the desired dialogue. The practice of

a political "clientele," dear to the Senegalese politicians, remains one of the great manifestations of this
discrepancy between occult political activities and development tasks.

To resolve these contradictions, in a country where
the structures bequeathed by colonization constituted
a great obstacle to modernization, the technique of
animation of a population has been devised. Simply
stated, its aims are:

1. to have the people participate directly in the
execution of the plan;

2. to diminish the action of the state and replace it
by spontaneous or induced initiative;

3. to favor voluntary leadership in the introduction
of techniques and modern organizations by mass-based
communities.

Once defined, *"animation"* must at once include three
more important considerations:

Among the factors of underdevelopment, we consider the social and cultural data of a country, what we
have agreed to call the human factors of underdevelopment. Sociology has demonstrated that the activation
of that planning on the operational level is less a matter of response to "command" from a central authority, than semispontaneous participation in a situa-
tional drama. But some in this situation act, while
others merely react, thus entirely vitiating the panacea
which had been obtained by the use of sociological
methods as well as the programmers' instruments of
measure. *"Animation"* did not help resolve the problem of developing a *strategy of development*.

After World War II, in a context which was peculiarly Anglo-Saxon, it was at last realized that the
problem of development strategy had to be cast in
terms of the "people's participation" in their own development. Based on the Anglo-Saxon principle of self-
help, the *community development* or *"amenagement
des collectivités"* became the great concept which the

UN propagated in Africa as well as in Asia. This system comprehended the entire range of means by which the inhabitants of a country joined their efforts to those of the government for the purpose of improving the economic, social, and cultural life of the collective units, to bring these collective units into a meaningful role in the life of the nation, and to facilitate their contributing to the progress of the country. This procedure, obviously, has definite weaknesses: first, it is merely a first step and it does not provide any perspective for social or even political change. Second, its strength is problematic, since, depending as it does in voluntarism of the people, in a very real sense it also demobilizes them.

My third remark bears on the experiments which are supposed to resolve the problems of rural development in technocratic terms. Here, one is primarily concerned with the methods which operate on the assumption that the technician is capable of transmitting to peoples the new techniques which will help them resolve their problems of production. The social and economic structures in which these peoples live matter little. What comes first is the injection of techniques into the rural communities.

This method seems to me very dangerous, because, whether we like it or not, no problems in rural communities are purely technical. They are technical problems which must be thought out and resolved within a given social and political framework. If we think otherwise and permit development to be sought under the cover of "technology" alone, the result will be a reactionary *depoliticizing* of the masses.

From this point of view, therefore, it seems to me that Senegal's choice of animation as the guiding spirit of development, operating within the limits stated, is in fact one which can be put in real revolutionary terms and which consequently allows for a certain doctrinal orientation in rural development.

Using Animation to Encourage a New Type of Relations between the State and the People

One of the authors of the animation movement, Ben Mady Cissé, said "The colonial period had left deep impressions in the peasants' attitude toward authority and administration. Subjected time and time again to the arbitrary authority of chieftainship, to the fraud and abuses of colonial functionaries in the context of pseudo-cooperative organizations set up by the colonial administration, and to the pressures pervasive in a controlled economy entirely beyond its influence, the rural world, by reflex, fell back on itself and became suspicious of any outside intervention. Independence of itself could change nothing under such crystallized conditions of isolated living."[8] Consequently, for the peasantry the government continued to be seen as an alien phenomenon; as Ben Mady Cissé points out; "Relations continued to be based on suspicion, not on collaboration." It was necessary, therefore, to undertake the re-establishment of dialogue with the people by coming face to face with them, by seeking them out in their own villages. It was the only way to release the force and vitality which had so long been repressed. In this manner, animation went to the heart of the national reality by awakening the population, by helping the people to become conscious of their economic condition, and by offering them the possibility of improving their own social and political lot—by providing the very means by which the action of the state could be oriented toward their liberation. Of course, this reorientation could not be automatic; responsible individuals do not automatically spring into

[8] B. M. Cissé, "L'Animation Rurale, base essentialle de tout développement," extract from *Afrique-document*, Nos. 68 and 69, 1963, p. 2.

being. Leadership consisted for the most part of traditional or modern elites whose concern for their personal stability contradicted the social evolution demanded by the concept of animation. However, freed from tribute to the interests which were at the heart of the existing political structure, the peasants were suddenly awakened to opportunity linked to responsibility. Only by breaking this link with the past could the way be cleared for a powerful democratic force which could vitalize and enlarge the process of political integration of masses of peasants.

Animation then appears truly as a political phenomenon in the sense that, above and beyond the real changes which it introduces into a given social group, that is, those of technical and economic progress, efficient and democratic co-operative management, etc., it creates structures which enhance natural solidarity. This is then the political dimension of animation: a reconversion of mentality of the people and their social structures which takes into account the freedom and initiative of the people.

What the Animator Is

Animation can be truly realized only if the people themselves initially choose their "animators." After that, others can be trained by the cadres of animators themselves. Without describing in detail the varieties of methodology used, let us remember the following motivating idea: the animator is a representative of the people who has come to realize the necessity of development and who has returned to his community. He is a peasant, and, remaining a peasant, he is indissociable from his group, which he leads in an effective plan of work. Rather than seeking to establish his position in the village, he is there because the village chose him. He discusses the problems of development with the technicians in order to make the program understood by and acceptable to the people he represents. This idea of representation has considerable importance. In both a historic and sociological perspective, we know that the traditional hierarchy had on the whole been unrepresentative. The colonial administration has for a long time imposed on the people the chiefs of cantons or villages. The people had no voice against their despotism. Through animation, these very communities now find their rights, but especially the *right of speech*.

Animation and Traditional Values

In examining the criteria for designating the animators, it seems to me that two points must be discussed: *the age of the animator and traditional influences at the village level.*[9]

In practice, the family situation plays an important role in the people's choice. In the peanut-growing basin, for example, dominated by the Ovolof and Serere ethnic groups, the power of decision belongs, in the end, to the head of the extended family: the extended family is the basic social organization, and at the same time, the basic economic unit. The elders of the village form a village council, a real political institution. In such a gerontocratic structure, age (twenty-five to forty) seems to me to be an effective criteria. Such is not the case, however, as soon as we deal with the *Diola* milieu, where social organization is based on the family. I have noticed that in the Ziguinchor Province, the animator's average age was between twenty-five and thirty.

Doubtless the most important fact to underline is

[9] For more details on these problems of method, see R. Colin, "L'Animation, participation des masses et des cadres au développement," *Dossiers Tendances,* No. 12, 1965.

that, in the act of choosing animators, factors intervene which are alien to methodological criteria of animation. It is, for example, the influence exercised traditionally by a family or a social group in the village that guides the people's choice. Two examples may illustrate this phenomenon. The first is borrowed from the river region. There, it often happens that a powerful clan will override the people's choice and send to "animation training" a man whose allegiance to the clan is sure from the start. The second example, from the Mouride milieu, illustrates this same phenomenon: the marabouts are, in fact, those who appoint the animators. In the case of Mouridism, it is important to underline the popular character of the guild organization. Mouridism has not only been a religious experience, but also, a "popular culture" movement, an archaic form of animation, which has already known some upheavals. If animation meets with its greatest difficulties in the Mouridized region, it is due solely to the fact that the adepts are already, in their own way, animated. Some of the values upheld by animation such as "the will to work," the free organization of the communities, and the modernization of certain aspects of the culture are already known to the Mourides. It is therefore necessary to find other motivations for them so that these values do not disappear under the weight of the guild authority structure. Contact with animation may revitalize them. What can be said at this moment is that the structures of mobilization born from animation cohabit artificially with the Mouride structures. It is doubtlessly because animation has not chosen facile methods that these difficulties persist in hindering its action. To destroy the "old" man so anchored in the rural milieu, to safeguard his personality, and at the same time respect the necessary stages of a progressive transformation are not easy aims to achieve.

By its action, animation has already made it possible to unify and to mobilize certain traditionally antagonistic social groups. Thanks to it, the privileges born with colonization, and which have become traditional (such as bribery), have been suppressed. The notables who persisted in upholding them are denounced by the villagers themselves, as these privileges hinder the evolution of the peasantry. No decree, no law could have ended them so swiftly. Repression especially could not be used at a time when the entire country needed to invest in itself. Animation, in proceeding to reconvert the peasant masses by utilizing psychological shock processes, was able, at the same time, to make the peasants confident in themselves: life without confidence is static and the outside world oppressive. In other words, it is what Ben Mady Cissé was expressing when he said:

"In order to defeat apathy . . . one had to begin immediately at the time of independence to bring to the peasants new and serious reasons for developing themselves and for having hope. While the state was setting into motion, on the national level, an entire organization destined to break the infernal circuits of colonial administration, Animation was penetrating into village communities, opening new horizons, and encouraging them to realize not only what their potentials were but how necessary it was that they implement their own development. Experience has proven it. The peasants, to whom free speech and initiative were returned, have not only revealed themselves to be open men determined to transform their economic situation, but they have retained an unknown wealth of creativity and especially an organizational ability which it is impossible to neglect."[10]

[10] B. M. Cissé, *op. cit.*, p. 8.

Co-operative Structure Bound to the Animation Movement

The "co-operative" structures set up by the colonial system have often been stigmatized, not without cause. Indeed, instead of strengthening the communal tendencies of African societies, they upset the existing economic and social organization. As M. Dia so aptly put it, "this concept of communal living everyone has seen as being a criterion of simplicity has brought on, in fact, a more complex social and economic organization than one has been willing to admit."[11] African society, therefore, in spite of the contempt in which its structures were held, had achieved the co-operative revolution which Europe only experienced later with the famous Rochdale pioneers. Their concept of a co-operative "republic" came to them from an experience which has been hitherto unrecorded: the Green Wood experience, which would have been the first kibbutz in the world, and which later inspired Engels' slogan "The experience of communal living and working."[12] Everywhere in Africa, the associative feeling had given birth to work communities based on mutual help. Even if the terminology of the co-operative was unknown to them, Africans nevertheless had their harmonious "village-co-operatives." Used as a reference, this situation has prompted the Senegalese to find in the co-operative movement one of the institutions able to favor rural modernization. Closely related to the Animation Movement, co-operatives will be the instrument of the economic democratization of rural communities.

[11] M. Dia, Contribution à l'étude du mouvement coopératif en Afrique Noire, *Présence Africaine* (Paris, 1958), p. 12.

[12] For more details, refer to the numerous works of H. Desroche, especially to the book entitled *Coopération et développement* (Paris, P.U.F., 1964), p. 121 and following.

The Co-operative Movement and the Commercialization of Peanuts

It was during the campaign of 1960–61 that all the new economic structures (Office of Agricultural Commercialization, Senegalese Bank of Development, Regional Centers of Development) began to function, working solely with the co-operatives which had also just been set up. It was, therefore, a real test for the government's policy of socialization. There were 712 co-operatives participating in the campaign, a rather small figure, but their output reached 188,000 tons, or one-fifth of the total peanut production. Jay Belloncle correctly described the situation when he said, "such a tonnage meant that the game had been won." Not only was the National Bank getting back its entire investment, but it was able to hand back to the co-operatives the sum of fifty million francs, representing the net profit of the project. In addition, the policy of reforming the retail trade, by officially recognizing and controlling a selected group of private stocking agencies, produced excellent results. The experience was therefore conclusive and, beginning with the following campaign, the government decided to intensify and extend the socialization of the peanut-market.[13]

The Office of Commercialization, through the co-operatives, was to control the whole circuit of peanut sales. The peasant, by the same token, found himself freed from the clutches of usurers and dealers, since he could sell his peanuts through the co-operative at an advantageous price. The export-import firms, linked with colonial domination, saw an important domain slip through their hands on August 8, 1961, when the government took measures forbidding the commercializa-

[13] G. Belloncle, "Etude du mouvement coopératif sénégalais" (Dakar, 1964), p. 9, mimeographed document.

tion of peanuts by any organization which had not received official authorization. As for the marketing of peanuts, only the O.A.C. was authorized to do it. Nineteen sixty-two, then, was the year co-operatives came into their own. Being almost identified with the producer, and able to buy peanuts from any point in Senegal, they handled, that year, close to 500,000 tons, or almost 50 per cent of the total production.

The Co-operatives as Instruments of Rural Development

If marketing is one of the principal functions of the Senegalese co-operative movement, it would seem that the co-operative movement ought to exercise this function to expand. In other words, it is through its role in the marketing of peanuts that it can develop other roles that will transform it into a "development co-operative." As M. Dia said, "the cooperative movement cannot be a technocratic or bureaucratic process endowed with a certain output coefficient and directed from the outside. It must be the basic level of responsibility in economic acts."[14] This evolutionary view of the co-operative movement is far from expressing the social feeling associated with certain popular movements in the initial stages of their development. The co-operative, according to Watkins, is an "educational movement through economic action." It can and must be a "school in the art of being human," as Claudel would say. As co-operatives of rural development, the peasant co-operatives aim at "progressively assuming all those activities required by a harmonious development of the peasant community under consideration."[15] However, and let there be no illusion here,

[14] M. Dia, *Circulaire no. 32 sur la doctrine et l'évolution du mouvement coopératif,* May 1962, p. 2.
[15] *Ibid.*

this conception of a "development co-operation" does
not mean that all the feelings of tension or opposition
that accompany any liberation have been overcome. On
the contrary, it is often that these tensions appear and
are crystallized from within analogous institutions. In
analyzing, for instance, the relations among fellow co-
operative members in a region such as the Baol, a
stronghold of mouridism, I discovered that the traditional relations of domination in the *marabout-
taâlibé contract* transfer themselves to the co-operative level. The presidents of co-operatives, and even
the weighers, are elected by a general assembly of
the members uniquely in function of the position which
they occupy within the guild organization. Generally
speaking, the president of the co-operative is the son
of the village marabout or his representative.

Does this deference given to formal leaders of the
religious organization, on the co-operative level, mean
that co-operative democracy, as a moral principle, is
absent? If "democracy" means conformity to decisions
of the majority, it is certain that the answer will
be no. If, on the contrary, we mean, by "democracy,"
a rational choice based on objective criteria of free
adherence and conscious participation, the Mouride
co-operatives would then be "co-operatives without
members." We are dealing here rather with a practical
rule, but one which is rooted in the values and symbols of mouridism itself.[16]

Rural Reforms and Rural Communities

Senegalese land was traditionally held collectively or
by family groups. Even if one can say there were no rich
farmers, meaning big landowners such as those in
Latin America, certain rights inherited from the pre-
colonial period still subsisted. It would be helpful to

[16] Sy, *op. cit.*

point out certain aspects of Baol rural customs. The most common of the traditional rights of ownership was, without a doubt, the *lamanat,* which could be found in all the states, except the Fouta. This institution (which probably comes from the Mandingues) had, initially, a purely fiscal character. The *lamanat* was conceded to nobles for services to the crown; the *lamane* was then responsible for collecting the rents due from the peasants. Rent had an essentially symbolic character: the farmers gave the *lamane* only a sheaf of millet. But by this gesture, peasants were reminded that they had no eminent rights to the land they farmed. "The country belongs to the king (*bûr*) and if you till the land, you must show him your gratitude," the *lamanes* would tell the peasants. Later on, however, probably in order to meet the expenses of the State institutions, the sheaf of millet was transformed into an actual rent.

During the entire life of the former Senegalese states, the *lamanat* was only an administrative function. It was only with the introduction of colonialism that these lords were recognized as being real landowners, and hereafter collected the same rents on their own behalf.

Other types of rights in this rather "feudal" system— the right of fire (*daay*), which might require the payment of a rent; the right of the ax, (*ngadio*) intended to be a land-clearing right; the right of the wooden shoe (*lew* in Wolof)—did not give real title to the land, at least in the Roman sense of the word (*jus utendi, jus abutendi, jus fruendi*). Here, again, it is the appearance of a mercantile economy which upset the entire rural system.

It was by a measure called "the national domain law" that the independent state of Senegal undertook to put an end to these persisting privileges. It was, in truth, a real agrarian reform bill whose first principle was to dispossess all those who did not farm the land.

The State, "heir to the ancient ancestral privileges," will hereafter be sole "master of the land," with the exception of those persons who, on the day the law was enacted, were already legally registered as land-owners.[17] This land reform raises some highly political problems. Intending, through its enactment, to democratize the administration of the national patrimony, the land reform measure implied that all abuses linked to ancient forms of land acquisition would be suppressed. President Senghor, in clear terms, relegated the problem to its proper domain. "It is vital that the people become aware of the fact that the enactment of these texts will bring an irremediable end to the former situation characterized by the payment of taxes to the *lamanes*. The persons occupying or personally working land attached to the national domain, at the time of the enactment of this law, will continue to occupy and farm it, but they do so by virtue of the authority of the State, who is the holder of the national territory, who attends to its distribution and who, in return, requires no rent."[18] President Senghor's concern is to end abuses committed against the producer, and especially to protect him. The creation of state lands will be a proper framework from which to proceed. Defined as a homogeneous body of land parcels required to develop the peoples in a given zone, the state lands must be able to "permit the proper functioning of a rural cooperative founded as a profit-making and self-managing enterprise."[19] Of a reduced size, and destined by the country's structural evolution to be the starting point for new communities, the state land should also be considered as tomorrow's basic economic cell. Its future is linked to

[17] *Loi sur le domaine national,* June 17, 1964 (article 1).

[18] L. Senghor, *Circulaire aux gouverneurs de région,* 1964.

[19] *Decret d'application de la loi sur le domaine national* (article 3).

that of the co-operatives, which may or may not democratize the management of the communities resulting
from these reforms. What can be said, at the moment—
and President Senghor touched on this problem at the
last convention of the "U.P.S."—is that the new rural
communities aim at progressively handing over to
groups of villages the responsibilities which the civil
servant has held for a long time. This phenomenon
seems to have considerable importance if we see it in
light of the idea that the future centers of decision will
not only be, as before, the state institutions but also
the popular structures born from the Animation Movement, from the co-operative system, and from the
dialogue with the State's technical institution at the
local level, the *Center for Rural Expansion*. This struc-
turation will allow populations to assume responsibility
for the three essential functions of rural development:
the *planning function,* vested in the rural council; the
function of economic acts, vested in the co-operatives,
and finally the function of animation or rural apprenticeship, left to the network of animators.

Conclusion: To Continue Structural Reform

It is important to point out the extent to which
efforts to modernize the rural world tend to destroy
the old peasant world. It appears that the chief objective of the policy of rural development carried out
by Senegal since independence is to guarantee the
peasants a minimum of physical well-being by breaking up all the old production and consumer circuits of
a barter economy. One must admit, however, that the
existing relations which still prevail in Africa, between
the dominant and dominated economies, present difficult problems. What matters, however, is the will of
the Senegalese people to resolve them progressively.

Another point to mention is that the policy of setting in place these development structures so as to

meet the needs and aspirations of rural populations is not done without difficulty. There are some major inconveniences, for example, at the operational level, due to the division of development tasks between several ministerial departments or their interference in the midst of the same ministry. Included among these structural problems is the most urgent one of the regrouping of tasks of rural formation since it is closely bound to the future of political modernization. To anyone familiar with Senegal, the necessity of an homogeneous machinery of rural promotion not only has absolute priority, but its creation determines the political integration of the rural sector. President Senghor is acutely aware of these problems since he has worked to resolve the economic problems of the rural communities by freeing the co-operatives and Regional Centers of Development Assistance from the too bureaucratic requirements imposed on them by certain ministerial departments.

Regrouped in one institution, the National Office of Co-operation and Development Assistance, these management roles must be supported by animation and rural formation. In this case as well, reform is necessary—and this is President Senghor's concern—so that socialism may finally become a tangible reality in the rural areas.

ANTHONY H. M. KIRK-GREENE

The Merit Principle
in an African Bureaucracy:
Northern Nigeria

QUALIFICATION AND THE ACCESSIBILITY
OF OFFICE IN THE SELECTION
OF PUBLIC SERVANTS

*Anthony H. M. Kirk-Greene was Supervisor
of the first Administrative Service Training
Course and seconded as Lecturer at
the Institute of Administration in Northern
Nigeria. He has had extensive experience
both as a teacher and as an administrator.
He was elected to the Senior Research
Fellowship in African Studies of St.
Anthony's College, Oxford, in 1967.
He has written numerous books and articles
including* This is Northern Nigeria *and*
The Emirates of Northern Nigeria
(with S. J. Hogben).

A Methodological and Glossarial Note

Leading on from a previous study of the social pressures brought to bear on individual members of the
new bureaucracy that had begun to develop between

1957 and 1962 in the conspicuously authoritarian society of Northern Nigeria,[1] this case study considers an institutional extension of the personalized conflicts inherent in the same Nigerian social context, advancing the scene to the no less formative years of 1962–67. At the same time it lifts the argument out of its earlier transitional stage of the new bureaucratic cadres' search for identity and legitimacy, and, in reviewing their consolidation as an established Civil Service, examines how this major institution of the development process has handled, and to what extent it has succumbed or triumphed therein, this confrontation with the forces of traditional authority that were previously observed in action at the individual level.

The approach has been contained within a generally Weber-derived terminological framework, but its motivation is less an a priori application of a theoretical model and more an empirical enquiry. Hopefully, the features of change and continuity—or, as was often said to describe the Northern Nigerian experience, "continuity in change"—among exponents of authority discussed herein may suggest relevance to selected variables in established models or help to evolve their own model for measuring clerisy behavior in similar societies experiencing similarly induced socialization.

Certain terminological caveats must be entered, and in doing so I wish to acknowledge the valued views of Professor C. S. Whitaker, Jr., on the essence of this chapter. One is to underscore the focal concern of this chapter with *recruitment* to public office in contemporary Hausa society: no premises are advanced on *postappointment* attitudes and values of the same civil servants. Indeed, I see no reason to deny the present possibility that, once a more open type of recruitment has been instituted, there may be a marked reaffirmation of certain Hausa norms within the behavioral patterns of even a meritocrat-recruited public service.

The bitter ethnic confrontation of 1965–66 in Nigeria could very well accelerate the cultural process of what may be termed "re-Hausafication." Secondly, despite the superficial polarization of "traditional" and "modern" as terms of reference, I have long held both to be a simultaneous process wherein nearly every traditional society is all the time "changing" and many a modern one is continuously "traditionalizing." Nor need change per se take the form of an upward or "forward" curve: a curve of a cyclical nature, dipping below the control axis as well as rising above it, is equally "change." It is indeed this cyclical interpretation of change that informs much of Northern Nigerian socialization and leads me to go along with the burden of Professor Whitaker's triple reformulation of the hypothesis of eurhythmism, namely that:

"1. Significant change in one important sphere or aspect of social activity may ramify in other aspects or spheres; however, such ramifications are not always consonant with the character and direction of the initial change.

"2. Change may offer novel opportunities for those adversely subjected to that change to defend, recoup, reaffirm, augment or facilitate antecedent activity or value, notwithstanding that such activity or value is manifestly or latently inconsistent with the character and direction of the initial change.

"3. Subjected to potentially transformative political change, a society previously characterized by political domination presents special opportunities for 'manipulative response' that limits the impact of that change."[2]

With these qualifiers, this essay, set within a broadly Weberian conceptualization, comprises a study of a bureaucracy (here viewed as a development institution but treated primarily on the personal level of practitioners of public administration; in transition from its formation as a predominantly (1) *ascription*-based (2) *hierocracy* of a (3) *traditional* society, where their (4) *appointment* as (5) *officials* of the (6) *king* operated through a (7) *closed* recruitment system, toward a predominantly (1) *achievement*-oriented (2) *meritocracy* of a (3) *Westernized* society, where their (4) *selection* as (5) *officers* of the (6) *State* operates through an (7) *open* recruitment system. Projected between these oppositions is the phenomenon of a threatened revival of traditionalistic authority, albeit disguised in some of the trappings of modern officialdom, where a charismatic leader momentarily appeared to be seeking to combine both these polarized elements into a bureaucracy based on personal rather than institutional loyalty. Translated into Northern Nigerian specifics, we have the opposition of traditional Hausa/Fulani court mores—and their perpetuation into modern Native Administration and political party behavior—and a twentieth century apolitical Civil Service ethos; the incipient acceptance of the latter confronted at one stage by the authority of the Premier in whose role there paradoxically converged the hereditary status and legitimate authority of traditionalism as well as the liberalising dynamic demanded in the leadership of a modernizing society. This challenge was symbolized in the interruption to the loyalty graph away from an individual, who enjoys his obedience-claim by virtue of his traditional status, to an institution, formalistic and impersonal—an interruption caused by a threatened diversion toward a situation which had overtones of patrimonialism.[3] In the event, the forces of education fulfilled their historical role of leveling and have brought about the advent of a fresh element in the ranks of the new bureaucracy: Coleman and Rosberg's "new assertive social groups and claimant élites,"[4] here styled the "meritocrats."

For ready identification of the major concepts employed in this chapter, the following terms have been adopted. Wherever appropriate, terminology sanc-

tioned by Hausa usage has been given. The choice of
the term "meritocrats" clearly owes a debt of acknowl-
edgment to Michael Young's revival of its currency in
his *The Rise of the Meritocracy* (1958), with its slogan
of rule by "not an aristocracy of birth, not a plutocracy
of wealth, but a true meritocracy of talent."

MERITOCRATS: The new generation of achievemen-
talist, university-educated civil servants, who insist on
higher education as a *sine qua non* qualification for
a senior bureaucratic appointment and undiluted merit
—here represented by Western-education patents—as
the yardstick for promotion. They hold scant brief for
the HIEROCRATS and their ascriptive criteria, and not
much more for many of their superiors in the public service who, though lacking in formal education as
identified by college degrees, often compensate by
possessing the administrative experience and know-
how absent among the MERITOCRATS. In some instances this group may be identified as *'yan zamani,*
"the mod. generation." Hausa has no exact word to
convey the semantic force of "merit" and "qualifications," so that public service advertisements have had
to build on paraphrases of the theme of *kokari,* "in-
dustrious effort," *ya cancanta,* "it behoves that . . ."
and *ilmi,* "book knowledge."

HIEROCRATS: Those who have carried over into Native Administration (local government) service and
party politics—and, according to the MERITOCRATS,
now and again into the civil service—unquestioning
acceptance of the creed that the ascriptive criteria
and hereditary authority of traditional Hausa society
should confer equal rank and status in modern society. Cf. the contemporary English "square" and
"Establishment."

The socio-occupational undertones of this confrontation, derived from traditional Hausa society, are expressed in the important Hausa opposition of *karda*

(ascribed status) + *asali* ("the old families") v. *shigege* (achieved status) + *'yan tsirge* ("the parvenus").

EMIRATISM: The beliefs and attitudes derived from the influences, mores, and expectancies of those traditionally holding authority (*masu-sarauta*) in the type Hausa/Fulani Native Administration. It has no pejorative overtones, save in the eyes of those MERITO-CRATS who see it as a force designed to perpetuate, at their expense, the traditional authority-structure through the agency of its exponents, the HIEROCRATS.

KADUNAISM: The projection of Emiratism at the level of national politics and government. In the Lagos press of 1912 this was identified as "The Nigerian System," and in the Southern Nigerian press of fifty years later it was dubbed "Ranky-Daddyism" (from a mishearing and misunderstanding of the traditional Hausa greeting of respect *ranka ya dade,* "may your life be prolonged").

The following abbreviations, common in the literature on the civil service in African states, have been used:

PSC = Public Service Commission
NA   = Native Administration
DO   = District Officer
ASTC = The concessional entry Administrative Service Training Course (Zaria).

Introduction

The quicksilver ratios of continuity in proportion to change have operated as a focus of fascination for social scientists working in the new area-discipline of African studies to an extent that a comparative reading of the Asian literature on nationalism and socialization does not at first suggest. The purposeful transfer of institutions and the incidental heritage of less tangible though equally valid phenomena by means of education and societal "neocolonialism" understandably remain a favorite topic of research.

Few would wish to challenge Reinhard Bendix's evaluation that "the central fact of nation-building is the orderly exercise of a nationwide public authority."[5] Those who exercise this authority are the administrators—Bendix's "formally instated officials"—who, as the executive arm of government, constitute the corps of bureaucrats internationally recognized as civil services. In the total process of decolonization and institution-building, no act has been so fundamental to postindependence success (one might, mindful of the Congo chaos, almost say survival) as that of bequeathing a public service adequately staffed, oriented, and trained to carry the administrative burdens of the new state. "As the Union Jack was lowered at midnight," writes a leading observer of the localization of the government services in such countries, "perhaps the principal question which the departing British asked themselves was what they had done to leave behind a stable framework of law and order and services."[6] Few institutions thus inherited by the ex-colonial territory from the metropolitan country have, at least in the Anglophone areas, been invested by the legatees with quite the same social prestige as the higher civil service.[7] There, it seemed, was where real power lay: to the vast mass of the people, "Government" had for years been symbolized in the familiar figure of the District Commissioner, *roi de la brousse* and hopefully lord of all he surveyed. Macaulay would today be more than satisfied were he to see the competitive careerism displayed in the new nations for securing a post in their English-model civil services, for had he not declared that the day when India demanded British institutions would be the "proudest day in English history"?[8] True, as African public officials have taken care to emphasize,[9] there had to come a profound change of attitude by and toward the civil service, now to be viewed as a positive instrument in the development of political and economic institutions of the new states rather than as previously the traditional guardians of law, order, and tax collection. But the predecessor Service's high traditions of loyalty, integrity, and hard work have seldom been questioned as the aim of every new indigenous civil service.

More often than not, this concept of a public service fills an institutional vacuum. Until the advent of the colonial power and its bureaucratic machinery, such a notion may have been unknown, and the limit of a civil administration was the host of courtly hangers-on, favorites, and royal household officials. In most cases, the establishment of bureaucratic cadres encountered only a negative resistance: if there was no institution to build on, at least there was nothing to replace. But what of those societies which meet the Fortes and Evans-Pritchard criteria of "states," political systems possessed of, *inter alia,* centralized authority and an administrative machinery?[10] Among these, the emirates of Northern Nigeria have long held the stage as an example of a polity marked by an advanced degree of administrative sophistication.

This case study seeks not to elaborate, but to extend, the current literature on the persistence of Hausa social rank concepts in modern political institutions, by examining their operations in the complementary sector of the civil service. In thus assessing the extent to which social forces control public service attitudes, it will be possible to measure the scale of disruption or restructuring in Hausa status hierarchy brought about by the shift in patterns of recruitment to public office from, in the Weberian typology, "traditional" to a "radical-legal" authority. If we accept the demonstrable thesis (see Tables II and III below) that traditional authoritarianism has successfully permeated the leadership structure and behavioral patterns of party politics in the emirates of Northern Nigeria—

seen by one of their closest political analysts as "traditional political entities whose salient common characteristics are hierarchical and quasi-theocratic authority, a high degree of social stratification, [and a] well-developed bureaucratic machinery . . ."[11]—we may ask to what extent has it made its mark on the parallel exponent of modernization, the public service. In tracing the influence of emiratism on the modern civil service from its domination at the pre-jihad Habe court through Fulani-governed Hausaland down to its operation within the post-1900 Native Administration system of local government, we shall notice one aspect of the situation that is atypical in the African context: the existence within a traditional society, long before the advent of a European colonial bureaucratic machinery, of a sophisticated and effective hierarchy of officials charged with the executive administration of the emirate. It will be evident that such an organization could clearly provide a challenge to the introduction of that kind of bureaucracy inherent in the legal type of authority, for the situation coincides with Weber's finding that the advance of the bureaucratic structure is "realized most slowly where older structural forms have been technically well developed and functionally adjusted to the requirements at hand."[12]

Stratification in Hausa Society

With the exception of the Tiv, Hausa society is probably the best-documented in Northern Nigeria. For most of this, scholars are indebted to the researches of Professor M. G. Smith. Under his impetus, there has emerged an impressive corpus of literature[13] on one of the most significant of Hausa phenomena, namely the manner and measure in which its traditional social stratification has permeated its modern life, including party politics: "Political authority among the Hausa not only arises from the total social system but gives rise to a system of ideas and beliefs which weld the political organisation into a coherent and comprehensible whole."[14] Because of the ready availability of this documentation, it will not be necessary to do more than summarize the points in it which relate to the theme of this chapter.

Aside from such facets of institutionalized social status as the correlation between political prominence and patrilineal descent, the distribution of authority within kindred on the basis of agnation and generational seniority, and the way in which among non-kin "relative social position is shown in different verbal greetings and physical gestures appropriate to relationships of equality, inferiority or superiority,"[15] there are two further important determinants among Hausa males: the elements of rank and of occupational class. Sociologists today support Smith's rejection of the earlier sociopolitical opposition within Hausa society of *sarakuna* ("the royal classes") + *masu-sarauta* ("those holding office") v. *talakawa* ("the peasantry"), as "an illusory antithesis which breaks down under examination."[16] Currently preferred is the categorization based on three broad occupational strata, coterminous with the dichotomy still recognized by the Hausa in the socioeconomic distinctions between *attajirai* ("rich"), *madaidaici* ("comfortably off"), and *matsiyaci* ("poor"). Here previous undertones of a Marxist-type class struggle within the emirates are replaced by a classification that carries the more valid assumptions of wealth rather than of power distinctions. Despite the limitations of this model, too, its practical value for the Hausa is accepted: "It is at once a description of their society, a guide to their behaviour, and a normative frame."[17]

For the purpose of this essay, however, attention must be paid to two of the most notable deficiencies of this revised categorization of Hausa society: its tendency to embrace all officials into one homogeneous status group and its blurring of Linton's fundamental analytical distinction of status as ascriptive or achieved.[18] In this context we may note the existence in Hausa not only of these two sociological concepts, *karda* and *shigege,* but of a number of proverbs that reveal their deep roots in society: *dan asali ya fi shigege,* "he who is to the manner born is better than the newcomer," or *harbi ga dan jaki gado ne,* "the art of kicking is something that the young donkey acquires through heredity."

Public Officials in Pre-1900 Hausaland

Thanks to the research of two Northern Nigerian scholars, we can derive from their translated *A Chronicle of Abuja*[19] an above-average understanding of the administration of Hausaland up to the nineteenth century; and from Professor Smith's reconstruction built onto this[20] we have a brilliant depiction of the administrative processes of the Fulani government in one of the principal Hausa city-states up to the twentieth century. Our concern here is with one aspect of such governments, namely the recruitment of public officials into the civil administration. Smith has identified three characteristics of these cadres relevant to our study: (i) Government was conducted through a system of ranked and titled offices (*sarautu*). (ii) Relations between offices of subordinate and superordinate rank holders were highly formalized. (iii) Very few of these offices were hereditary. The offices of the type Habe state have been classified into eight rank orders, each forming a separate unit differentiated in terms of its status and responsibilities. These are kingship, inner chamber officials, royal household officials, public officials, vassal chiefs and royal officials, slave officials, and the *malamai* (clerics and scholars).[21] It is no more accurate to interpret the socio-occupational distinctions discussed above as prohibiting some degree of mobility than it is to regard these rank orders as closed to promotional opportunities. There was an acknowledged order of precedence among titleholders, and the closed series of groupings were defined only by the four horizontal status divisions (royalty, freedom, eunuchry, slavery), the last three of which cut right across the eight vertical orders. Within each order of rank there were ascending titled offices. These did not form an unbroken serial scale, but any official could aspire to a higher office within his own social status group, i.e., free nobles in the household order might hope for promotion to the junior military offices reserved for freemen, from among whom the senior military official would be chosen, always a freeman.

The two groups of public officials were known as the *rukuni* (lit. "group") and, junior to them, the *rawuna* (lit. "turbans").[22] To these groups, comprising freemen, eunuchs, and slaves, was entrusted the civil and military administration of the emirate. They were responsible for the territorial administration of the fiefs which they held and for the maintenance of law and order. They oversaw the slave officials who held the lesser civil service posts. The officials of the royal household were headed by the *Sarkin Fada,* himself a freeman and a civil administrator but junior in rank to the *Madawaki,* the senior public official. On behalf of the king, the *Sarkin Fada* kept an eye on the slave officials through his agents the *Hauni* or executioners, while the *Madawaki* supervised the slave officials through the *Sata,* a slave promoted to the *rawuna* class of public officials. Within the *rukuni* class, the *Madawaki* was responsible, with his fellow freemen, for military affairs and was himself captain of the cavalry[23] and army commander, while the civil administration proper, such as the markets, supplies, communications, prisons, and police, were in charge of the *Galadima* assisted by fellow eunuchs. Recruitment into these public official orders was from household official into the *rawuna* and thence the *rukuni*. If, however, one excludes from the civil service category all those administrators involved in political decision-making, then Smith considers that the slave and *malam* orders alone exhibited a purely administrative character.[24]

Since much of our subsequent discussion of contemporary civil service behavior is valid for other areas of Northern Nigeria, exposed to the Muslim cultural influence but not within the confines of Hausaland *pur sang* (e.g., Nupe, Kanuri), it is worth remarking that this embryo bureaucratic administration was not restricted to the original Hausa states. Revealing glimpses of effective government through avocational nobles and trained slave officials are found in the narratives of nineteenth-century travellers like Clapperton, Barth, Staudinger, and Monteil. Among the Nupe, Nadel has shown how three groups of officers of state were identified at the rank level immediately below the *ena gitsuzhi,* the royal nobility group from among whom the king is chosen.[25] Each *ena,* or social order, of these *ticizhi,* "the titled ones," was unmistakably delineated: the *sarakinzhi* comprised the civil and military nobility; the *manzhi* comprised the Koranic scholars who made up the judiciary, the clergy, and the scribes; and the *ena wuzhi,* or order of court slaves (the other rank orders were both *egi,* "freemen") who, though lowest in rank, nevertheless wielded considerable political influence within the state's administration. Again, in Bornu, the traditional Kanuri administration is said to have been based on numerous officials, thirty-two of whom were *maina* or royal princes, twenty-three kogana or freeborn, eight *malams,* and forty-two slaves and eunuchs. The last-named were generally subdivided into three grades of military

specialists, but all were fief holders. Under the rule of
Rabeh in the 1890s, the territorial administration took
on a different shape, with "strangers" appointed as district (*ajia*) and village (*lawan*) heads, superordinate
to local agents (*bulama* and *mbarna*) at the hamlet
level.[26]

The structure of Hausa public administration after
the Fulani conquest underwent modification in its details, especially in its system of appointment to office, though the Habe framework of government remained easily recognizable. The senior officers of
state, the *hakimai,* became territorial administrators
and now combined both civil and military functions.
In Zaria titled slaves no longer enjoyed fiefs, which
were exclusively allotted to freemen. In nearly every
emirate, the political system was bedeviled by competing royal dynasties—Table I gives an impressive example of the zigzag pattern of royal succession—each
with its groups of adherents (*'yan sarki,* or those eligible for the throne; *jikokin sarki,* or grandchildren of
previous rulers in the dynasty; *barori,* or clients and
family followers) all avid of office. To play one off
against the other by the tantalus of office became
every emir's game, and so step by step the Fulani
rulers appropriated the former Hausa offices for persons of royal or noble status. Eunuchs and slaves were
now eliminated from holding territorial office, and in
order to accommodate their administrative talents
within the royal court and household, fresh titles had
to be created.

Two points bearing on our total argument may be
observed here. One, in view of what we shall be saying
later about the reaction of the meritocrats to the
familial, personalized, and hierocratic system of appointments and promotion within the native administrations (subsumed under the rubric of emiratism), it
is significant to note how the Fulani reign was stigma-

Table I

A: THE EMIRS (LAMIDOS) OF ADAMAWA

(1) MODIBBO ADAMA
1806-48

LAWAL 1848-72 — MANSUR — (3) SANDA — HAMIDU — (4) ZUBEIRU — (5) BOBBO AHMADU

SUDI — (6) IYA — AHMADU BOBOA — (7) ABBA 1910-24

(8) MUHAMMADU BELLO (MAIGARI) 1924-28 — (9) MUSTAFA 1928-46

(10) AHMADU 1946-53 — (11) ALIYU 1953-

B: THE EMIRS (ETSUZHI) OF NUPE

MALAM DENDO

(1) USMAN ZAKI — MAMMAN — (2) MASABA

(4) MALIKI 1884-95 — (3) UMARU MAJIGI 1873-84 — (5) ABUBAKAR 1895-1901 — MAMUDU

(7) BELLO 1916-26 — (6) MUHAMMADU 1901-16 — (8) SAIDU 1926-35

BAGUDU — (9) MUHAMMUDO NDAYAKO 1935-62 — (10) USMAN SARKI 1962-

[Adapted from the dynastic genealogies given in S. J. Hogben and A. H. M. Kirk-Greene, *The Emirates of Northern Nigeria* (London 1966)] tized by a growing instability of promotional patterns. Smith, unconsciously echoing the scornful plaint of patronage made by many a meritocrat of the 1960s to whom service with his local NA may be suggested, has described how "officials of Fulani Zaria were appointed, promoted, transferred and dismissed at the king's pleasure, and without any formal restrictions, hereditary or otherwise, limiting the ruler's freedom of action. . . . Not only were office-holders liable to peremptory dismissal on the death of their patron, their offices also were liable to be transferred to another rank and given to persons of different status, since the allocation of office was governed by the king's political situation and needs," and concludes that "political offence, defined by the system as attachment to the king's political rival, was the principal ground for dismissal, and political solidarity with the king . . . was the principal ground for appointment."[27] Secondly, mindful of what we shall be discussing further on about the threat of a personal loyalty towards their leader being expected of civil servants instead of an institutional one to their service, comment must be made on the phenomenon of *barantaka,* or clientage. Appointive officials of state were accustomed to identify themselves as *barori* (sing. *bara*) of the king. There was naturally competition for office, and this largely took the form of appointment based on one qualification, not of open merit, but of closed social status or clientage. Social scientists can still discern clientage as coterminous with Hausa society and consider it an institution whose significance in the political organization it is hard to overestimate.[28] Among the Nupe, too, "attachment to a man of rank and influence is a way to secure social promotion, the chance of becoming 'somebody,' of being lifted from the ignominy of a commoner's life into the sphere of rank and importance."[29] Here, indeed, social symbols and

the protocol of formal etiquette have remained substantial and almost inviolate. If it was only a generation ago that Nadel was talking of how "the social
stratification stretches beyond the formalized rank system embodied in the political structure—it embraces
the whole country and absorbs and reinterprets in its
own sense the cultural configuration of Nupe at large,"
and of the noticeably "submissive behaviour of a client
towards his patron, or a member of the lower class
towards a man of rank,"[30] it is less than a year ago
that one group of Nigerian "leaders of thought," to
use the current idiom, identified among the root causes
of their country's political catastrophe of 1966 the
"national traits of sycophancy, deference support and
pathological craving for praise."[31] An acquaintance-
ship of any depth with Hausa, Kanuri, Yoruba, or Nupe
society reinforces these observations; their incompati-
bility with the principles of the meritocracy is apparent.

Having discussed the differentiation of status in
Hausaland as expressed in its recruitment of its administrative officials, we can now proceed to examine
to what extent this phenomenon of a particularist privileged group has been projected into the twin development institutions of the emirates in the twentieth century, those organisms exhibiting the new political and
administrative processes. In the political sector, scholars have provided a vivid illustration of the persistence with which Hausa social divisions have carried
over into the contemporary political life so that all
that is necessary here in depicting the political scene
against which to set the bureaucratic one is to note
the results of such research. Thus Dudley, analyzing
the impact of traditional status patterns on the membership of the Northern legislature, has shown that
among the Northern People's Congress (NPC) party
members returned at the 1951 and 1956 regional elections (the ones which carried it into self-government)
the following percentages obtained:[32]

TABLE II

*Familial Status of NPC Members of the
Regional Legislature*

	1951	1956
Sons of Chiefs	8%	6%
Brothers of Chiefs	9	3
Nephews of Chiefs	1	1
Cousins of Chiefs	1	2
District Heads*	30	29
NA Officials*	69	32

(*Some such officials were at the same
time relatives of chiefs.)

Coleman, comparing the Northern Regional with
the federal legislature, calculates that for 1952 as
many as 89 per cent of the former and 95 per cent
of the latter house were NA employees, and in 1956
district heads still accounted for 20 per cent of the
Northern membership of each house.[33] Again, Whitaker has produced a tabulation[34] which shows that
in 1959 over 75 per cent of the members representing
the "emirate" provinces (Sokoto, Kano, Katsina,
Bornu, Zaria, etc.) in the Northern House of Assembly derived from the traditional ruling class. Among
ministers, the score was seventeen out of nineteen!
In the Federal House of Representatives elected in
1959, which carried Nigeria into independence, Dudley
reckons that almost one-fifth of the 134 NPC members were sons of ruling emirs and another 10 per
cent were District Heads.[35] Taking the two emirate
provinces *par excellence,* Post has calculated that in
the same federal election thirteen of the twenty-one
NPC candidates in Sokoto were NA employees/coun-
cilors and another five were district/village heads,
while in Kano eighteen of the thirty NPC candidates

belonged to the first category and a further seven to the second.[36]

It would be otiose to seek further proof of the perpetuation of traditional Hausa special patterns in the modern political system. The case appears amply proved. The inference is inescapable that the power pattern of contemporary Hausa society reflects as much continuity as it does change.

The Conversion of Hausa Court Officials into Native Administrative Staff

In now turning to the complementary strand in the woof of nation-building, the behavioral patterns not of the politicians but of the civil servants as representatives of a fundamental development institution, we are entitled to ask whether we can discover any trace of the dynamics of the antecedent Hausa/Fulani system of recruitment to public office—still so vivid in the strictly political sector—within the bureaucracy of its modern government. In putting this question, we must distinguish the two aspects of the introduction of the modern bureaucratic process into Northern Nigeria: the local government scene, represented in the establishment and growth of native administrations from 1910 onwards, and the central (in the Nigerian federal case ranked as regional) civil service scene from 1954 through today.

Granted the basic rationale of the policy widely recognised as indirect rule, whereby Great Britain decided to govern her new protectorate of Northern Nigeria, acquired in 1900-3, through its indigenous institutions, it should not be surprising to find that Hausa social hierarchy, duly modified by the Fulani overlordship of the past hundred years, so established its position that it was able to influence and infiltrate the appointment of the new public administration officials almost undeterred. True, the statuses of slavery and of eunuchism were quickly abolished by the British government on the humane plea of being repugnant to natural justice. Additionally, there was now an extra tier of authority, the resident and the district officer, always appellate and often executive: however "advisory" their legal role, in practice few could avoid the seeming need to play that of kingmaker or administrative catalyst into the bargain, and all were expected, by those in authority above as well as below, to do something more than sit with their feet up and wait for the emir to seek their "advice." True, again, the British deplored the custom of absentee landlords and insisted on a redistribution of fiefs (H: *gunduma*) and on the *hakimai* or fief holders returning to their districts (exceptionally, in Bornu they had always lived there) instead of leaving them in the charge of rapacious agents, *jekadu,* while they resided in the capital, rotating like satellites around their mini-Sun King.

But by and large the administrative structure was, in so far as the recruitment of its officials was concerned, very little changed. Thus, while actual titles and order of precedence vary within each emirate, it was a common experience to find within the new native administration system the erstwhile *Sarkin Fada* became the intermediary or liaison officer between the emir and the DO and the emir's letter writer retain his function and title as *Magatakarda.* At the other end of the scale, the *Santali* emerged as the official charged with holding the emir's staff of office through the automobile window instead of beside the royal horse. The *Sarkin Dogari* and the *Yari* have continued unchanged in their respective police and prison responsibilities as well as in title. The *Alkali* remained as leader of the Moslem judiciary within the emirate, as did the *Ma'aji* when he took over the native treasury. The *Waziri* has in most emirates (notably not in Kano) retained his *sarauta* as the senior representative of the emir. Royal chamberlains like the *Makama,*

Turaki, and *Barde* became the appointive inner councilors in name that they had always been in practice,
and military titles like *Sardauna, Mayaki, Sarkin Yaki,*
etc., were redistributed to civil officials.[37] The *malam*
class in general became the clerical grade without
which bureaucracy cannot function, and to this very
day have retained their faintly Pickwickian appella-
tion of "scribes," often headed by the *Sarkin Malamai*
or Chief Scribe. Yeld is quite blunt about this non-
change: "Political status and channels of mobility
have remained virtually unchanged within the
Emirates."[38] Even the inferiority attached to slave
status is recorded as persisting in the emirates,[39] while
the unexpected welcome given by the emirs to the
British plan to widen the base of the bureaucracy by
appointing heads of technical departments in the NAs
is an example of Hausa assimilation at its best. The
Zaria experience of the British introduction of technical staff into the native administration shows how, far
from showing reluctance to appoint a new class of
officials that might be open to *'yan tsirge* entrants, the
emir seized upon this God-sent opportunity to create
more titular offices and distribute them to the claimant
sons of rival dynasties, while the departmental heads
so appointed found a no less welcome source of valuable patronage at their disposal. In a like manner,
the emirs of a later generation were able to maneuver
themselves into a position whereby nomination of a
local man by the party executive to run for political
office at the national level required the personal consent of the (nonpolitical) emir, so that election to the
legislature became virtually another perquisite in the
gift of the emirs.

A further example of the adaptation of Hausa court
culture to the demands of modern political life is to
be found in the partial modification of the conventions governing the award of traditional titles.

It is possible to discern here an interesting sociological reformation wherein emirs have been compelled to confer on *arriviste* persons who have achieved eminence on the political ladder traditional ascriptive titles and commensurate advancement in the NA scale which were quite outside their expectation had they remained in the NA. Not only have some of the *shigege* politicians used the political ladder to short-circuit the emirate closed promotion system and thus acquired the *asali* reward of titles otherwise beyond their reach, but they have also had titles and offices created or revived like those of Wazirin Shendam, Sardaunan Bida, Walin Muri, Ciroman Jos, Madawakin Yola, Wazirin Katsina.[40] In the event, these NA posts have proved a valued haven after the military coups of 1966—an earlier recourse to this insurance against loss of political office than was anticipated. The message of such an interacting situation has been expressed in a perceptive passage by Sklar and Whitaker: "Some NA officials now occupied a dual role as local administrative subaltern in a traditional bureaucracy and politician in a modern elective parliament. Given the political influence of emirs and other traditional notables on the one hand, and their command of the local native bureaucracies on the other, these roles became interdependent. Consequently, one of the rewards for loyalty and service to one's superior in the context of the local administrative bureaucracy was the support of that superior in one's candidacy for elective office. Conversely, one's adherence to the cause of traditional institutions in the context of this new regional legislative body enhanced one's security and prospects for advancement within the local bureaucracy."[41] This interlocking activity is emphasized if one recalls that Northern Nigerians elected to the legislature and even appointed ministers were, unlike their civil service counterparts, never required to resign their NA posts but were carried on the establishment as being "on leave without pay." (At the time of writing, in mid-1967, a major political revolution is foreshadowed in the Northern Military Government's decision to ban NA officials from all forms of participation in party politics, thus bringing their regulations into line with those prescribed for central and regional government officials.) In contrast to the politicians, the civil servants derived from an NA background have preferred the favor of the usual bureaucratic honours system (both the British awards like O.B.E. and the Nigerian ones like O.F.R.), and I can recall only two cases where NA titles have been conferred on them while in office: one was an outstanding agricultural officer appointed as an NA councilor, the other was a former chief scribe given a local title.

Nadel once summed up the undeflected persistence of traditional social values of Northern Nigeria in a notable passage that still carries some validity in its NA relevance: "The Nupe kingdom and its society still exist, not only very vividly in the memory of the people but to a very large extent in concrete reality. . . . There are no more wars, raids and conquests; slaves and feudal fiefs exist no longer. But ranks and titles and state offices linked with ranks and titles still exist. Slaves have turned into *bara* or Native Administration officials; fiefs into administrative districts in the charge of royal princes. That the framework of the political organization could survive almost unchanged is in large measure due to . . . Indirect Rule and its tendency to utilize as far as possible the traditional social system."[42] So acutely has it been possible in Hausaland for the social past to be felt in the present and so intense has been the persistence of Hausa culture as an almost tangible way of life that it has long seemed to me that were a Hausa Rip van Winkle to return to Kano today, a century after his 1867 pilgrimage to Mecca, he would (provided he were blind to *realia* like buildings and deaf to linguistic neologisms) at once feel at home within the essential Hausa behavioral matrix. The tenacity of Hausa culture to survive and its genius to absorb rather than be assimilated are formidable indeed.

If, as it seems logical to assume, the colonial government hoped that it would be able to train a bureaucracy, recruited on merit and without regard to social provenance, so as to staff the NAs, it must be held doubtful whether during the first fifty years they achieved very much in the way of relaxing the hierocratic Hausa conventions governing recruitment to the highest public offices. Perhaps it was a matter of realistic priorities by the British. With "law and order" established, rationalization of the emirate organization and the inculcation of competence and honesty in office became their primary preoccupations. Attention to the widening of the recruitment base of the NA staff and their training was of less concern (there was no school of administrative instruction till 1954, and not a single NA scribe was officially taught even to type until 1946) than attempts to broaden the top of the NA pyramid by persuading the emir to enlarge his council through the admission, first, of nontraditional titleholders, and, next, of educated men, often commoners and *'yan tsirge*. Any abrupt step by a British administration committed to noninterference with the state religion of Islam could easily be countered by the emir's objection in the name of religious tradition: *wannan ba al'adammu ba ce*, "it is against custom." A native authority could—and did—put up a convincing case that certain of the senior administrative posts like district headships were customarily in the emir's personal gift or were a familial office, without regard to other qualifications. Despite the *harmattan* of change that swept so draftily through the North in Sir Donald Cameron's breezy wake, progress was slow in inculcating a more liberal attitude toward

NA staff policies. Thus each appointment of a non-traditional or educated man to the emir's council was a matter of proud achievement, duly signaled with self-congratulation in the annual provincial reports of the 1930s,[43] while the eventual admission of Christo-pagan, non-Fulani elements to such councils in the 1950s were invariably the subject of a special press release. Fifteen years after the unarguable directive from the Secretary of State for the Colonies that attention must be given to "means of securing an effective place in local government for those Africans who are best qualified to be real leaders of the people,"[44] such emirates as Kano, Sokoto, and Katsina still retained traditional, nonelected members in over half the seats in their policy-making councils. The point made is not so much that the colonial government was wrong in its policy of gradualism—that depends on the measure of one's acceptance of the motive of indirect rule[45] as an insurance of guaranteed stability rather than as an instrument of induced modernization —but that it had, maybe unconsciously, encountered a highly resistant sociocultural force in the persistence of Hausa emiratism. Along with this, of course, went the classic dilemma of indirect rule, poignantly rephrased to spell out how "the very logic of British policy, which involved upholding a certain discretionary power on the part of traditional rulers, precluded elimination of that ample measure of royal patronage around which the government largely revolves to this day."[46]

The year 1954 brought two important changes to this image of the largely unimpeded erosion of the British bureaucratic concept favoring the appointment of merit-based local government officers over birth-based NA officials. One was fresh legislation for handling the NAs, made under the new Native Authority Law. At last some measure of control over the appointment and discipline of NA staff was to be accepted.

From here, the administration was able to push the setting up of appointments boards and establishment committees within each NA, and the newly formed Ministry for Local Government urged the establishment of NA staff officers and issued a succession of regulations designed to relate NA appointments at all levels, from councilors and district heads down to treasury scribes, to the qualification of merit rather than of status within the traditional system.[47] Statutory provision was made requiring the approval of the regional governor for the appointment of anybody to an NA post carrying a salary of over $1300, a level which included most of the senior middle-management posts.

The second major influence was the opening of the Institute of Administration at Zaria, invested with the express objective of raising the standard of NA staff by a variety of courses from elementary typing up through committee proceedings to developmental planning and execution. Although these courses have subsequently been criticized for failing to achieve their maximum potential of ensuring that henceforth only certificated staff should be appointed to NAs, their contribution to local government up to 1962 (when the institute became a semiautonomous body within the new university and the philosophy of its local government training was rethought) was a notable one. Three forces militated against greater success in this sphere. One was that some NAs took advantage of the renewed emphasis on the advisory rather than executive role of the district officer during the upsurge of national politics and were able to lobby successfully enough on the political level to gain acceptance of staff who were sometimes unacceptable by absolute standards. Some of these were "disqualified" rather than "unqualified," such as the dismissed government accountant or the convicted scribe, both of whom found their way into senior NA posts. Another was the giddy job mobility, whereby a trained forest guard would, because of his hierocratic connections, suddenly be appointed a district head, or a sanitary inspector would be sent on a professional course and on his return be promoted to deputy chief scribe.[48] Thirdly, there was the traditional reluctance of NAs to open their ranks to employees from outside their own NA area. In some instances where a strong-minded DO persuaded a smaller NA to recruit key trained staff from other NAs, trouble (? instigated) often followed, so that the Moslem chief scribe has soon resigned from the Christo-pagan NA and the Christian convert cashier has had to be hurriedly moved on from the Moslem NA.[49] Against these obstacles, however, must be set the gain realized from the belief that by promoting the concept of trained staff and by insisting that acceptance on a course demanded a prescribed minimum educational standard, the institute would make a progressive breach into the hitherto closed recruitment processes of the NAs.

It was, in sum, the rejection of the straight transfer of this closed society of inbred and self-perpetuating emiratism into both the new sphere of political recruitment as well as the older area of appointments to the native administration staffs that prompted the major opposition group in Hausaland to include in an early manifesto the assertion that "the shocking state of social order at present existing in Northern Nigeria is due to nothing but the Family Compact rule of the so-called Native Administrations in their present autocratic form."[50] Political analysts have found the NPC guilty of this charge, maintaining that the party was founded so as to defend the ruling groups against forces threatening their interests: ". . . its leaders spoke with the authority of a 'party in power,' but they spoke also as men associated with traditional sources of power."[51] Small wonder, then, that the new generation of "educated elements" despaired of breaking through. They began to seek other channels to public office. The promise of derestricted promotion opportunities to NA office held out by the conciliar expansion of the 1930s in the emirates and by the positive local government reforms of the 1950s had disappointed. So, too, had the fresh sector of political participation created by the 1951 constitution, for it was now evident that traditional authority had succeeded in retaining a high degree of influence on the new political institutions so that "the hierarchy of the dominant party had been fused with a pre-existing indigenous administrative hierarchy."[52] Peter Lloyd paints the founder membership of the NPC in bold colors, as a party primarily composed of persons "most of whom were either Fulani by birth, or were the sons of slave officials and thus in position of clientage to the emirs."[53] It was only the minority who gained foundation admission to the political machine despite their lack of ascriptive status, and even they first had to demonstrate their unequivocal loyalty as "good NA men."

In such a situation of creeping traditionalism, widely sanctioned and upheld, what, the meritocrats were now asking themselves, would be their chances of participation in a third new sphere of participation that opened up in 1954, namely a Northern Nigerian civil service. To what degree would the aspirant meritocrats, eager to escape the inhibiting influence of emiratism, find both a sanctuary and an outlet in a civil service that was now dedicated to opening its ranks to Northern Nigerians? Would they find that the judgment of one observer of the sociopolitical scene, how "in the norm, with the exception of some cities, identification with the traditional ruling element, regardless of personal qualification, is a fundamental prerequisite for securing admission to elite status,"[54] would prove as true of the new civil service as it had disenchantingly done in political and NA recruitment? In what measure would the Schumpeter thesis of "Social structures, types and attitudes are coins that do not readily melt,"[55] remain paramount here too? Or would the Colonial Civil Service tradition of "open status groups, united by a common education, outlook and discipline, and open to mobility"[56] succeed in establishing itself in an atmosphere hitherto characterized by the entrenched acceptance of traditional perspectives on access to office?

The Northern Nigerian Civil Service and Its Public Service Commission (1954)

Incited by the constitutional showdown of May 1953, the three groups of provinces had pressed for separate identity within a federal framework, and under the new 1954 constitution each regional government was granted its own legislature, judiciary, and executive. This regionalization of the previously unitary Nigerian Civil Service had a profound impact, above all on Northern Nigeria. It was now clear that in the immediate future the recruitment of indigenes to replace expatriates in the higher ranks of the public service could not afford to overlook the issue of regional prevenance. Localization of the bureaucracy in the North no longer meant Nigerianization; it now meant Northernization.

Localization of the Nigerian civil service had received its first major recognition with the appointment of the Walwyn Committee, but, unlike Ghana, where two Africans were appointed as administrative cadets in 1942, the process did not really get under way until the Foot Commission was set up in 1948. The implications of a purposeful and accelerated Nigerianization of the civil service were exhaustively examined in 1952,[57] but the firm decision in favor of a single unified service was overtaken by the pace of constitutional development. Perhaps the most far-reaching recommendation to emerge from the milestone Phillipson-Adebo report was that calling for a genuine Public Service Commission. (In the light of the constitutional regionalization decision, this became four Public Service Commissions, one for the federal and one for each of the regional services.)

Civil service morality in Anglophone Africa derives from the famous Northcote-Trevelyan reforms of 1853. These have their American counterpart in the Civil Service Reform of 1883. The establishment of Public Service Commissions in colonial territories can be traced to a 1946 policy paper aimed at dovetailing Colonial Service reorganization with political advance toward self-government: "Public Service Commissions should be established in the Colonies . . . It is desirable that the Governor should be advised in those matters [appointment to posts in the local service] by a Public Service Commission appointed by him and so composed as to command the confidence of the Service and the public."[58] The relationship between a Civil Service and a Civil/Public Service Commission may be likened to that of a student body and the university authorities in so far as these exercise the joint functions of what Oxbridge calls admissions and moral tutors: on the wisdom and standards of the latter depend the commonweal and reputation of the former.

Throughout the recent history of localization of the Asian and African civil services, credit is due to the Public Service Commissions in each country for their role as the jealous guardian of the Guardians—the answer, if you wish, to the classic question of *quis custodiet ipsos custodes?*

The importance of the establishment of a body of this nature must receive special notice in our context, for in the Northern Nigerian setup its functions would sooner or later encounter the expectations of emiratism, already paramount in the parallel service of native administration employment and now no less influential in the realm of political recruitment. In the same way that the emirs and chiefs were looking askance at the notion of having a Minister for Local Government[59]—for were not they, the native authorities, local government in law as well as in fact?—so the hierocrats and the traditional elements may well have pondered over the extent to which this new, independent body might impinge on the tradition-sanctioned principles and provenance of recruitment to public office. For such a British-inspired instrument was clearly going to promote the very criteria so far unaccepted in the NA context: open recruitment, based on the qualification of ability and merit rather than the acceptability of familial and occupational status. Despite the naïve view of some of the top British colonial officials in Africa and Asia during 1945–55 that the civil service could serenely operate in a nonpolitical role and virtually close its eyes to the rough-and-tumble of party politics played à l'africaine, the PSC was well aware that it had a duty to perform when cast in the role of Defender of the 1853 Faith. This responsibility was to maintain the morality of the civil service, and hence the morale of its officers, by resisting any pressure toward an out-and-out politicization of the bureaucracy and its personnel, and by discouraging any tendency (which may not always have been overt) to fostering the recruitment attitudes of emiratism. The time is not yet ripe, nor the data available, for a definitive study of the role of the PSC in Northern Nigeria. Yet some preliminary assessment may suitably be attempted, within the context of this inquiry, at the end of the commission's first decade of existence. For this essay maintains that in the dissemination and acceptance within the new Northern civil service of an alien ethic of open recruitment through merit, one contrary to a traditional code the PSC successfully promoted—often in the face of built-in cultural resistance, implicit as well as explicit—a spirit that has withstood the forces of emiratism (so effective in other aspects of the development process in Nigeria) and thus won from the new meritocracy support for their principle of derestricting the qualification for access to office.

The PSC's first test came within a year. Wishes for Northernization of the civil service rather than straight Nigerianization had crystallized in the evidence presented to the Phillipson-Adebo commission. In 1955 this was adopted as the government's official policy.[60] The PSC was the body charged with the first major implementation of this Northernization policy, the emergency training over a five-year period of 1000 Northerners as government clerks.[61] This was essentially a civil service operation. In later years, however, as the genuine fear grew of being swamped by the South's far greater educational resources, the policy assumed more openly political overtones. Its responsibility was removed to the Premier's Office, a special implementation committee was set up under a minister charged with its supervision, and a senior administrative officer was seconded to run its secretariat and maintain close liaison with the awards of the Scholarship Board and with civil service training institutions. The existence of such a committee underscores the influences to which the civil service and its guardian PSC were liable to be exposed in the context of a society that had inherited not only an inflexible attitude toward authority, but also a traditional system of public officialdom. Despite obvious temptations to play politics, however, credit must go both to the NPC for taking so few rather than so many of its opportunities to infiltrate the civil service with its own code of emiratism, and to the PSC for its considerable success in holding the ring.[62] Politically, the notion of an independent, quasi-judicial body responsible for the maintenance of recruitment standards in the civil service proved acceptable enough for the elected government to write the status and functions of the PSC into the region's constitution.[63] Regarding the civil service, it can be established that the PSC did mitigate the danger of traditional Hausa authority patterns reproducing themselves in recruitment into the bureaucracy in the same way as they had been perpetuated in recruitment to political office. This is best shown in Table III, which contrasts the socio-occupational origin of cadet entry into the Northern Nigerian Administrative Service during the first six years of its deliberate civil service training programs, with those of Northern members of the Nigerian legislature in its foundation years.[64]

TABLE III

Comparative Family Status in the Recruitment of Political and Bureaucratic Elites in Northern Nigeria 1951–61

	POLITICAL		BUREAUCRATIC		
	NPC 1951 (90)	NPC 1956 (130)	ASTC 1957–61 (120)	EGTC 1960–61 (70)	DPA 1962 (40)
Royal	21	11	1	3	0
Alkali	26	3	11	3	2
Trad. title	33	30	23	15	15
Karda	80	44	35	21	17
NA	77	32	13	12	19
Others (*talakawa*)	12	23	52	67	64
Shigege	89	55	65	79	83

Notes.

1. All figures are expressed as percentages. The actual size of each sample is given in brackets.

2. Under NPC 1951, some members were simultaneously royal scions, traditional titleholders, and NA officials. Such pluralism has been eliminated from the other data.

3. No native court judge (*alkali*) was allowed to run for office in 1956.

4. NPC = party membership in the Regional House of Assembly.

   ASTC = intake into the concessional training courses for entry to the Administrative Service.

   EGTC = intake into the special training courses for entry to the executive grade.

   DPA = intake into the first degree course in public administration (graduated 1965).

Why emiratism did not prevail in the staffing of the civil service to anything like the same extent that it did in politics and the NAs is less obvious than the fact that, as Table III demonstrates, it did not. It is a subject we shall return to after we have examined the significant process of administrative recruitment since the formation of the Northern civil service in 1954. Such a historical focus may provide the cumulative evidence demanded of an analytical enquiry of this nature.

The Six Stages of Recruitment into the Administration

We now turn to an examination of how the PSC implemented its responsibility of recruiting Northern Nigerians into the senior cadres of the administration. It would seem to have made a realistic appraisal of the limited educational resources available and so decided to adopt the characteristic Northern policy of gradualism. This policy, it may be noted, was one that not only expressed a fundamental tenet of indirect rule under the colonial regime, but one which, under an independent government, became tantamount to recognition as a Northern cultural trait and as such appeared as a frequent theme in the Premier's speeches. A refusal to correlate civil service recruitment with output, actual and anticipated, from the higher educational institutions could only result in a service motivated by patronage (cliental or nepotistic) or manipulated by an oligarchy (feudal or party). In the North few wished this. But in order to regularize the status of administrative staff, care had to be taken to forestall any crude emiratist attempt to treat the civil servants as, in the Weberian phrase, "a group of persons who are from time to time assigned *ad hoc* missions by the chief."[65] Because of its administrative traditions, Hausa society was peculiarly exposed to the pursuance of bureaucratic control along these lines. Whereas in its recruitment to professional and technical offices the need for recognition by professional bodies was sufficient insurance against infiltrated recruitment unless one was prepared to see bridges collapse and patients die on the operating table, in the administrative service the amalgam of forces at work —namely the Hausa tradition of personal clientage to the ruler and the British faith in the brilliance of the gifted amateur—could have played up the belief that administration was an art rather than a science and thus bedeviled any attempt to recruit on open lines. Fortunately for Nigeria, the rationalization of the Northernization imperative took into account wider issues, and the task of not only recruiting but also of training the country's administrators was taken very seriously.

An appreciation of the limiting effects of the North's underdeveloped educational system is vital to an understanding of the recruitment pattern in that most sensitive and influential sector of every African civil service, the administration. Over the decade 1956–66, five separate stages, each conditioned by the availability of educated manpower, can be distinguished (and a sixth envisaged) in the PSC's graduated implementation of that basic criterion in the conduct of a modern bureaucracy, namely that "only persons who have the generally regulated qualifications to serve are employed."[66]

The first phase came in 1956, when recruitment of

career-term expatriate officers to the administration ceased and an *ad hoc* scheme was devised whereby half a dozen Northerners in the junior ranks of government service were attached, one each, to handpicked British officers in the field. They were expected to acquire through this "Big Brother" relationship—so very British in its pragmatic, untutored informality and in its firm belief in the Aristotelian principle that the best way of learning to play a flute is to learn to play a flute—a knowledge of the functions and conduct of a district officer. The whole philosophy was that of the traditional apprenticeship of Britain's medieval craft guilds, where an apprentice was attached to a master craftsman in the expectation that he would be intelligent and enthusiastic enough to pick up what he could by observing. Nor did the craftsman in this Nigerian instance have any brief other than the unwritten assumption that since he was held to exemplify the *beau idéal* of a district officer, any cadet attached to him would inevitably if inexplicably acquire the same aura of ability. The era of training courses and of acceptance that administration can be taught rather than acquired had clearly not yet arrived. In the event, out of the six "guinea pigs," two within ten years reached the top administrative rank (staff grade), one became Class I and two Class II administrative officers, and one fell by the wayside.

The second stage came a year later, with the introduction of a crash program to train Nigerian administrative officers at the Institute of Administration in Zaria. A modest body of literature on this Administrative Service Training Scheme exists,[67] important partly because the latest analyst of localization programs in the civil services of new states considers that the Zaria project "might almost be said not only to have saved the administration of Northern Nigeria, but to have saved those of East Africa by its example,"[68] and partly because it reveals that some of the

personnel division dangers of such accelerated programs now being felt by African civil services were
not totally unforeseen by those involved, even though
their advice was, rightly or wrongly, unacceptable at
the political level.[69] There were no more men of the
first, "Kid Brother" category available; there was a
brave and correct decision not to accept high school
seniors but to encourage them to go on to the university; there was eventual agreement not to divert all
Northern graduates or final year students, whatever
their discipline, into the administration, despite the
seductive argument that without a competently managed administrative infrastructure no technical and
professional development plans would ever get off the
drawing board. So the new training course was made
up of men personally recommended by serving district
officers. The influence of emiratism was thus largely
discounted, but other ills beset the selection: failure
to take up further references resulted in the removal
of over 10 per cent of the first intake of students for
reasons of their past catching up with them. For the
subsequent training courses of this nature, applications were invited by public advertisement, and the
PSC ended up its annual processing with a full-dress
interview of the final short list comprising four times
the twenty-five to thirty candidates eventually selected.
It was still not possible to aim for anything near the
desired educational standard of a university degree,
but the wording of the advertisement constituted a
piece of judicious flexibility and achieved its object
of progressively raising the permissible minimum each
year.[70]

The third stage came with the Kingsley-Rucker report,[71] which in 1961 recommended the establishment
of a special two-year diploma course at the Institute
of Administration, organized in conjunction with one
of the American schools of public administration. Initially, these *diplômés* were to be recruited into the

executive (i.e., subadministrative) grade of the civil service, but as soon as the institute became part of the new University of Northern Nigeria in 1962 (plus the hard fact that the opening of such a diploma course must inevitably cancel the coexistence of the earlier A.S.T.C. output of men with *lower* educational entry standards qualified for admission into *higher* civil service posts after a *shorter* training period), it became clear that it was only a matter of time before this scheme logically developed into a full-scale baccalaureate in public administration. In the event, this occurred before the initial intake completed their course, and entry to the degree course in public administration has since 1963 demanded the same standard of advanced secondary education as does admission into arts and social science degree courses in most other Anglophone African and all English universities.

The fourth stage in the recruitment of administrators into the Northern civil service is best treated as a whole, though to a certain extent it overlapped the first three stages. In essence, it was an extraordinary transitional stage, brought about by the need to supplement the earlier sources of recruitment while awaiting the major source of degree men promised under the revised third stage. Administrators, if not the less patient politicians, were aware that an administrative training program was not a seven days' wonder. Yet it was imperative to continue feeding Northerners into the civil service, especially during the threatened "hungry season" between the closing of the special entry source (A.S.T.C.) in 1962 and the first group of public administration graduates due in 1965, a period which coincided with a steep running-down of expatriate officers due to premature retirement. To supplement the minuscule trickle of Northern graduates in other disciplines from the Universities of Ibadan and Fourah Bay as well as a handful from British universities (barely a dozen administrative cadets in all, spread over the three years), traditional civil service expedients like acting appointments and supernumerary posts were utilized, in addition to less traditional ones such as advertising promotion posts and offering lateral entry into the senior grades of the service. In view of the resentment of today's meritocrats at most of the nongraduate appointments made under this phase,[72] suspecting that this was a deliberate attempt by the emiratists to pack the service with loyal hierocrats, it is important to ask how far this was a revival of emiratism in the civil service hitherto largely held in check by the PSC.

Four kinds of alleged emiratist appointment may be distinguished during this transitional period. One was the direct transfer from NA service. Effectively withstood at the administrative level, it was publicly advertised at the next level as one of the channels of recruitment for the executive grade—a decision that caused much heart-burning among up-and-coming meritocrats, whose unyielding rejection of the standard civil service principle of promotion to the administrative class for experienced officers through a limited entry competitive examination has at times been alarming in its arrogance. Two, the officer thus recruited into the executive grade could be sent to Lagos, on promotion, to fill the Northern quota in the federal civil or foreign service, and then in course of time be brought back to the North to hold an administrative post. After a while, this leapfrogging practice was curbed by a civil service ruling, born from discontent at the loophole, that promotion in the federal service would be offered only to those who transferred to it, not to those "lent" on secondment. Three, lateral intake from the statutory corporations, or its concomitant of appointment to a corporation or to a quasi-administration post, e.g., the legislature or a statutory corporation, followed by the early gazetting of the incumbent as a supernumerary administrative officer. Since supernumerary appointments were always in the end absorbed, such chickens eventually came home to roost in the promotion nest. Four, the occasional attempt to justify the feeling that "we cannot afford to waste even one educated man"—a sentiment that often led to greater wastage in the long run by undermining the whole institution's discipline—such as the urged acceptance of flunked-out military cadets and "semigraduates" or the attempt to appoint directly certain ministerial protégé aides who were barren of other qualification. On the whole, it is fair to acknowledge that such cases were rare, nor did the government infiltrate many career politicians into the civil service. Information available records only one top-ranking administrator and two more at the senior level who had first enjoyed a substantive political career. NPC sympathizers—as opposed to practitioners—were naturally legion, among expatriates as well as Northerners, and there is plentiful documentation to show that few job opportunities were made available to opposition sympathizers while they continued in their would-be willful ways: the Hausa act of *tuba,* repentance, could rapidly bring its reward of office on the administrative as well as the political scene, and many learned the wisdom of the adage of what to do if you cannot beat 'em.

Thus the advancement of the fifth, and present, stage, where since 1962 recruitment into the Northern administration has required the possession of a university degree, preferably (but not exclusively, save in the eyes of some of the more aggressive public administration undergraduates!) in public administration. This completes the phased raising of recruitment standards, always within an open merit system, implemented by the PSC between 1956 and 1966.

Though the sixth stage has not yet occurred in Northern Nigeria, it already obtains in the Eastern and Western Regions, and the North could shortly be in the happy position of at least being able to foresee the possibility of raising its upper-echelon recruitment sights even higher. This opportunity arises when there are more graduates seeking admission to administrative posts than there are posts available. In the other Nigerian civil services, the general practice of an open competitive examination has obtained for the past three or four years. This may be further refined in two ways. One, as in the Eastern Region, where eligibility to sit such an examination demands a first- or second-class honors degree, those with a lower class then requiring a compensatory postgraduate diploma in public administration. Two, as in the Western Region and in the former British Colonial Administrative Service,[73] where acceptance by the PSC is provisional and subject to successful completion of a probationary course in public administration before taking up an actual appointment.

It will be clear from this section that, in so far as the primary and secondary school admissions basis is genuinely broadened, the phased raising of educational admission standards into the civil service will have been in inverse proportion to the opportunity for the continued injection of emiratist principles of favoritism, clientage or family at the appointment level. (Their recurrence potential in the subsequent interpersonal roles within the civil service is not argued here.) The greater the intake into secondary schools, the wider the basis of recruitment that should become available to the PSC. Bretton's generalization that in the North there obtain systems that "rely on favoritism rather than merit in their employment and promotional practices"[74] would not seem to stand up to an application to the Northern Administrative Service. Table III has already indicated this truism, and it is possible to cite several personal instances both where "court favorites" who had in the early days satisfied the PSC selection board but failed the actual training course were not in fact appointed by the PSC (despite minor emiratist storms) and others who, despite their royal birth, had come up the "open" way of impartial examinations at school and university level in order to qualify for office on accepted modern criteria. It would be hard to overemphasize the signal achievement of the PSC in its successful establishment of modernist qualifications for appointment to public office within a society which traditionally held very different views and which managed to promote them in the other aspects of contemporary political life such as party candidature and local government office.

But if, as we have shown, the spirit of emiratism did not prevail in the recruitment of civil servants, it behooves us to ask why the traditional recruitment patterns did not persist when the situation, of a society short of meritocrats but strong in hierocrats, lent itself so well to the opposite development. It seems likely that, had the hierocrats been intent on perpetuating their emiratist philosophy into the formation of new bureaucracy, they could, given the dearth of meritocrats in those ten formative years up to the first output of public administration graduates in 1965, have done so with a fair measure of initial success— until, that is, the effects of a deliberately expanded system of higher education began to assert themselves. We must accordingly seek reasons why the hierocrats did not wish to.

One was the genuine admiration of the colonial civil service tradition of, if not always brilliance, at least undoubted integrity and devoted, hard work. Though later politicians, reared on the slogan that he who is not for us must be against us, may have been suspicious of its inculcated virtues of neutrality and impartiality— qualities publicly condemned in the postindependence years by national leaders like Nyerere and Nkrumah[75] —there is little evidence of any wholesale rejection of Western-type bureaucracy in the early stages of its establishment in Nigeria beyond, it must be conceded, a somewhat mocking amusement at the strange advocacy of the British principle that a civil service must be equally loyal to a hypothetical successor government drawn from opposition parties. A case could, however, be argued that this respect for the bureaucratic machine may have been truer in the North than in the South, for there relations between the civil servant administrator and the local chieftaincy (long since institutionalized in the Hausa language as *di'o* [DO] and *e'ne* [NA] respectively) had in the generality been happy—to some extent based, it may be, on the gentleman's agreement of mutual social noninterference which can be shown ever to have been a link between the privacy-respecting Moslem and the my-home-is-my-castle Englishman.[76] Two, there was the feeling in the cabinet that, even if the civil service did rear its ugly head of hyperimpartiality (hastily reinterpreted as obstructionism), the political machinery would be strong enough to meet such a threat in the same way as it had disposed of the handful of expatriate administrators who would not move with the times and dared to hinder the political will of NAs or even insist on local opposition leaders getting a fair hearing—that perfidious Albion trait of British support for the underdog.[77] Three, given the shortage of even minimally "qualified" (in the sense of formal education, not of administrative experience) people, the order of priority was to fill the political offices first—and their fertile breeding ground, the NA bureaucracies—before turning to the civil service. The latter could in the meantime be staffed by expatriates, who were seldom averse to a Northernization policy in the service and could generally be brought to heel by the political whip in those rare cases where such discipline was called for. They would keep the office seat warm and could be ousted much more easily than a *soi-disant* "brother" Nigerian civil servant from the South.[78]

Fourthly, there were available to the party caucus

alternative channels of patronage either for those Northerners who were qualified for the civil service but were not entirely acceptable to the new government or for those who were not qualified for such employment but whose services in quasi-bureaucratic posts were desirable. In the first category, it is possible to point to a number of university-trained men who were persuaded to take up appointments in the federal rather than the regional civil service. By and large, these new meritocrats were either graduates from the non-Hausa provinces or were relatively ultraradical Hausa reformists. Sometimes they had to be persuaded by offers of "transfer on promotion" or, to quote the supreme political blandishment made to a group of Middle Belt graduates who protested against their exile to Lagos, "the North must send in its best XI to bat against the South on the Lagos wicket."[79] Interestingly enough, during 1964 and 1965, the tendency reversed itself and there was a marked urgency among graduates from the emirates to enter the federal or Foreign Service and "breathe the freer air of Lagos or London." Events since 1966 appear to have again reversed the trend.

A variation of the earlier theme, however, was the possibility of syphoning off the eager non-Hausa meritocrats into politically peripheral posts within the Northern civil service which few Fulani would be qualified, if indeed they ever wanted, to hold for several years to come. Thus, an examination of the Staff List reveals a preponderance of Middle Belt men in the higher ranks (though not always at the very top) of the professional departments like Forestry, Public Works, Education, Medical, and also the Army,[80] while the senior echelons of the administration remained predominantly Fulani-oriented until the advent of the meritocrats. Lloyd has suggested that "within the emirates the educated Fulani youth tends to seek employment in the NA, where his birth offers him better opportunities."[81] Although this is no longer the sole pattern, it is true that the educated Hausa-Fulani has continued to find a seller's market while his Middle Belt counterpart had by 1965 begun to encounter signs of a buyer's market, especially in the award of scholarships. Such students appearing before scholarship selection boards relate how they were quickly made aware of this discrimination. Such a situation is an important element in any consideration of the problems and process of national integration in Northern Nigeria. Even though skillful politicking overcame the 1958 threat of a new region being carved out of the North, the educational superiority of the area was such as to make Kaduna recoil in horror from any suggestion of a simple merit ladder in recruitment among Northerners, even within the Northernization policy. Thus it was decided to direct the top government high schools to take in quotas of pupils equally from all the provinces, regardless of the headmasters' protests that this unfairly kept out many Middle Belt boys who were far brighter than some of the Hausa entry. In the same way, the PSC was unable to accept applicants strictly on the merit of their qualifications, as up to 90 per cent of the qualified applicants for advertised posts came from the Middle Belt. In the interests of the development of "one North," most institutions bore such ethnoprovincial issues in mind when considering their admissions lists. Nor is it by any means certain that such political sensitivity was misplaced in the circumstances: ethnic arithmetic was a glaring fact of Nigerian life and as such had to be lived with.

Under the second category of alternative avenues of office comes the rich source of patronage over, first, appointments to such bodies as the statutory boards and corporations, whose personnel selection makes such a revealing source of study; and secondly, recruitment to the business sector, where firms and banks were genuinely anxious to take on "dry Northerners"[82] but for a variety of reasons at first found it impossible to retain those of merit. The result was that too often a jumped-up manager had a prior civil service or NA record of disqualification, and in the early days of the Department of Public Administration before the Business School found its feet at Zaria this state of affairs was held by students to be a serious obstacle to seeking a respectable career in commerce. Interestingly enough, the reverse swing took place a few years later when the government was suspected of recruiting hierocrats to alleviate its fear of the growing corps of meritocrats within its own ranks, and there was an unexpectedly vigorous reaction against government service in favor of a business career.

Fifthly, some of the senior emiratist men whom the politicians might have wished to see in civil service posts were those who preferred a straight NA or statutory corporation post, where perquisites and opportunities of concurrent political office were up to 1967 recognized as standard fringe benefits, in contrast to the General Orders ethos of the civil service already accepted by a growing number of the new bureaucracy.[83]

Sixthly, it is possible to discern a stage when the meritocratic ranks were about to become numerous enough, and hence significant, in the bureaucracy, and in order to redress the balance in favor of emiratist principles it was necessary for Kaduna to reduce the prestige of the influential Provincial Administration, whose members—Nigerian as well as expatriate—did not always accept the type African equation of public administration as synonymous with political government. This was done by demoting the Resident and appointing over him a politician as the government's senior agent within each province. This temporary victory of emiratism was publicly symbolized in the physical quitting of the residency by the senior civil servant, now allotted the "second best" house in the government residential complex, and the privilege of flying a flag in his compound and on his car now became the prerogative of the political appointee. Such a thesis of being one of the reasons for the introduction of the provincial commissioners—part of the general politicization of local administrative systems in Africa by the creation either of parallel posts or of superordinate party offices—carries a firmer tenability when reconsidered in the light of the growing conflict-potential between the hierocrats and the meritocrats in the administration discussed here.

Yet, if the PSC was successful in holding in check the blatant self-perpetuation of Hausa social stratification that had made its mark in political recruitment, the civil service training establishments experienced their own teething troubles in their uncomplicated intent of substituting civil service behavioral ethics for the institutionalized deference of Hausa society. Here, with its deliberate awareness of the need for correction, the ASTC played a valuable role in its training motivation, one that has not been available to the broader, nongovernmental functions of a university department concerned primarily with educating. A primary concern was the reconciliation of Hausa behavioral traits in the junior-senior relationship with the standard practices of face-to-face encounters in the type civil service. Nor can this well-intentioned brainwashing be divorced from another field of concern within the total Africanization process: in its enthusiasm for a meritocratic, classless, and casteless system of recruitment into the public service, and in its belief in the inculcation of a British civil service code of behavior as the *sine qua non* of a modern bureaucracy, to what extent were the civil service academicians producing a brand of bureaucrat who might not find himself acceptable to the equally emergent type of political leader whom he would be expected to serve? Quite aside from the conscious danger of such tutors turning out young men in their own stamp, not because they were unaware of the need for a new philosophy for a new administration but because the politicians would neither endorse a fresh one nor reject the old, there is evidence in the removal of certain prominent African civil servants to international organizations outside their own country to suggest that politicians were beginning to question whether they really wanted such an uncompromising civil service ethos. This stemmed, as we have seen, direct from the puritanical reforms of 1853. These had been effected in the halcyon days of an England cushioned in its belief that with Queen Victoria on the throne and a fleet of gunboats to chastise those who perversely showed signs of not wanting the benefits of civilization, God was in his heaven and all must surely be right with his Britain-centered world![84] How valid, some asked in passing, was such a civil service charter in the *brouhaha* of contemporary political Africa?[85]

The March of the Meritocrats

We have seen how the PSC ethos came to be accepted by the new civil service of Northern Nigeria as the code of behavior that they desired to follow in their own bureaucracy. This was achieved despite the possibility of interference along emiratism lines and despite the two obstacles to a wholesale system of recruitment through open competitive examinations —the dictates of the Northernization imperative and the imbalance threatened from the educationally advanced Middle Belt. We are now in a position to examine today's situation in so far as it concerns the attitudes toward the relevance of qualifications in accessibility of office within the ranks of the Northern civil service. What we find is a stage beyond wholehearted support for the PSC ethos of open recruitment and promotion on considerations of merit. Presently, we find a threatened friction on this very issue, not on whether these strict standards should be relaxed but on the suspicion that in the past they have been breached. In consequence, there are signs of friction within the Northern civil service directly connected with our central theme of qualification for office; nor is this going to be confined to the Northern Nigerian context.[86] Today's meritocrats (and tomorrow's too) in most sub-Saharan bureaucracies accuse yesterday's neomeritocrats of hierocratic leanings, of revisionist tendencies, and of educational inadequacy. Yesterday's radicals have, in the eyes of tomorrow's meritocrats, become today's Old Guard and have betrayed the true spirit of recruitment through merit. This concept of merit has as its exemplar the possession of a university degree. Those without such a qualification are seen as unfit to hold high office in the civil service. Any attempt on their part to argue the value of experience as something that cannot be acquired in a university course is summarily dismissed; and any attempt to legitimize their status by acquiring university patents later in their career is seen as a plot to entrench themselves in office and an obstacle to the "rightful aspirations" of the meritocrats. Link this feeling of superiority with the growing economic specter of being deprived of a post commensurate with graduate qualifications, invoke the shibboleth of "lowering academic standards," and we are presented with the instance of the recent riot at the very university which had for a whole decade pioneered public administration programs in Africa, its students now demonstrating against the award of "mature student status" to established civil servants enabling them to complete a baccalaureate program in two years.[87] It is on these attitudes that it behooves us to fix attention in the final part of this essay, for here the expression of anti-emiratism reaches its climax among even Hausa undergraduates. And, given the nature and pattern of the process of Africanization, this reaction could be repeated in the civil services of all those Anglophone African new states[88] (especially Zambia, Tanzania, Malawi, Kenya, and to some extent Uganda and Sierra Leone) which have lacked either the I.C.S. and Ceylon tradition of steady localization of the Administrative Service by graduate cadets, or an infrastructure of experienced junior administrators, such as the *effendi* of the Sudan Civil Service, or the immediate availability of substantial graduate manpower (e.g., Ghana, Eastern and Western Nigeria).

The principal motive-springs of meritocratic aggression are discernible at their clearest in their negative contexts. This is not to suggest they have no positive qualities. On the contrary, they have; but within the framework of the civil service as a development institution, which is the boundary of this paper, their incentives are most easily assessed in their expressions of "anti-ness."

One is their "anti-ASTC" bias, that is to say, their opposition to those of their colleagues recruited under the second method of Northernization of the civil service, in the period 1957–62. Because of the inescapability of crash training programs in the accelerated Africanization of civil services, and because of the related event of the pioneer Zaria program having been imitated as a model elsewhere, this division of loyalty is one that may be anticipated in many other countries as they reach the next stage of their Africanization programs, that marked by the availability of an ample graduate entry for the higher civil service. The salient establishment problem is what to do with the older, educationally underqualified but experiencewise well qualified administrator at the time when younger and graduate administrators enter the service and soon decline to respect their seniors on this very ground of educational distinction. Here is a rejection of the assumption of synonymity, carried in proverbial lore across the African continent, in the aphorism enjoining obedience to one's "elders and betters."[89] In its worst realization, this attitude reveals an impatience of office, an unrealistic discounting of the value of experience or the worth of past performance, and a blind devotion to the Mammon of Diplomaism. In fairness to the certificate-conscious youth of the new states, it should be pleaded that much of the blame attaches to the British. In the colonial days, one of the standard procedures to reduce the clamour of local indigenes for entry into the administration was to insist on the possession of a university degree as a minimum qualification. This persisted during the postwar period, through the time when a fair proportion of those recruited by the Colonial Service after 1945 did not have a degree (yet many made admirable administrators) and when the Premier of one colony was able wryly to point out how "the fact that at one time none of the three Lieutenant-Governors had acquired degrees seemed to be of little consequence in practice, and did not appear to vitiate the argument."[90] The misjudgments of the past need not concern us here, nor their possible solution other than the obvious one that at some stage a ruthless pruning of any dead wood in the bureaucracy will be necessary.[91] The existence of this antipathy and its origins in the suspicion by the meritocrats that here may be a vestige of emiratism which by definition is not conducive to the well-being of the civil service remain our interest.

A second focus of attack by the meritocrats is the class of appointment to the administration that did not even undergo the relative merit tests of the ASTC (which did its best with the material sent to it by the PSC) and which the meritocrats uncompromisingly label as emiratist appointments. These officials, mostly of lateral or "irregular" (in so far as they by-passed the conventional, but never officially defined, channels of administrative recruitment) entry, today hold high —and often honorable—office in the civil service. Yet this very fact of seniority aggravates their original appointment in the eyes of the meritocrats, so that criticism is voiced of even the Permanent Secretary grade in Kaduna (much of it, let it be stressed, of excellent quality) because over 75 per cent of the posts are held by nongraduate Northerners and none has the formal qualification in public administration so cherished by a majority of the present meritocrats. This is, of course, strongest in their criticism of the appointments of former committed party agents or candidates (very few, in the event) and of those many more who jumped from a junior post in government—or worse, as they see it, in the NA service—to a senior administrative position on the strength of a nine-month noncertificated course at a university or staff college overseas. The question of competence and experience often does not enter into their arguments; formal educational qualification appears as the be-all and end-all.[92] Allowing for his evident anti-Northern bias, this would seem to be the class of appointment that Bretton had in mind when he castigated "the training of an indigenous cadre of Northern administrators and skilled technicians, as well as of professionals, all, of course, loyal to the traditional rulers and dependent upon them."[93]

In both these categories, the antagonism is exacerbated by the fact that the holders of such posts have not only risen rapidly to the top with the flowing tide of nationalism and Africanization—at a speed that cannot ever hope to be repeated[94]—but are now, given their comparative youthfulness, likely to remain there for almost a civil service generation—or more, if proposals to extend the compulsory retirement age in keeping with the realities of an *African* civil service are implemented. Cumulatively, these attitudes help to explain the typical demand of the meritocrats, that governments should "prevent people who already occupy jobs advertised for graduates, and who are not graduates, from blocking the appointment of graduates."[95] This reaction typifies the self-conscious self-assessment of the new clerisy, recently identified as a social class in its own right, "based on education, occupation, and source or amount of income."[96] Table IV draws together selected attributes of age and university education of Nigerian holders of the top administrative posts in the federal and regional public services just before the January 1966 military coup:

TABLE IV

Selected Attributes of Age and University Education Among Top Nigerian Administrative Officers in the Federal and Regional Civil Services, 1965

Permanent Secretary Grade	Total Posts	University Qualification	Age Groups 30–35	36–40	41–50	50+
Federation*	15	9	0	2	11	2
North	16	3	3	5	6	2
East	13	9	0	2	8	3
West	9	n.a.	0	0	7	2
Adm. Off. Class I Grade						
Federation*	19	14	9	3	6	1
North	11	4	7	4	0	0
East	11	7	1	4	3	3
West	7	n.a.	1	1	4	1
*Northern Civil Servants Holding such Federal Posts						
Perm. Sec. Grade	4	2	0	2	2	0
Adm. I. Grade	6	3	3	1	2	0

Source: Based on data abstracted from the official Staff Lists. The Western Region information is valid for 1964; its Staff List carries no key to educational attainment.

The third target of the meritocrats is the NA system. Leaving aside their general attitude toward the institution of chieftaincy, this antipathy takes two forms. The first manifests itself in an implacable rejection of local government service, so that no Northern NA can yet point to any graduate among their hundreds of administrative posts. The reasons advanced for this rejection are several. One is because of the prevalence of nepotism—a phenomenon at the local government level which shares many features with what emerges at the national level as tribalism. Another is the acceptance of corruption in its form of, to quote an official committee of leading NA officeholders, "a governmental system where an exchange of presents in conjunction with an appointment or promotion to administrative office is a legitimate and sanctioned social practice."[97] A third is the persistence of *karda/shigege* discrimination within the working of the typical emirate bureaucracy. Whereas an analysis of birth and occupational status of families suggests that the PSC was not concerned with such criteria as qualification for office in government employ—sons of cooks and messengers are today in the administration, though the traditionally lowest classes of butchers and musicians, along with their modern counterpart (largely because of their common political affiliation) of bicycle hirers, have not registered much of a score—the social distinction has remained a valid one within NA service. All three of these objections can be traced to the continuation of traditional Hausa social norms into modern life and the frequently demonstrable irrelevance of qualification to jobs. A fourth objection, that of refusing to serve under an educationally less qualified superior, is often common to service in government, while the fifth, the claim that no NA can afford to pay a graduate his self-assessed worth on the national employment scale, is easily remedied by the government subvention of such graded posts as has been authorized for the employment of superiorly qualified personnel in Native Treasury and Native Court posts. It is worth pointing out that this rejection of NA service is not confined to potential administrators. Equal resentment was caused among would-be secondary teachers when it was announced that the products of the Advanced Teachers Colleges would be liable to a posting to NA Provincial Secondary Schools, and they have held it significant that within eighteen months government was obliged to convert all such schools into government secondary schools. The assumption of indirect rule, that service in the NA would provide an essential corpus of experience for those eventually destined to govern an independent Nigeria (of what constitutional shape few bothered to imagine in those balmy days of "indefinite time ahead"[98]) at both the administrative and political levels was not demolished till 1948, when a forthright administrator declared "it is idle to expect an educated African gentleman, eager to work for the self-government of Nigeria, to fritter away his efforts in argument with yokels round the parish pump."[99]

The other manifestation of the meritocrats' attack upon the NA system of personnel management will be touched on only briefly here, but it will doubtless attract closer study in the course of time. It may be expressed in the assertion that the process of party political government adopted in Northern Nigeria was in many respects a macrocosm of the traditional political process of the emirates; in brief, "Kaduna" became the mirror-image of an emirate and was run as a super-NA. Scholars have accumulated a growing quantity of evidence to identify this phenomenon of Kadunaism, from the minor but significant desire of the government to reform the local government system of Kaduna by the creation of a Kaduna Native Authority and a new chieftaincy title, Sarkin Kaduna, to the observations of inside writers cited earlier. The aspect of this institutional convergence—the phrase is

C. S. Whitaker's—referred to here is the alleged role
of the late Sardauna of Sokoto in his relationship with
the new bureaucracy. He has been identified by Dame
Margery Perham as a "super-emir."[100] Most of the
evidence for the assertion that the Premier's attitude
toward the senior civil servants began more and more
to reflect signs of the traditional Hausa ruler's expectancy of the correct behavioral norms in his court
officials lacks the documentary support that could be
wished for, but interviews have hinted how during the
declining years of the political life of the First Republic there were many moments when socialization
seemed far away to the meritocrat. Statistical data
based on elective course preferences expressed by
university students indicate as a cogent reason for
joining the Foreign Service and commerce[101] the wish
to escape from "official" interference in their private
lives and enjoy the status of being an individual, behavior that in much of Africa has been traditionally
looked upon as deviant and antisocial.

What interests us in this connection is the crystallization of this emiratism into an implicit expectancy
that civil servants owe a personal loyalty to the
Sardauna and not an institutional one to the service.
This is strikingly in keeping with the Weberian model
that sees such a demand as the negation of the primary
principle of bureaucracy, namely the depersonalization
of administrative management. "The patrimonial character of a body of officials is above all manifested in
the fact that admission involves a relation of personal dependency,"[102] he has noted, so that an official
might often degenerate into a *puer regis*. Obedience in
traditional authority Weber defines as not something
owed to enacted rules but directly to the person who
occupies a position of authority sanctioned by tradition. Such traditional authority tends to develop into
"patrimonialism," characterized by a purely personal
administrative staff, or in its extreme cases into the

permissive wide discretion by the ruler categorized by Weber as "Sultanism."[103] The parallel is there, and without pushing it too far it does seem that there was a time when the new bureaucracy was approaching the stage of giving, not altogether unwillingly though sometimes with private resentment, to the Premier, who was endowed with immense charisma and filled the acknowledged role of "the Saviour of the North in its Defence against the South," a personal loyalty. In brief, they were bound to him by largely genuine "affectual ties," in the Weberian phraseology. Certain it is that there was about this time (1964–65) a check in the growth of a full civil service ethos of institutional loyalty and its "spirit of formalistic impersonality, *sine ira et studio*,"[104] which had a marked effect on the career goals of those university students who had earlier looked on a civil service appointment as the highest desideratum. And in June of 1965, as again in the demonstrations of March 1967 against the admission of established civil servants into the student body, they made outspoken allegations of emiratist influences at work and the anxious belief that Kadunaism was responsible for the grossly delayed offer of appointment in the regional civil service (in unfortunate contrast to the prompt offers from the federal PSC) because it did not welcome the advent of a large group of new meritocrats. Student complaints were rife and reached the state of despair exemplified in the assertion by Hausa graduates themselves that "Kaduna prefers the NA types to us graduates, it only wants yes-men who will say *ranka ya dade*" (1965) and "Government wants to cheat us students and keep us out of our rightful jobs" (1967). However unfounded the suspicion, it had been born; and that is significant enough.

To the more sanguine observers it had seemed that this patrimonial hold could be broken when there were enough of the "new Northerners" in the civil service to form a diplomatic but firm pressure group which would wish to cleanse the spirit of Kadunaism from the Nigerian system. This would have been in harmony with the Weberian typology of a high level of personal absolution being maintained for only a short period; "The rule is for important limitations on the chief's power to be imposed through pressures exerted by the administrative staff."[105] But the bloodshed of January 1966 violently forestalled the sophisticated method, and today the meritocrats have even turned their feelings against the erstwhile radicals, whom they now dub as conservative and hierocratic emiratists.

In concluding this section, confirmation is appropriate that no evidence has come to light to suggest that, once there are more candidates than there are vacancies in the civil service, the Northern meritocrats would not welcome the full-scale open competitive examination for admission into the administrative class that has now become an annual feature of the other regional civil services. It is erroneous to see the student agitation in May 1966 against the Ironsi regime, both on the Zaria campus and in London demonstrations,[106] as a sign that Northerners felt inferior to Southerners in an open competition for civil service jobs and therefore wanted the continued umbrella of a Northernization policy. If its roots are to be sought in the job sphere, they must be looked for in the Northern student reaction to the two promotion lists announced in Lagos, one of army officers and the other of permanent secretaries. Few meritocrats are admirers of the previous system at, for example, the Military Academy and in the Foreign Service, where some of their own people were admitted with embarrassingly lower educational qualifications than those demanded of Southern applicants.[107] The Northern graduate knows he is as good as a Southern graduate, and his resentment was often turned against his leaders for allowing the North to be held up to scorn for the low caliber of some of its civil servants sent abroad and to the center on what he saw as spurious promotion.

Conclusion

We must now try to draw together the threads of this case study of the growth of meritocratic principles in the selection of public servants, viewed as an element in the development process.

From the time of their entry into the Western-based educational system, the potential meritocrats have been exposed to a standard of success equated with merit and ability and divorced from family or occupational status. This ethos is embodied in the continuing series of examinations (school entrance, university entrance, degree finals) and achievements (school prefect, football captain, student prize winner), in all of which the lesson is learned that individual effort alone will bring success and that familial or status connections are of no account in the impersonalized objectivity of such an educational system. Secular education has historically acted as a primary agent of socialization, and in its Western form its radical effects on African society present a catalytic phenomenon that is still under exciting analysis by social scientists of all disciplines.[108] In contrast to traditional patterns of Hausaland, the self-made man is now assuming some of the glory of the hero, so that the proverb *dan asali ya fi shigege* no longer seems to carry its earlier validity of "some divine right of birth." An extension of this open-merit philosophy into the realm of public appointments leads naturally into the Weberian concept of modern bureaucracy where "the possession of educational certificates are [sic] usually linked with qualification for office . . . such certificates or patents enhance the status element in the social position of the official. . . . Today, the certificate of education becomes what the test for ancestors has been in the past, at least where the nobility has remained powerful: a pre-requisite for equality of birth, a qualification for state office."[109]

This education does more than provide a new road to accessibility of office. It also widens that road to accommodate all who walk it. Here is a conspicuous example of the acknowledged egalitarian effect of education, its social consequence distinguished, in another Weberian definition, as "the tendency to 'levelling' in the interest of the broadest possible basis of recruitment in terms of technical competence." In the shift of this foundation for access to public office, from a closed society of officials to one opened to officers on merit, Northern Nigeria presents a signal laboratory for study.

We are presently witnessing, in the recruitment to public office, hereditary rank and status giving way to patents of education as the recognized hallmark of eligibility for office. Once the floodgates of the schools are fully opened, with their insistence on total equality of opportunity in selection and examination, there can be no more societal control over who are to succeed. Any attempt to do so in contemporary Africa, to disenfranchise the new generation of their "right" to govern earned through their educational attainments, would probably lead to a noisy revolution rather than, as in the Asian experience, to a withdrawal of the intellectuals. This withdrawal is more typical of the tertiary stage of the localization process, when there is such a superfluity of meritocratic talent that graduates are glad to find employment even as clerks, chaprassis, or taxi drivers. Such an educational inflation is an experience that Africa has so far been spared, though its possibility cannot be ruled out if the high school and collegiate expansion of today reaches tomorrow's destined conclusion without the economy keeping pace.

Most political scientists who have worked in Northern Nigeria agree that its exceptional stability up to 1966 depended on the wide acceptance of its favorable sociopolitical climate and its deliberate policy of phased modernization recognized as "Northern gradualism." Whitaker has added to this kind of assessment the compensatory absence of the supreme catalyst of industrialization.[110] This paper suggests that in the bureaucratic recruitment sector a comparable catalysmal phenomenon has now appeared, in the shape of the clamant exponents of a Westernized higher education. It may be conceded that in the literature observers tend to have been so fascinated by the perpetuation of the traditional Northern social system at the political level that they have failed to pay adequate attention to its increasing rejection at the bureaucratic level. Many, however, were uneasily aware of some of the conflicts developing at several levels within the system, and some perceived the trend without documenting it: "Given a favourable social and political environment, the elite recruiting system developed in the North is rather effective. It permits a certain status mobility at the top with a minimum of dissent. . . . But the environment will not be favourable much longer. The introduction of universal franchise—however restricted in practice in the North—tends to interfere with the prevailing elite recruiting system because it introduces legitimate alternatives for claimants to positions of power and influence. The availability of new sources of wealth, education and training in administrative skills, no matter how circumscribed and ideologically restricted, will interfere with traditional methods of elite recruitment."[111] The study of bureaucracies in Africa is soon due to advance from its preliminary stage of the statistical Africanization of the cadres to its secondary one of the ideological and generational conflicts inherent in the recruitment of a new, graduate, entry into a service still predominantly

staffed by men of lesser formal qualifications and sometimes recruited on a narrower social basis.[112]

We have seen the development of a bureaucratic
ethos of appointments, fostered by the PSC, in a civil
service which inevitably ran the risk of perpetuating
the cultural traits of the society from which it emerged
yet which, unlike its counterpart in the development
process, party politics, managed to survive them. We
have seen this emancipation consummated by the advent of the new graduate generation of civil servants,
the meritocrats, often impatient of their senior colleagues and certainly suspicious of what appeared to
them as the momentary threat of a relapse into emiratism manifested in the demand for a personal rather
than an institutional loyalty. The contrast in the social
provenance of those recruited to office at the political
level has now been pointed up. At the bureaucratic
level, the meritocrats have triumphed, strong in the
faith that Western higher education induces an upward social mobility which none of the traditional
forces can now deny them. That all is not yet plain
sailing is evident: there are storms to weather,[113]
but at least they are out of the dreaded Roaring Forties
of Emiratism. Whether they will carry their meritocratic
principles of qualification for office over into their
behavior in office, or whether the forces of Hausa culture, long recognized as being exceptional in their
tenacity to absorb and revive, will re-emerge predominant remains to be seen. It also remains to be seen
whether they are also able to assert their meritocracy in
the political sphere, either directly by mobilizing their
forces and ousting the ultratraditionalists from political
as well as bureaucratic office, or indirectly (as has
been the experience in Senegal,[114] and long since
class-stratified Britain) by increasing their influence in
proportion to the extent to which the political leaders
lean on them to execute their modernization programs.[115] The rise of the African meritocracy has led

to the creation of a fresh dimension in the structure of society.

In the administrative processes of development few institutions are so influential as the civil service. For most of the new nations, the bureaucracy is the operating scene of the new clerisy. The extent to which in Northern Nigeria this institution has handled the confrontation between traditional forces dedicated to a belief in recruitment to leadership from a closed status group and those Western-oriented forces intent on the universal accessibility of office has been the focus of this study: it is a major aspect of elite formation brought about by the socializing influence of the colonial experience as transmitted in its program of secular education. This exposure of the areas of internal friction in the next stage of the Africanization of the civil services, accentuated in the authoritarian Northern Nigerian context but often valid elsewhere in Africa, may have some relevance for a constructed study of the type of impediments likely to be encountered by these bureaucratic cadres in seeking to make their optimum contribution as a development institution in the new states. An open-recruitment system has enabled the emergence of a class of professional bureaucrats and we are left with the contemplation of the new, bureaucratically articulated, meritocracy engaged in an ideological, semisocial struggle with its predecessor personnel, both elders and equals. Often the aspirations and values of such a struggle are ambivalent: such is the fate of the man of two cultures. In the event of absolute victory for the meritocrats, this clerisy could establish its own brand of elitist hierocracy, replacing the earlier qualification of birth by a no less rigid qualification of university education as the passport to office among the new oligarchy. Thus the wheel could turn the full circle, and bureaucracy, which Weber sees as normally coming into power on the basis of a reduction in economic and social differences, could next set up criteria of ultra-refined educational attainments (already achieved by those in power), which might then take on an ascriptive status of the same exclusiveness as the earlier criteria of social and occupational stratification. In thus substituting one *karda* for another, Weber's postulate of democracy's fear that, having ousted traditional authority, "a merit system and educational certificates will result in a privileged caste," would be amply realized.[116] The achieved status of university education could become the new ascription.[117]

There is, too, evidence to suggest that the current rejection of traditional Hausa societal values with respect to accessibility of office might well be followed by a renaissance of related Hausa values during behavior in office: once the gates to public office have been opened through Western education, they could be closed again by the new cadres of Hausa elites eager to re-Hausafy the mores of their fresh-structured society. Such, indeed, would not be out of keeping with the remarkably absorptive nature, at all levels, of Hausa culture. Proud and persistent, it is strong in the will to survive. Here we have sought to analyze one aspect of the contemporary Hausa social, and hence political, power struggle, setting the scene among the tensions within the bureaucratic cadres. For as Weber said of the Chinese mandarin class, whose rise to power makes such a compelling parallel with the march of the meritocrats in today's African concern, "the total political situation of the *literati* can be understood only when one realizes the forces against which they had to fight."[118]

Footnotes

1. A. H. M. Kirk-Greene, "Bureaucratic Cadres in a Traditional Milieu," in James S. Coleman, ed., *Education and Political Development* (Princeton: 1965).

2. C. S. Whitaker, Jr., "A Dysrhythmic Process of Political Change," *World Politics*, XIX, 2, 1967, 216–17. In this connection, too, I would recall Apter's flexible and important definition of "traditionalism" as "validation of current behavior by reference to immemorial prescriptive norms. That is not to say that traditionalist systems do not change but rather that innovation—that is, extrasystemic action—has to be mediated within the social system and linked with antecedent values." David E. Apter, *The Politics of Modernisation* (Chicago: 1965), p. 83.

3. "Where authority is primarily oriented to tradition but in its exercise makes the claim of full personal powers, it will be called 'patrimonial' authority"—Max Weber, *The Theory of Social and Economic Organization,* trans. A. M. Henderson and Talcott Parsons (New York: 1947), p. 238. This will be referred to in citations as Weber I. Quotations from H. H. Gerth and C. Wright Mills, trans. and ed., *From Max Weber: Essays in Sociology* (London: 1948) will be cited as Weber II.

4. James S. Coleman and Carl G. Rosberg, Jr., eds., *Political Parties and National Integration in Tropical Africa* (Berkeley and Los Angeles: 1964), p. 3.

5. Reinhard Bendix, *Nationbuilding and Citizenship* (New York: 1964), p. 18. See also Karl W. Deutsch and William J. Folz, *Nation-Building* (New York: 1963); William B. Hamilton, ed., *The Transfer of Institutions* (Durham, N.C.: 1964); Sir Charles Jeffries, *The Transfer of Power* (London: 1960); and, on a wider and more theoretical scale, Joseph La Palombara, ed., *Bureaucracy and Political Development* (Princeton: 1963) and David E. Apter, *op. cit.*

6. Richard Symonds, *The British and Their Successors* (London: 1966), p. 13.

7. In the same class of the legacies of imperialism are the English language, the social assumptions of higher education, the Sandhurst ethos, perhaps the Westminster model, and, more cynically, the breath-taking financial opportunities offered by the system of popularly elected parliamentarians. On a lesser plane I have heard quoted among the heritage of British colonialism football and public sanitation—but certainly not, in American eyes, municipal public transportation!

8. House of Commons debate of 10 July 1833, quoted in Symonds, *op. cit.,* p. 18.

9. E.g., A. L. Adu, *The Civil Service in New African States* (London: 1965), pp. 22, 217, 235.

10. M. Fortes and E. E. Evans-Pritchard, *African Political Systems* (London: 1941), p. 5.

11. C. S. Whitaker, Jr., "Three Perspectives on Hierarchy," *Journal of Commonwealth Political Studies,* III, 1965. See also his *The Politics of Tradition,* unpublished Ph.D. thesis (Princeton University: 1964).

12. Weber II, p. 228.

13. Important contributions to the study of the Hausa-Fulani social system include:

D. W. Ames, "Hausa Drummers and Their Drums," *Ibadan,* October 21, 1965, pp. 62–80.

——, "Music and the Musician in Hausa and Igbo Societies," unpublished paper, 1967.

D. P. L. Dry, "The Hausa Attitude to Authority," in *Proceedings of the First Annual Conference of the West African Institute of Social and Economic Research* (Ibadan: 1952).

Billy J. Dudley, "The Nomination of Parliamentary Candidates in Northern Nigeria," *Journal of Commonwealth Political Studies,* Vol. II, 1963–64, pp. 45–58.

——, *Parties and Politics in Northern Nigeria* (London: 1967), *passim.*

A. H. M. Kirk-Greene, "Bureaucratic Cadres in a Traditional Milieu" in James S. Coleman, ed., *Education and Political Development* (Princeton: 1965), pp. 372–407.

J. Schacht, "Islam in Northern Nigeria," *Studia Islamia,* Vol. VIII, 1957, pp. 123–46.

R. L. Sklar, *Nigerian Political Parties* (Princeton: 1963), pp. 321–37; 365–78; Ch. XI.

R. L. Sklar and C. S. Whitaker, "Nigeria," in James S. Coleman and Carl Rosberg, eds., *Political Parties and National Integration in Tropical Africa* (Berkeley and Los Angeles: 1964), pp. 612–24, 633–36.

——, "The Federal Republic of Nigeria," in Gwendolen M. Carter, ed., *National Unity and Regionalism in Eight African States* (Ithaca: 1966), pp. 11–17; 65–94.

M. G. Smith, "Slavery and Emancipation in Two Societies (Jamaica and Zaria)," *Social and Economic Studies,* 3, 1954, pp. 239–88.

——, *The Economy of Hausa Communities of Zaria* (London: 1955).

——, "The Social Functions and Meaning of Hausa Praise-Singing," *Africa*, XXVII, January 1957, pp. 26–45.

——, "The Hausa System of Social Status," *Africa*, XXIX, July 1959, pp. 239–52.

——, *Government in Zazzau*, 1800–1950 (London: 1960).

——, "Kebbi and Hausa Stratification," *British Journal of Sociology* (Jamaica), Vol. XII, March 1961, pp. 52–61 (reply to *Yeld*, infra.).

——, "Historical and Cultural Conditions of Political Corruption Among the Hausa," *Comparative Studies in Society and History* (The Hague), 6, 2, 1964, pp. 164–94.

Mary Smith, *Baba of Karo* (London: 1954).

J. S. Trimingham, *Islam in West Africa* (London: 1959).

C. S. Whitaker, "Three Perspectives on Hierarchy," *Journal of Commonwealth Political Studies*, Vol. III, 1965, pp. 1–19.

——, The Politics of Tradition: *A Study of Continuity and Change in Northern Nigeria*, 1946–60, unpublished Ph.D. thesis (Princeton University: 1964).

L. R. Yeld, "Islam and Social Stratification in Northern Nigeria," *British Journal of Sociology*, Vol. XI, June 1960, pp. 112–28.

14. Dry, *op. cit.*, p. 15.

15. Yeld, *op. cit.*, p. 115. She goes on to observe how "social equals stand and touch hands when greeting, while an inferior crouches before a superior and removes his shoes before entering the superior's compound. Only social equals may eat together and therefore the sexes eat apart, while an inferior goes to greet a superior at his or her home and not vice versa." It was on the etiquette described in the first sentence, which *inter alia* had caused anxiety to Hausa civil servants expected to "advise" their emirs as government agents, that Hausa district officers calling on the emir in their official capacity were officially directed that they were not expected to remove their shoes.

16. Smith, 1959, p. 247.

17. *Ibid.*, p. 250.

18. Ralph Linton, *The Study of Man* (New York: 1936), p. 115.

19. M. Hassan and S. Ma'ibi, *A Chronicle of Abuja* (Ibadan: 1952; repr. Lagos, 1964). This is a translation by F. Heath of their vernacular *Makau, Sarkin Zazzau na Habe* and *Tarihi da Al'adun Habe na Abuja*, both published in 1952.

20. M. G. Smith, *Government in Zazzau 1800–1950* (London: 1960).

21. *Ibid.*, and diagrams at pp. 36 and 47. A complete list of all titleholders by categories is given as an Appendix to Hassan and Nai'bi, *op. cit.*

22. *Rukuni* seems to imply a special decision-making character of a group, without which it would recede into the generality of groups. This is also expressed in its secondary usage, e.g., *shi ne rukuni a cikinsu*, "he is a key person in the group." The public ceremony of the emir winding a turban round the head of a newly appointed official (Hausa: *an yi masa rawani an nada shi*, "he has been appointed") is still of importance in Northern Nigeria and is frequently described in the newspapers. In Nupe (see Nadel, below) the Hausa word has been taken over as the generic term for "titled nobility," *rowni*, and is used coterminously with the vernacular word *ticizhi*.

23. Hausa: *ma-da(wa)ki*, "owner of horses."

24. Smith, *op. cit.*, p. 56.

25. S. F. Nadel, *A Black Byzantium* (London: 1942), esp. chapters VII–IX and the rank tables at pp. 100–8.

26. District administration data assembled in O. and C. L. Temple, *Notes on the Tribes, Provinces, Emirates and States of the Northern Provinces of Nigeria* (Lagos: 1922).

27. Smith, *op. cit.*, pp. 9, 106, 116.

28. E.g., Smith, Whitaker, Dudley, cited in Note 13.

29. Nadel, *op. cit.*, p. 123.

30. Nadel, *op. cit.*, pp. 130–31.

31. *Memorandum of the Mid-Western Delegation submitted to the Ad Hoc Conference on the Nigerian Constitution* (Benin City: 1966), Para. 7.

32. Condensed from Dudley, *op. cit.*, p. 50. These are repeated, in tabular form, in his "The Northern People's Congress," in J. Mackintosh, *Nigerian Government and Politics* (London: 1966), p. 361.

33. James S. Coleman, *Nigeria: Background to Nationalism* (Berkeley and Los Angeles: 1958), pp. 380–83.

34. In his unpublished thesis (see note 11 above), cited in his "Three Perspectives . . ." Note 18.

35. Macintosh, *op. cit.*, pp. 89–90.

36. Condensed from tables in K. Post, *The Nigerian Federal Election of 1959* (London: 1963), p. 427.

37. In some measure the scene recalls the Ethiopian experience—so attractive for an exploratory comparison between emperor and emir—where "the entire staff of government officials has been the direct sociological descendant of the traditional court retinue"—Donald Levine, *Wax and Gold* (Chicago: 1965), p. 185.

38. Yeld, *op. cit.,* p. 123.

39. See especially Smith: 1955, *passim,* and 1960, pp. 253–61. Present day instances can be quoted of the same social rejection by royal families of the suits of *shigege* and *talaka* politicians aspiring to marry into them.

40. Whitaker has identified no less than eight ministers who raised their status thus, gaining higher title without office in their respective NAs—"A Dysrhythmic . . . ," p. 211.

41. Sklar and Whitaker, *op. cit.,* p. 609.

42. Nadel, *op. cit.,* p. 157.

43. Cf. the gubernatorial rebuke: "In a few [NAs] recently there has been some delegation of powers to members of the Emir's Council . . . it has been thought that this was quite an extraordinary advance, offering another reason for complacency."—Sir Donald Cameron, *The Principles of Native Administration and Their Application* (Lagos: 1934), Para. 22.

44. Dispatch to the governors of the African Territories, February 25, 1947, Para. 5.

45. Recent useful analyses of this philosophy of colonial administration include L. Gray Cowan, *Local Government in West Africa* (New York: 1958) and A. H. M. Kirk-Greene, *The Principles of Native Administration in Nigeria, 1900–1947: Selected Documents* (London: 1965). Margery Perham's *Native Administration in Nigeria* (London: 1937) has just been reprinted. See also the long introductions to two 1965 reprints from Frank Cass and Co. (London), Sir F. L. Lugard, *The Dual Mandate* (1922), and C. W. Orr, *The Making of Northern Nigeria* (1911).

46. Whitaker, 1965, p. 3.

47. For a summary of these controls, see M. J. Campbell, *Law and Practice of Local Government in Northern Nigeria* (London: 1963), pp. 120–31. They were eventually brought together and printed, with amendments from time to time, as model *NA Staff Regulations.*

48. Personal field notes indicate that had a close survey of such mobility even been undertaken, the wastage figures might

have seemed disquietingly high. A possible compensation lay in the reflection that, at the NA level, any training at the institute was bound to have some general effect, even if its specifics were never utilized. The same loss was at one time perceptible in the lack of correlation between government training bursaries and subsequent employment. For an introduction to this problem of unrealized skills, see the useful article by P. A. O. Dada, "Evaluation of Local Government Courses in Relation to Careers of Staff Trained at Zaria 1954–1964," *Journal of Administration Overseas,* Vol. V., No. 4, pp. 268–70.

49. This was one of the prices paid for the lack of a unified local government service like that obtaining in Western and Eastern Nigeria. Resistance to the establishment of such a scheme in the North can be helpfully explained in the light of the closely knit demands of personalized emirate loyalty implicit in the general theme of continued hierarchical sentiments developed in this essay.

50. *Declaration of Principles* (Northern Elements Progressive Union), 1952.

51. Post, *op. cit.,* p. 52. See also Sklar, *Nigerian Political Parties,* pp. 365–66.

52. Coleman and Rosberg, *op. cit.,* p. 678, Note 22.

53. P. C. Lloyd, "Traditional Rulers," in Coleman and Rosberg, *op. cit.,* p. 400.

54. Henry L. Bretton, *Power and Stability in Nigeria* (New York: 1962), p. 57.

55. Joseph Schumpeter, *Capitalism, Socialism and Democracy* (New York: 1947), p. 12.

56. Lloyd Fallers, "Equality, Modernity and Democracy in the New States," in Clifford Geertz, ed., *Old Societies and New States: The Quest for Modernity in Asia and Africa* (New York: 1963).

57. S. Phillipson and S. O. Adebo, *The Nigerianization of the Civil Service* (Lagos: 1954).

58. *Organization of the Colonial Service,* Col. 197, 1946, p. 4. Cf. "The institution of Public Service Commissions is comparatively new to the civil service in African states. It was not heard of before constitutional changes brought about self-government and independence"—Adu, *op. cit.,* p. 130.

59. Cf. Ahmadu Bello: "After many searchings of hearts and with much doubt a Ministry of Local Government was created

. . . uncertain of the effect such a Ministry would have on the great Emirs"—*My Life* (Cambridge: 1962), pp. 94–95.

60. The original declaration, cited in the *Annual Report of the Public Service Commission, 1954–57* (Kaduna: 1958), Para. 18, was repeated in the Regional House of Assembly in 1964: "First Northerners, second expatriates, and thirdly non-Northerners on contract"—*Debates* . . . , 1964, p. 435.

61. In 1952 there were approximately 1,500 Northerners in the junior grades of the civil service and twenty-five in the senior; over 80 per cent of the region's clerical posts were held by Southerners. By 1956 this had risen to 2,400 and sixty-two respectively: these figures represented less than 10 per cent of the senior posts established. For a full statistical analysis of Northernization see the tables compiled by A. H. M. Kirk-Greene, "The Higher Public Service," in L. Franklin Blitz, ed., *The Politics and Administration of Nigerian Government* (New York: 1965), p. 231.

62. This is not the kind of situation that is easily documented. Indeed, here as in more and more instances these days, the telephone is robbing the future scholar of the minutes, telegrams, and policy decisions on government files that today fill the public archives and are the very stuff of historical research. In a closer study of the personalities involved, it would be appropriate to consider the influence exercised on the development of the new public service ethos through the leadership of the permanent heads of the civil services and chairmen of the PSCs. In the North, an outstanding officer held the office during the crucial years before and after independence. In the West, observers commented upon the deterioration of civil service morale once its brilliant Nigerian head left for another post and the service, previously acknowledged as the most competent in the country, began to drift. The amalgam of traditional Hausa *ladabi* ("good breeding and good manners maketh the good man") and intellectual radicalism combined in the personality of one of the chairmen of the Northern PSC in this period would be a no less influential factor in such an evaluation. Overall, of course, there dominated the charismatic, compelling personality of the region's premier.

63. Sections 66–72 of the Constitution of Northern Nigeria Law, 1963. These were drafted to give expression to the recommendation of the 1957 Constitutional Conference that "the Public Service Commission should be insulated from politics, and

provision for its appointment should not only make its independence a reality, but also be clearly understood to do so."

64. Adapted from the tables in Dudley, *op. cit.,* p. 50, and Kirk-Greene in Coleman, *op. cit.,* pp. 384–85. It must not be thought, however, that during the decade before the expanded secondary school program in the North began to bear fruits (ca. 1960) that the terms "Member of Parliament" and "uneducated" were synonymous. This is far from the truth, and Whitaker has shown how the Northern parliamentarians constituted an elite in terms of Western education as well. His figures of those holding political office in the 1956–61 legislature reveal a mean seven and a half years of formal Western-type schooling, a figure that rose for the average of Northern Nigerian cabinet ministers. (Whitaker, 1964, p. 408, cited in Whitaker, 1967, p. 215). The heavy weighting of graduates in the Western and Eastern Regional Cabinets tends to push the Northern picture out of perspective.

65. Talcott Parsons' introduction to Weber I, p. 67. In a well-known passage Weber has identified the five behavioral areas which distinguish a traditional bureaucracy from a modern one: see Weber I, pp. 343 ff.

66. Weber II, p. 196.

67. Much of the basic documentation is to be found in a series of articles appearing as a follow-up to A. H. M. Kirk-Greene, "A Training Course for Northern Nigerian Administrative Officers," *Journal of African Administration,* Vol. XI, 1, 1959, pp. 41–72, covering not only the Nigerian experience, but also that of its East and Central African successors. This literature is supplemented by a number of mimeographed conference reports.

68. Symonds, *op. cit.,* p. 262.

69. Two of the gravest and most far-reaching were: (a) the frustration caused to the teaching staff by the failure of the cabinet to evolve a new spirit of provincial administration to match the new corps of administrators under training, so that, to quote the view of two of them, "we were aware of the danger of turning out replicas of the expatriate District Officer of an earlier decade" but could do little about it; and (b) the realization that by thinking only of the immediate stopgap problem, trouble was being stored up against the day when the new meritocrats would emerge with their college degrees and look askance at a service whose top posts were held by men who,

regardless of their administrative experience, held considerably lower educational qualifications. In the parallel Malayan situation, warning was also given of the imbalance resulting from such uneven recruitment and the dangers of a "saturation of a bureaucracy with servants probably less competent than later applicants" (Robert O. Tilman, *Bureaucratic Transition in Malaya,* Durham, N.C.: 1964, p. 76), while for the Tanganyikan service A. L. Adu unpopularly recommended the creation of a new grade of administrative officer rather than a wholesale acceptance of obviously temporary recruits into permanent promotion posts.

70. E.g., Notice No. 135, *Northern Nigerian Gazette,* February 6, 1958.

71. J. D. Kingsley and Sir Arthur Rucker, *Staffing and Development of the Public Service of Northern Nigeria* (Kaduna: 1961).

72. Two cases are of interest because they are often cited by the meritocrats. One was the appointment of a well-connected Fulani holder of a nongraduate overseas diploma in public administration to an administrative post at a time when a degree was already accepted as the minimum qualification. The other was the curious case of two classmates. One obtained a first-class nongraduate diploma in public administration but was told that to secure appointment as an administrative officer he must next undertake the nine-month special training course. He refused, went to a university, and three years later returned qualified for a direct appointment. His classmate failed the diploma course, accepted a place on the special training course, and was appointed an administrative officer two years before his classmate—with all that this meant in the way of eligibility for promotion.

73. There is something of value in the precedent of training approved for H.M.O.C.S. which placed no restriction on the degree subject offered and retained all professional training against the special Administrative Probationers' Course.

74. Bretton, *op. cit.,* p. 67.

75. "We cannot afford the luxury of civil servants who are neutral"—Julius Nyerere quoted in *The Observer* (London, June 3, 1962). For Ghana see one furor following one dismissal of the Chief Justice in early 1964. It was once asserted in the House of Representatives in Lagos that the specially trained

elite corps of Nigerian senior civil servants was nothing less sinister than a Trojan horse left by the departing British! (*Debates,* November 22, 1960).

76. Cf. F. A. O. Schwarz: "The traditional system of the North had weathered the British era well because of indirect rule and the North's educational isolation . . . The Northerners were less humiliated and uprooted by the colonial experience though they did not benefit from colonialism nearly as much as the Southerners"—*Nigeria* (Boston: 1966), pp. 77, 232.

77. One of the most pungent of the NPC's across-the-board vilifications (they were more often personal than general, and even then few by the usual decolonization standards) was the Premier's public ascription of blame for the anti-Northern Nigeria vote in the Trust Territory plebiscite of November 1959 on the "subversive activities of British officials."

78. Apart from the oft-quoted bogy that an Ibo civil servant would on the departure of the British fill all junior posts with his own family, there was the more reasoned realization that in "one Nigeria" there would be serious difficulties in the way of dismissing Nigerian nationals from government service (cf. Ahmadu Bello, *op. cit.,* p. 111), whereas in the last resort the cry of "Europeans go home" could always be raised. In the event, this was rarely heard as an xenophobic generalization in the North, only in individual cases of conflict of personalities.

79. This and the following quotation are both from personal communications. The vast scarcity of university-trained men in the regional quota of posts in the federal services simplified the rationale of such an induced exodus of meritocratic talent, where junior Northern officials would have to work side by side with graduate colleagues from East and West; as such, there was a case for sending graduates to fill such posts where educational egalitarianism was a live issue to which all were liable to be sensitive.

80. A breakdown of the parade-state of one of the infantry battalions *after* the regional regrouping of troops in the fall of 1966 showed eighteen of the twenty-two Northern officers in the unit as Christian and only eighty-four of the 681 other ranks as Moslem (Colin Legum, *The Observer,* October 23, 1966). One of the North's pleas to the Minorities Commission of 1958 was that the Middle Belt's educational manpower was vital to the creation of a truly Northernized civil service.

81. Lloyd, *op. cit.*, p. 399.

82. The terms "wet" and "dry" were popular with students at the Institute of Administration, Zaria, as a substitute for the officially disapproved "Middle Belt/Holy North" dichotomy. "Riverain" and "far" became acceptable to officialdom.

83. Notable instances include the acceptance of the call by his people of M. Muhammed Tukur, who renounced his civil service appointment as commissioner in the UK to become Emir of Yauri, and the rejection of local office by the eldest son of the ex-Emir of Kano, M. Aminu Sanusi, in preference for remaining in his career post in the Foreign Service. The high prestige accorded to chiefs among Ghanaian secondary school children's perception of occupational hierarchy is striking—see Foster, *op. cit.*, pp. 268–69. It is also interesting to recall the relatively high score of ministers who gave up their political office in preference for the accustomed laurels of NA office. The obverse of this coin invites reflection on the attitudes of that handful of *'yan sarki,* royal scions, who have accepted the civil service ethos but who may well be called upon to succeed as chief in their emirates.

84. The mid-Victorians' self-assuredness in imperial expansion has been succinctly depicted by Ronald Robinson and John Gallagher, who speak of how "in the exhilaration of their achievements they not unnaturally gave praise for the industrial philosopher's stone to their own domestic arrangements and virtues"—*Africa and the Victorians* (London: 1961), p. 1. "Few doubted," they write later (p. 3) "that *gesta Dei per Anglos.*"

85. Bretton, never one to stand on ceremony with appearances, has been one of the political scientists to raise this query openly in Africa: "The British are concerned with strengthening the integrity and efficiency of the bureaucracy and with separating the bureaucracy from political partisanship, the African rulers view the administrators very much as their predecessors did in Britain prior to the [1853] reforms: they expect the bureaucracy to be a tool in the power processes, including those outside the limits of legality."—*op. cit.*, p. 86. But for many he spoils his case by implying that Nigerians are not *ready* for such a sophisticated brand of bureaucracy.

86. The word "friction" is advisedly used in preference to the term "cracks" sometimes heard in this context. The latter could infer a weakening of the civil service competence: to the contrary, the behavior of the Nigerian civil services during 1966

and 1967 has been beyond praise, for they have carried on their shoulders the executive running of the federation. The Army appeared neither qualified nor, after its internal massacres, able to command sufficient talent to "run" the ministries with its own personnel.

87. It is against this sort of profound anxiety that must be seen the rowdy demonstrations by students at Zaria protesting against the introduction of an abbreviated BA program for civil servants granted "mature student" status. See *The Times* (London, February 20, 1967), and the perceptive contributed article "Anxious Administrators," *West Africa,* March 25, 1967.

88. And perhaps Malaya, given the constitutional guarantees of fixed percentage quotas of civil service posts by ethnic groups—see Tilman, *op. cit.,* pp. 109–10.

89. Cf. Zolberg: "The claims of youth in its various forms are particularly intolerable because many African societies place some importance on age as a criterion for political authority: although, traditionally, young men often had an institutionalized place in the system, it was strictly defined and was not allowed to interfere with political control before authoritative roles were vacated by the death of their incumbents."—*op. cit.,* p. 74. What has happened is that education has encouraged the meritocrats to jump the authority-race gun. Cf. Apter, *op. cit.,* 45 ff., on the particular effect on youth of the accessibility of innovative roles created by education.

90. Bello, *op. cit.,* p. 110. See also K. E. Robinson, *The Dilemmas of Trusteeship* (London: 1964), p. 63, for an interesting statistical note on the education and experience of colonial governors.

91. The Colonial Service itself handled a similar problem of underqualified recruitment and blockages in the promotion ladder by men who had failed to make the grade by "Harraginization"—the power to enforce premature retirement but without forfeiting earned pension rights recommended in West Africa's Harragin Salaries Commission of 1945.

92. One is reminded of the witty speech of Malcolm Muggeridge on his installation as the Rector of Edinburgh University in February 1967, when he spoke of how "in our society the belief that the road to paradise is paved with A-levels is held at least as tenaciously as any article of Christian dogma in the days of Torquemada."

93. Bretton, *op. cit.,* p. 65.

94. Cf., the assessment by an inside observer of the civil service scene: "The fact that those giddy days of jet-propelled promotion are past, for Ph.D. holders as well as for secondary school men, is hard to grasp, and few will accept the fact that in the old Colonial Service it was only the flyer who became a Senior DC in ten years or reached the Staff Grade in under twenty"—"Anxious Administrators," *West Africa*, March 27, 1967, p. 403.

95. From a letter by a Sierra Leonean student published in *West Africa*, February 25, 1967, p. 272.

96. Zolberg, *op. cit.*, p. 71.

97. *Report of the Exchange of Customary Presents* (Kaduna: 1953).

98. The phrase is taken from Sir Andrew Cohen, *British Policy in Changing Africa* (Evanston: 1959).

99. Brigadier E. Gibbons, *African Local Government Reform in Kenya, Uganda and Eastern Nigeria* (1949, unpublished), Para. 93. Cf. Ken Post's conclusion that "the nationalists, while regarding these [LG] reforms as desirable because of their 'democratic' nature, in fact successfully concentrated their efforts upon winning control of the central government. The foundation for parliamentary government, theoretically regarded as essential, was in practice never fully laid."—*The New States of West Africa* (London, Penguin: 1964), p. 97.

100. Foreword to A. H. M. Kirk-Greene, *The Principles of Native Administration in Nigeria* (London: 1965), p. xii. In the discussion of "personalism" that follows, the emphasis is more on genuine personal loyalty than on the autocracy described in Henry Bretton's *The Rise and Fall of Kwame Nkrumah* (New York: 1967).

101. This backlash has been documented by an analysis of the specialization preferences (government, business, Foreign Service) of the first three groups of students at Ahmadu Bello University registered for a degree in public administration. Those electing for government at one time fell away to under 20 per cent—they endured the sobriquet of "government stooges" and one of them was publicly mocked for winning a cup presented by the Premier for good conduct—from an earlier 75 per cent. Cf. the suggestion that the administrative service was no longer attracting the cream of graduates in two specially contributed articles "Northern Nigerians as Today's DOs," *West Africa*, November 1963, pp. 1234, 1259. Although there is

no suggestion of anything approaching India's experience of the withdrawal of its intellectuals from public life, so intimately analyzed in the writings of Professor E. Shils, it was significant how in 1964–65 a trickle of Northern graduates began to ignore the many government service vacancies and move into commerce, banking, and academia. The events of 1966, however, reversed this trend once again, and with the removal of the inhibiting superemirate atmosphere of "Kadunaism," government service looks set fair to regain its popularity unless the current [February 1967] resentment of civil service proposals linked with Zaria's Institute of Administration results in another rejection of such a career (see Note 87).

102. Weber I, p. 386. Rupert Emerson has formulated a valuable discussion of the personalization of loyalties and movements in the new nations—see *From Empire to Nation* (Cambridge, Mass.: 1960), p. 281.

103. Weber I, pp. 341, 347.

104. Weber I, p. 340.

105. Weber I, p. 63.

106. The influence of these demonstrations is asserted in the Federal Government's *Nigeria 1966* (Lagos: 1967), p. 8.

107. Cf. their angry dilemma over the kind of situation which could permit a Lagos University lecturer to write how a drastic modification of the ideal that a degree was a necessary prerequisite to joining the administrative grade "made it possible for Northerners, among whom it is difficult to find graduates, to participate, *however inadequately,* in the upper echelons of federal administration" (italics added)—Eme O. Awa, *Federal Government in Nigeria* (Berkeley and Los Angeles, 1964), p. 172.

108. Typical is Levine's experience of the Ethiopian situation: "High among these new values is that of rewarding an individual solely on the basis of performance. Although the long arm of 'connections' has occasionally reached into the school system, to save, for example, the relative of some dignitary from dismissal despite substandard performance, the day-to-day operation of school life follows general standards which are applied without regard to family connection, class position, or tribal and religious affiliations."—*op. cit.,* p. 113.

109. Weber II, pp. 200, 241.

110. Whitaker, 1964, *passim.*

111. Bretton, *op. cit.,* p. 68.

112. Although not within the specifics of this essay but certainly relevant to the broader theme of the reciprocal acculturative effects of a formal Western education on an African group having its own traditional social structure, reference is invited to Philip Foster's major study, *Education and Social Change* (London: 1965).

113. Some of the institutional ones have been discussed by Kirk-Greene in Coleman, *op. cit.,* pp. 401–2 and in Blitz, *op. cit.,* pp. 244–47, and some of the personal ones in my "Some Problems of the African Administrator Today," *African Affairs,* October 1967, pp. 40–52. The philosophy and practical problems of the reorientated civil services of the new states in their positive role as a development institution have been analyzed by such writers as Adu and Symonds (*op. cit.*), by J. Donald Kingsley, "Nigeria," in La Palombara, *op. cit.,* pp. 301–17, and by Guy Hunter in his *New Societies of Tropical Africa* (London: 1962), his "The Administrative Machine," *African Affairs,* Vol. 65, 1966, pp. 129–234, and his "Development Administration in East Africa," *Journal of Administration Overseas,* Vol. VI, 1, 1967, pp. 6–12. See also Aristide R. Zolberg, *Creating Political Order* (Chicago: 1966), p. 73, and the unsigned article of wide relevance throughout Africa, "Anxious Administrators," *West Africa,* March 25, 1967, pp. 401–3.

114. See Deutsch and Foltz, *op. cit.,* pp. 124 ff.

115. The irony was seen by some in the personification of much that was good in emiratism, a man who was then appointed chancellor of the very university whose tutored meritocracy was devoted to destroying the principles of accessibility to office that he so notably stood for. Parallels can be discovered in the chancellorial status of Haile Selassie, Nkrumah, and Nyerere, who preside over the very universities that breed disaffection and rejection of the power patterns which they themselves represent. Whereas riches, political office, houses and cars and gorgeous robes and women might historically lie in the gift of "the Chief," be he traditional or new-political, education is totally inalienable. As an Ethiopian student put it: "The Emperor will have to learn that our education is not a plaything he can turn on or off as he pleases"—quoted in Levine, *op. cit.,* p. 214.

116. Weber II, p. 240. There was a hint of a preliminary instance of this kind of status entrenchment in the allegations by graduates from the American-patterned Nsukka University that

the Federal PSC was rating their BA lower than that of graduates from the other, British-patterned Nigerian universities when
considering appointments to the public service.

117. A remarkable instance of how the qualification for recruitment into a modernizing civil service can be firmly based
on achievement factors yet operate just as firmly on standards
based on the ascriptive orientation of the actual training course
is to be found in the experience of the Malay College for Administrators—Robert O. Tilman, *Bureaucratic Transition in Malaya* (Durham, N.C.: 1964), p. 127.

118. Weber II, p. 443.

LEONARD W. DOOB[1]

Facilitating Rapid Change in Africa

Leonard W. Doob is Professor of Social Psychology at Yale University and a member of the Yale University Committee on African Studies. He is the author of Becoming More Civilized, *and has edited a recent anthology of African poetry.*

In spite of many bright spots above and below the surface, it is clear that all is not well in Africa. It would be sadistic and useless, though, to catalogue the difficulties and evils now plaguing our African friends. In order to consider with equanimity some of the theoretical issues involved in rapid social change and then in particular to focus upon an attempt to mitigate tensions arising from two border disputes in contemporary Africa, however, it is necessary only to secure assent to a single proposition: whether or not accelerated change of peoples and groups is indeed necessary or desirable at the present time. Many African leaders seek to produce such change and ask for assistance in doing so; and they certainly agree that their own border disputes are wasteful and evil. The evaluation and the values are theirs, therefore; here is no neocolonial attempt to urge (or not to urge) anyone to remake Africans in a Western image either efficiently or rapidly.

Gradualism

Let us, then, assume that African leaders and their advisers are impatient: they want, they need change fast. What should they do? Other than slaughtering those who oppose them—a solution not to be recommended, though sometimes practiced and not always on a small scale—most planned change rests upon an assumption subscribed to, undoubtedly, by the majority of social scientists, humanists, and men of good faith: build on the basis of people's present culture and ways of behaving. Do not introduce fertilizer, even though experts tell you the soil needs just that, until you become acquainted with people's present mode of agriculture, the ways in which they view their own agricultural practices, and their probable reactions to chemicals brought in from the outside. Do not begin teaching a new system of mathematics in the schools until you have learned how pupils conceptualize numbers and sets; otherwise they will experience numerous traumatic difficulties, and the educational innovation will be a failure. Do not change the legal system abruptly, for the traditional ways of trying cases will persist and must be taken into account as new courts acquire jurisdiction and greater power.

The evidence in favor of a gradualist approach is almost completely overwhelming. Virtually every anthropologist who deals with the problem makes the point that social change is slow and that elements of the old culture survive when people seem to have changed markedly on the surface (wearing European clothes, going to church) or even when they have been uprooted themselves (urban migration). If need be, moreover, psychology and psychiatry can be invoked to provide supporting assertions: old habits are tenacious, childhood traits pervade adult life. This approach, it is almost wasteful to say, is also most congenial from a philosophical and political standpoint. The planner, the agent of change, disregards at his peril people's current values and practices; he bows respectfully to the nuances of their culture and their personalities.

It is quite obvious, nevertheless, that people do change. In fact sometimes the change occurs with respect to values or behavior which in principle seem least likely to be affected. Among American college students, for example, truisms that are supposed to embody the wisdom of the culture and hence to be heavily reinforced have been found to be vulnerable to change in large part because, never having been challenged, they are not encased in supporting beliefs and arguments.[2] Refined analysis,[3] moreover, suggests that what are loosely called attitudes can perform the most varied functions within people and hence they can be variously changed sometimes, though perhaps rarely, with relatively little difficulty. Brainwashing, whether polite or impolite, allegedly induces fast alterations in personality. On an anecdotal level, finally, all of us think we can provide instances of sudden, even permanent change: ". . . afterward he was never the same."

In appraising change and planning in Africa, in short, the pendulum has been thrust far away from the earlier conceptions of most (but not all) colonial administrators and missionaries who were partially convinced that Africans could be trained or forced to modify their heritage and themselves by fiat. Here a mild effort is being made to suggest, however obnoxious the phrase, a middle ground between the glib swiftness advocated by the archcolonialist or missionary and the cautious gradualism proposed by the anthropologist or Freudian psychiatrist. The way of all flesh need not perpetually continue; under some circumstances change through a jerk is conceivable.

Actually everybody has to traverse such a middle ground. Any policy-maker knows, even if he suffers from megalomania, that he cannot disregard utterly the persons whom he would make the beneficiaries of his planning: some gradualism is necessary. And the most conscientious conservative realizes that facts about persons cannot by themselves give rise to planning; he must make some sort of value judgment transcending the momentary values at hand.

The Possibility of Rapid Change

There is no systematic treatise to which one can go to discover even a crude taxonomy of rapid change from the viewpoint of personality. In its absence, a heavy dose of intuition—perhaps clinical judgment in more respectable terms—must serve as a substitute. Three kinds, then, seem discernible:

1. *Conversion:* a general change in motivation and central values, with the result that numerous new goals are sought. Changes in scores of habits, in short, follow upon the adoption of the new philosophy or way of viewing the world or oneself. The supreme example is religious conversion: more conscientious adherence to the practices of the faith follows when faith itself has been acquired. The delinquent or criminal leads a different way of life with respect to many of his previous habits when he has acquired a new philosophy,[4] perhaps by becoming attached to a model he can respect or a person he can love. During World

War II, the Manus in New Guinea had contact with American soldiers, as a result of which they "grasped the idea that there was a total civilized way of life, not an unrelated assemblage of detailed superior weapons, gadgets, and religious beliefs, etc., about which the civilized man knew and they did not"; at that point, they followed one of their leaders and increased markedly the speed with which they were willing to accept Western ways.[5] In Africa a similar phenomenon is sometimes observed: the traditional man no longer merely desires some of the appurtenances or practices of Western society—such as a metal roof for his house, a bicycle for transportation, a cigarette for his jitteriness, or medicine for his pain—but seeks instead to become a Western man, the prerequisites and consequences of which include not only the roof, the bicycle, the cigarettes, and the medicine but also much, much more. Available autobiographies and biographies of African leaders, which are official and not to be trusted, point to some sudden change in the life of the person which has had far-reaching consequences; for example:

Kenyatta: at the age of ten, he ran away from home, appeared at a mission hospital, was operated upon for a spinal disease which "probably saved his life," was then accepted in the mission school and baptized.[6]

Mboya: at the age of eighteen, he attended a vocational school outside Nairobi where for "the first time he became really aware of the grievances of his own people and of European privileges. He was suddenly able to rationalize the sense of injustice and bitterness that his childhood days had hinted at."[7]

Nkrumah: around the age of seventeen, he was attracted to an African assistant vice-principal of the secondary school he was attending: "To me he seemed the most remarkable man that I had ever met and I had the deepest affection for him. . . . It was through him that my nationalism was first aroused."[8]

2. *Transformation:* a specific change in predisposition, with the result that an aspect of the milieu or of the self is perceived and evaluated differently. The child looks at a mess of black lines drawn upon a flat white surface; embedded in the surface he suddenly notices the face of a woman, or his attention is called to it; forever after he always sees, he cannot avoid seeing the face. Or the adult for years has felt anxious and insecure in certain situations; then he is taught, perhaps by a psychiatrist, that these feelings of his should be, can be labeled differently (they reflect, he discovers, latent courage), as a consequence of which he reacts quite differently in similar situations from then on. Such a shift may involve almost any aspect of living. The strange woman is no longer a sexual object or goal when it is discovered that her lineage is the same as the observer's and hence makes her taboo. A person with a white skin is not a stranger on hand to exploit the African; he is there with the permission of the African government in power and hence must be working toward some good end.

The literature on community development in Africa spills over with incidents suggesting that the physical stimulus, the environment, becomes transformed as a result of some experience or instruction gently administered by a central authority. In very general terms, an official with wide experience in West Africa has stated: "A community achieves a real sense of participation and ownership through a building which it has helped construct; and the community learns that it is really possible for it to obtain an improvement which it desires if it works itself to achieve it."[9] A building is thus transformed, it is being asserted, when people themselves have contributed to its construction. Or here is a somewhat detailed summary of a specific incident:

In a grazing area of what is now Northern Somalia, herds-men during the fifties increased future misery for them-selves through their mode of surviving during famines: they ruthlessly gathered whatever vegetation they could in order to provide food for their starving animals, but they thus curtailed the source on which the animals were normally dependent; and they chopped down trees to earn money, illegally, by selling the wood in the form of charcoal, but they thus cut off another livelihood. Then a community-development team held discussions "with the people, in particular the religious leaders and chiefs" concerning the ultimate folly of such practices. "Gradu-ally," as a result, they began to recognize "the fact that their own negligence was primarily responsible for the poor condition of their livestock and, so, their own pov-erty" and that this problem was " 'their' problem." When this occurred, they could be encouraged to make con-servation barriers that would slow down the flow of water during rainstorms and hence would "increase water pene-tration." Then that technique was copied in other vil-lages. "When the people . . . had seen the recovery of vegetation brought about by their efforts, they realised that no pasture improvement work was possible so long as there were some members of their community con-tinuing to burn live trees for making charcoal, and others who continued to cut trees down for animal fodder. It was in this way that a solution to this vital problem was accepted as a community responsibility."[10]

3. *Transplantation:* a general or specific change in the milieu, with the result that the perception, the evaluation, or the behavior occurs in a new context. The transplanted person may of course panic, but he may also adapt to the new circumstances, that is, he may change. "Paper cups," it has been asserted, "may be accepted more readily if an unfamiliar beverage is served in them."[11] Tribal habits may persist when Africans move into urban areas, but it is reported

again and again that some behavior changes,[12] in part of course because circumstances compel them to adopt new ways but also because separation from the familiar setting has a liberating influence.

Clearly conversion, transformation, and transplantation refer to processes that are closely interrelated but that can occur separately. Conversion and transformation describe changes in the person which may cause him also to change his milieu, and transplantation may lead to general or specific changes within the person characterizing, respectively, conversion and transformation. Conversion includes but is not confined to transformation and need not involve transplantation. Transformation can occur without conversion or transplantation but is facilitated by either. Transplantation may produce the general change of conversion or the specific one of transformation, or it may result in striving toward new goals as well as the perception and evaluation of new objects or persons.

As ever, no thought or no trio of concepts is completely novel; rather it springs out of the thought of its time. In this instance others toiling in the vineyard of social change have been making a distinction between slow and rapid or between difficult and easy social change, and thus they point to the possibility of nongradualism. A political scientist considers the values associated with "traditionalism" to be of two kinds: "instrumental," or "those in which ultimate ends do not color every concrete act"; and "consummatory," or those which are "part of an elaborately sustained, high-solidarity structure in which religion is pervasive as a cognitive guide."[13] The former he thinks can be relatively easily changed, the latter only with difficulty. Consummatory values, the assumption must be, ordinarily require a gradualist approach unless—unless there is conversion.

"A man from Mars might be led to observe that personality change appears to be very difficult for those who think it very difficult, if not impossible, and much easier for those who think it can be done," a psychologist[14] observes as he begins to argue for the possibility of "motive acquisition." By following various techniques during a period of from one to three weeks, he and his associates have been able to induce managers or teachers of managers in the United States, Mexico, and India to increase the intensity or scope of their achievement motivation. His evidence is admittedly of a preliminary kind, but it seems very clear that some kind of conversion is involved. For he explicitly tries to connect the need for achievement with other powerful or "superordinate" sources within the person, such as his self-image, his cultural values, and his reference groups. To create the proper atmosphere for this kind of change, moreover, he advocates a congenial atmosphere and hence he suggests that the training take place in some isolated place, such as a resort hotel; apparently this type of transplantation is facilitating.

Techniques for Producing Rapid Change

So far the processes of sudden change have simply been categorized. Now attention must be shifted to the theoretical and practical problem of ascertaining the conditions under which conversion, transformation, and transplantation are likely to occur. Paradoxically, perhaps, the first hint must come from the gradualist approach to change: conditions promoting slow change at least produce change, and slow change is a step in the direction of rapid change. Propositions from gradualists, however, are too abundant and contradictory to be, respectively, conveniently and profitably summarized here.[15] By a supreme and ruthless effort, this writer recently has tried to isolate the psychological processes which may be involved under headings indicating the psychological conditions antecedent to change, the psychological consequence of change, and the interaction between the two.[16] In the present context, only the antecedent ones are relevant; individuals, it is believed, are likely to accept a proposed change:

1. When it is not in conflict with traditional beliefs and values which are proving satisfactory.

2. When it appears to have advantages which can be intelligibly demonstrated in the present or which are anticipated in the future.

3. When it is introduced by people whom they consider important and competent and who have adequately consulted them or their respected leaders.

4. When it is in accord with the modal personality traits of their society or with a goal they are seeking.

5. When it makes demands whose components they have already learned or feel confident they can learn.

On a purely common-sense basis it should be immediately clear that these principles can be twisted to suggest how changes can be produced more rapidly. All five of them, for example, are humane, again in the democratic, progressive-movement, religious tradition: treat these good people gently and they will change with the least amount of grief. But a rough-and-tough approach may also be recommended: make them undergo a trauma, yes a painful one, if it is dramatic or rapid change that you seek. Torture them, literally or figuratively, quite painfully, and you will have instant (if not enduring) change. More systematically—and more humanely—it is possible, by weighting their variables in particular ways, to employ the five gradualist propositions as a basis for evolving tentative principles of radical social change:

1. *Conversion* is likely to occur when the individual is markedly dissatisfied with or frustrated by the traditional beliefs and values of his society and/or by his own habits and practices; when the advantages to be

gained from making the total change appear to him, or perhaps in fact are both numerous and beyond question; when whatever loss of social support or approval which will ensue seems to him unequivocally counterbalanced by corresponding gains from other people; when his personality is either so nonrigid that the required shift seems congenial or so rigid that the shift is tolerable only because it is violent; or when he is given an opportunity to learn the new components and to convert them into satisfying actions.

2. *Transformation* is likely to occur when the individual as a result either (a) of general dissatisfaction with his mode of existence or specific dissatisfaction with the situation at hand or (b) of willingly accepting tutelage from others not only desires but is also able to perceive an aspect of his environment or himself differently; and when he possesses the capability or potentiality of such perception.

3. *Transplantation* can occur only when people are provided or provide themselves with a new context or new surroundings; the initiative is likely to come from them either when general or specific dissatisfaction is great or when in the interest of another goal the change in context evokes desirable expectations.

Again, no miracle can be expected from the statements above. First, they are of necessity highly abstract, and each in turn or in practice must generate a host of operating principles if it is to be realized. Consider, for example, "the advantage to be gained from making the total change," part of an hypothesis under the heading of "conversion." How are such advantages to appear or to be in fact "numerous and beyond question"? Many of the techniques employed by McClelland and his associates, as previously indicated too briefly, seek to accomplish just that. Or similarly, how can the individual be "given an opportunity to learn the new components"? Again, new principles are needed to suggest the ways in which the setting might be controlled or the impulse could be rewarded once it has been aroused. As ever in social science, one reaches only a certain depth, never rock bottom, before calling a halt to the digging.

Then, secondly, the more specific a principle of change (any kind, slow or rapid), the less sure our knowledge becomes, either because relevant research is insufficient or trivial or because the interrelationships among the numerous variables in real-life situations cannot be glibly disentangled. Here, for example, is undoubtedly the best summary of available knowledge, pitifully inadequate as it is, concerning the role of an important motivational factor in attitude change:

> The relationship between the degree of fear aroused by a threat appeal and the degree to which the communicator's recommendations elicit sustained acceptance is generally curvilinear: as the level of fear is increased, motivation to accept reassuring recommendations about ways to cope with the danger will be increased; but, as the level of fear mounts higher and higher, resistances are mobilized that can interfere with long-run effectiveness. . . .[17]

It could well be that in certain African societies some Africans would not follow the above principle: high anxiety might not produce resistance; the factors associated with high anxiety in Western society or in other African societies or in unspecified situations within their own society would not give rise to such anxiety among them; or simply on occasion, because of the arousal of different impulses, the conditions declared equal for the principle to be formulated simply do not operate.

Then, finally, the principles are difficult to apply because changes, whether in individuals or their society, so often have repercussions. Again the area of community development in Africa provides an illustration. Among the Turu, who live in the Central Province of Tanzania, an attempt was made in 1959 to institute a community development program which emphasized, among other goals, the improvement of diet from a nutritional standpoint. At first, demonstrations were staged to show how available ingredients could be easily and inexpensively prepared. People enjoyed the samples they were given to eat, in part because from their standpoint this was "Swahili" cooking, that is, exotic but tasty combinations which they associated with the higher status of more acculturated urban dwellers. Up to this point there was certainly gradualism. But when information about the new food had diffused, change became more dramatic and rapid. "Incidents" like the following occurred:

Early one morning two men came to see us from Itongo. They said that they had heard that we could teach their wives how to cook food which would make their children strong and healthy. Could we not also teach them how to cook food which would restore youth and strength to their husbands?

Two women with babies on their backs woke us at 6 a.m. to ask us to come and demonstrate how to make *mchuzi* [the Swahili food] out of green vegetables where there is no meat. They begged so hard, saying that their husbands had put up a shelter yesterday and everything was ready, that we went with them and found 22 women and 12 men waiting, the fire all ready and all the food provided . . . When everything was ready, the women cooked millet porridge and served the dishes to their husbands. The men were delighted, and shook hands with all of us, saying "Very sweet! If we eat like this every day we shall have all those vitamin things you have been talking about." The men's team were also there, so the men asked them many questions and then promised their wives that when the rains came they would plant groundnuts, tomatoes, and vegetables.[18]

What, then, may we conclude as a result of these complexities and difficulties? My own feeling is that our knowledge enables us to locate most of the parameters of slow or rapid change and perhaps a few of the principles; *but* each situation, like every person, is more or less singular. We have guides that inevitably are somewhat uncertain. We dare not be surprised by surprises.

The Workshop

From the heights or depths of theory I would move now to the depths or heights of applied social science in order to consider in some detail but in broad perspective a technique which seeks to produce rapid change in small groups of persons and which, it will be shown later in this chapter, may prove useful in connection with two border disputes in Africa. That technique has no universally accepted label—laboratory in human relations, laboratory training, sensitivity training, the Bethel or Tavistock approach, self-study group, group dynamics, group psychotherapy, etc., have been variously employed—but here the common designation *workshop* will be invoked. A workshop, in brief, consists of a number of persons, motivated by some problem usually connected with their work, who come together, often at an isolated site, for a period of a week or more, and there under the supervision of trained experts learn about themselves and their difficulties in large part from one another. Frequent opportunities are deliberately provided for the participants, who for this purpose are subdivided into smaller groups of around a dozen persons (called T-groups, T for training), to experience most varied, intensely emotional, and very frank interaction. Conventional means for disseminating information, such as lectures and films, may supplement the group learning situations. Over a protracted period, therefore, activities in this temporary community are scheduled for every hour of the day, all of which are more or less focused—though often in an unfocused manner —upon the problem at hand.

Workshops have been employed in the West by industries, laboratories, and other institutions to improve their own functioning; more recently, government has seized upon the approach to try to make key personnel more sensitive to some of their own leadership problems. The most famous workshop, held during the summer at Bethel, Maine, has trained heterogeneous people who have been attracted for reasons as diverse—and as pure or as impure—as those that lead patients into psychoanalysis. At first workshops appeared in the countries of origin, the United States and Great Britain, but more recently they have diffused to other European countries and also to Latin America, India, and Japan. The experts have their own professional organization; and, as might be expected, a host of publications on workshops exists, ranging from those promoting the dissemination of the technique in the tradition of American advertising[19] to those offering objective descriptions of it[20] or an analysis of its importance in a more general framework.[21]

Perhaps the easiest way to portray the spirit of the workshop is to outline its advantages as a mode of experience and learning; some of these features have been modestly trumpeted by its enthusiastic advocates; others have been added by this writer on the basis of the literature on learning and attitude change[22] and small groups.[23]

1. The workshop provides an opportunity for the participants to have close and prolonged contact with one another and thus, minimally, at least to perceive diverse viewpoints. On the level of a general principle it has been stated that "common sense, together with most of the available research data, suggests that, the

more contact one has with a group, the more clear one's image of it becomes."[24]

2. The workshop offers a stimulating and intense experience in which the participants learn more about themselves, their relations to other persons, and hence about their own behavior and roles in real life; they acquire self- and social awareness. The emphasis is upon the presence of other people since they compose the social situation in which ordinary learning frequently occurs. In fact, one reason why the workshop is referred to loosely as a laboratory is that:

> . . . human relations problems can be experienced and analyzed and possible solutions evolved, tested, and practiced. Within a heterogeneous group of from twelve to sixteen persons there exists potentiality for most, if not all, of the kinds of human relations and organizational difficulties which people encounter in working and living together.[25]

In a different sentence: a workshop follows not the parliamentary procedure of formal meetings but the kind of chaotic, informal, and stimulating routine of everyday existence.

3. Learning during a workshop is likely to be facilitated by the variety of techniques that are employed. In the first place, some persons respond more readily to a lecture or a film, others to the T-group. There are usually opportunities for practicing the skill to be acquired, such as exercises in leadership; concrete demonstrations of administrative or psychological problems; sessions featuring role-playing in which persons experience within themselves another viewpoint by being compelled to be its protagonist without making fools of themselves. Gains from role-playing, whether in a workshop or as part of group psychotherapy, are thought to be especially significant.[26]

During a given session or from session to session critical communications are repeated and also varied, and thus any of the devices associated with manipulating stimuli to produce attitude change—such as drawing vs. not drawing a conclusion from salient facts—can be invoked. Unquestionably strong emotions are aroused during the give-and-take of the T-group, and the arousal of such emotions is said to satisfy two of the crucial conditions underlying most theories of personality change, viz., "some sort of intense affective or feeling process" and "the context of an ongoing personal relationship."[27] Finally, in the course of the workshop deliberate efforts are often made to facilitate transfer of what is learned by attempting to foresee how the new experiences and knowledge can be applied in the real-life situations to which of course everyone returns at the end of the workshop.

4. A workshop makes "feedback" inevitable: through close and prolonged interaction with his fellows each person is more likely than in normal life to perceive his implicit and explicit reactions and to receive their criticisms and evaluations. Learning is thus usefully guided as it proceeds. Feedback challenges pre-existing positions or transmits a set of discordant facts or viewpoints; thus dissonance arises, and dissonance can lead to changes even in moral values.[28] Participants in a workshop react emotionally—the experiences are "real" ones for them—but simultaneously they are made to feel secure (or as secure as people can ever feel) since they know that others are in the same situation. As a result, they become:

> . . . at the same time both experimenters and the subjects of experimentation. They may thus learn skills in inducing change in a group of which they are also a part. This is a typical life situation. An individual who seeks to help a group improve is normally also a part of the group. . . .[29]

5. A workshop provides a favorable setting for learning: participants are literally isolated from their normal environment by living together in a common building such as a hotel or estate which is removed from their normal habitat; and they operate under rules which leave the situation unstructured so that they may interact almost in whatever ways they see fit. Hopefully, they feel less defensive or, in the phrase of the day, they are able to "unfreeze."

6. A workshop stimulates initiative in a psychiatric sense: the experts remain in the background but subtly bring it to pass that the participants themselves gradually diagnose the difficulties they have been experiencing in the real-life situations which initially brought them into the workshop or the ones which it is designed to ameliorate or anticipate. At the start, the participants are likely to be disturbed: they have no agenda and no leaders in their own ranks, they observe the experts who remain relatively passive, they cannot imagine what they will be doing throughout the long interval of time ahead, they have too much freedom. In the midst of this despair they may be told that they must evolve their own procedures. What is sought, in short, is progression from dependence upon the leaders to more or less complete autonomy. Then they are made to experience new techniques instead of merely hearing or reading about them; there is, for example, a vast difference between discovering the futility of polarizing judgments into black or white categories and discovering instances of that tendency within oneself or one's intimate associates in the T-group. Finally of critical significance is the fact that rewards and punishments administered on a here-and-now basis by peers in a group situation are likely to be overwhelmingly meaningful: no man, probably, is totally immune to feeling some joy from social approval and some pain from social disapproval.

7. A workshop encourages the kind of learning likely to effect changes in action. Practice in transferring the experiences in the restricted area of the workshop to real life has been mentioned above. Creative ideas may arise in the course of the sessions; in fact, one of the original inspirations for the technique has been research, almost completely with American subjects, demonstrating just that. A recent "summary proposition" on "group and individual performance"—which tries to sound universal in scope but is largely derived from restricted, atypical samples of Americans and Europeans—states that "group members may collectively achieve more than the most superior members are capable of achieving alone"; and with a similar cosmic-sounding sweep the same writers claim that among the "conditions associated with high consensus in groups in either substantive or affective conflict" are "little expression of personal, self-oriented needs," "a generally pleasant atmosphere," the recognition by the participants of "the need for unified action," and "problem-solving activity" by the group that is "understandable, orderly, and focused on one issue at a time."[30] All those conditions are realizable in a workshop. Participants who achieve creative solutions are then tempted to demonstrate their ingenuity through appropriate action. They also are inclined to carry out a group decision since they are identified with it and hence feel a sense of ownership and responsibility; and they may wish to provide additional proof of their own wisdom, in the sense of a self-fulfilling prophecy, by converting their experience into reality. When they come from a "natural" group and hence have not assembled more or less fortuitously—they belong, for example, to the same factory or government bureau where ordinarily they interact and co-operate—the transfer is likely to be easier and richer: practice in the workshop is more realistic

and later fewer modifications are required in the normal setting.

The mere recital of these seven claims perhaps establishes their connection with the principles producing rapid change suggested above. The participants are transplanted to a new milieu in order to attend the workshop. Once there they are subject to a variety of experiences which psychologically seem designed to transform the way they perceive themselves, their fellows at hand, and hence perhaps most people. The experience, especially the T-group, can be so dramatic that change may occur at a level central within their personalities, that is, they can be converted to another way of behaving, at least in their institutional settings.

Alas, the subject of workshops in general cannot be ended without striking a sour note as the devil's advocate. Every single statement concerning the glorious learning opportunities provided by the technique can be ripped into and twisted in such a way as to suggest that indeed learning is impeded by the workshop. Obviously, for example, the technique enables people to have contact, but just as obviously that experience can produce an unfavorable impression. People perceive one another, yes, but they may do so selectively: they hear only what they wish to hear. What has been called a mote-beam mechanism (perceiving traits in others which we do not perceive in ourselves) can operate to produce estrangement in a small group. Proactive and retroactive inhibitions can, respectively, prevent or blot out the necessary learning. Too much or too little anxiety can be evoked. And so on—but no device is perfect.

Workshops in Africa

Sporadically since 1961 an American group financed by the Ford Foundation has organized and conducted workshops in Africa. The principal Training Institutes in Staff Development and Human Relations, as they are called, assembled in Nigeria and Ghana and drew Africans and a few non-Africans from government, industry, commerce, and institutions of higher learning.[31] The ultimate aim has been very practical; for example, the one in Western Nigeria aimed to help "the Western Nigerian Civil Service to develop a training program to meet growing needs in a period of rapid social change."[32] A similar goal was sought by the Uganda Electricity Board. These workshops perforce draw Africans from various tribes within the same country, but in 1963 one conducted in Northern Nigeria included not only Africans from different countries but also Europeans, Americans, and Asians.

Those inspiring and guiding the workshops have indicated certain differences in the reactions of the African participants as contrasted with Americans and Europeans, all of which they consider minor and unimportant, though interesting. To a greater extent than in the West, the organizer of the African T-group must be active. Trust among participants is greater. Inconsistent behavior is more conspicuous; for example, the position advocated by a participant may shift markedly from one session to the next. Insights gained in one situation are transferred less easily to similar situations. More surface lightheartedness can be noted. Sometimes participants appear to experience greater difficulty in speaking about one another. The relatively passive role assumed by the organizer occasions more surprise, perhaps because leaders in traditional African society clearly exercise their authority. For some participants, the activity and especially the initiative required throughout the workshop is believed to be stranger and more unusual.[33] At some workshops the invited participants arrive with a formal agenda which they would have the "conference" adopt.

The use of English as the medium of communication at the workshops has created, it appears, no special difficulties, which fact "speaks for their intellectual capacities and the universality of the problems of human relations."[34] Africans with experience in workshops informed this writer, however, that in their opinion Africans who have studied abroad, or even perhaps those who have been to the United States and have absorbed its allegedly empirical mode of thinking, are more promising participants.

By and large, the available evidence suggests that the workshops in Africa function smoothly. Reports on whether the participants themselves become happier or better adjusted persons or whether they later function more effectively in their regular positions are necessarily scattered, largely anecdotal, and hence not very conclusive. Such information, however, would not be relevant for the present discussion since, as will be indicated below, the interest in workshops here involves not the benefits they bestow on the participants but the kind of solution to problems at which they arrive.

The question, then, is a simple one: are there any special difficulties arising from the fact that the participants are Africans? Three experts have offered this testimony concerning T-groups in Africa: they "presented no problems uniquely different from those experienced in American and European groups, though in highlights and shadows there were at times distinct variations."[35]

The most concrete data at hand come from a follow-up study in 1963 of a carefully selected sample of 102 Africans who represent half the number participating in workshops in West Africa. They were interviewed by a European and, according to him, they eagerly co-operated. Only relevant highlights of the qualitative and statistical analyses are given here.[36] Many stated that they had been confused, at first, by the T-group technique since they had attended British schools, which tend to be based on lectures and independent study. Informants were asked, "What thing about the workshop do you remember most vividly?" No matter how the replies are analyzed, "demonstrations and skill exercises" come first, followed by T-groups and films; this result which shows a "rather clear preference . . . for the more structured aspects of the training design is in rather sharp contrast to the reaction of participants in similar kinds of workshops in the United States," where the T-group in a comparable study was rated as "the most vivid event." Those reporting relatively high benefits from the workshop tended, to a slightly greater extent than those reporting less compelling benefits, to consider that the trainer had participated quite actively. Finally, "the reaction of the African participants to the American staff members (who were white) was not only favorable but . . . some commented that they felt they could be more open and free than they could have been if Africans had been on the staff."

At the close of two of the Nigerian workshops in 1961, participants answered open-ended questions concerning their experiences. The testimonials thus obtained illustrate again and again two of the processes of rapid change, one example for each of which is herewith reproduced:

Conversion

It was the most wonderful training experience I have ever had in my life. It has made a completely different man of me and I wish I could successfully impart the knowledge gained into this new generation to put them on the right track before it is too late. I am happy that those who attended the course have been able to identify most of our problems, and pray that we could all be able to tackle these problems one by one with a very realistic approach.

Transformation

My experiences of this training are that my whole mind has been reframed in the way I deal with people from now onwards. I have learnt that the other man is not a fool and that there is something new to learn from him. I have also understood the need for cooperation more fully. Thinking about a person's actions as a way of seeking improvement of one's standards is very important.[37]

Naturally such declarations, in spite of their ring of sincerity, cannot be taken at their face value.

The final relevant word concerning workshops in Africa comes from the experts who produce a generalization apparently applicable anywhere: "As it is with individuals, no two T-groups develop in exactly the same way."[38]

Ethiopia vs. Somalia, Kenya vs. Somalia

In the spring of 1966, it occurred to me that the technique of the workshop might be employed to try to induce very rapidly a change desired by the Africans themselves, viz., the ending of overt and costly conflict over territory in the East African Horn. So far as could be determined then—by consulting existing literature and important practitioners of the craft— the workshop had probably never been so utilized; later that year, however, one was convened in modified form in connection with a trouble spot in Europe. The two disputes in East Africa appear to offer a worthy and relevant challenge to the workshop as an instrument of change.

Those disputes must first be briefly described; and of course it is to be anticipated, as always happens when there is conflict, that no description can possibly be considered complete or impartial from the viewpoint of all the antagonists. The best we can do is to offer a set of references in which the contentions of the three countries appear.[39]

The Republic of Somalia, composed of what formerly were Italian and British Somaliland, achieved independence in 1960. The nation, unlike any other sub-Saharan country, is virtually homogeneous, for almost all its inhabitants can be said to belong to a Somali culture, loosely defined.[40] For reasons varying from historical and nationalistic to the humane and the political, Somalia seeks to "unite all those Somalis now living in French Somaliland, the Ogaden and other Somali-inhabited areas of Ethiopia, and in the Northern Frontier Territories of Kenya."[41] French Somaliland does not enter directly into the disputes being discussed here, except that its ultimate status obviously is of practical and symbolic importance to Ethiopia since, among other things, Djibouti, its capital, is the terminus of the railway line from Addis Ababa and hence that country's only outlet to the sea.

It is the areas of the Ogaden, the Haud, and the Northern Frontier District (N.F.D.) that are in dispute. According to the Somali definition, people of Somali culture are in the majority in both places, and it is certain that bands of Somali nomads use the areas as grazing lands. Armed conflict breaks out from time to time along the borders and inside the territories, small numbers of men are killed, and all three countries spend a not inconsiderable part of their budgets in defensive or offensive operations by their police and military forces. Here an effort will be made—impartially, it is hoped—to summarize directly the arguments and counterarguments which leaders of the three countries employ in their own mass media and at international conferences.

Somalia

1. Most inhabitants of the two areas are Somalis, they are our kinsmen, they should join us, the only

reason they are now separated from our nation is that these lands were given by the colonial powers to Ethiopia and Kenya.

2. Let the people in the two areas decide their own destiny; undoubtedly, since they are Somalis, they will decide to join us; an impartial investigation by the British in 1962 clearly showed that five of the six N.F.D. districts wished to become part of Somalia and to leave Kenya.

3. We need the areas for our people who as nomads must find water and grazing land for their herds; and perhaps oil will be discovered in the N.F.D.

4. Ethiopia and Kenya are acting like imperialists, black imperialists, when they prevent these lands from being given the opportunity to be reunited with us.

Ethiopia

1. We have legal and historical rights to occupy the lands we do: our boundaries were established with the Italians for their part of Somalia according to various treaties, especially those of 1897 and 1908, and with the British for their part, also according to various treaties, particularly that of 1897; like Eritrea (now part of Ethiopia), the Ogaden and the Haud as well as most of Somalia are lost provinces which belonged to us in ancient times.

2. Ethiopia is a multiracial state, and nationality need not be determined by language or culture (for example, the German-speaking Swiss are not part of Germany); the Somalis in the Ogaden and the Haud are our people; we treat them well, they live happily with us, they intermarry with neighbors in our country.

3. The areas are important to us economically; if only Somalia would co-operate with us, we could arrange mutually beneficial economic pacts since for purely geographical reasons our two countries are interdependent.

4. The Somalis are a threat to our security: they send into those lands troublemakers disguised as nomads, their own government is receiving military supplies from the Soviet Union.

Kenya

1. Kenya also is a multiracial state in which different peoples live in harmony with one another; we cannot begin to give away our territory (especially the N.F.D. which is one-half our land area), for then our entire nation could be dismembered; just as the occupation of the White Highlands of Kenya by European settlers did not make that area British, so the presence of Somalis in the N.F.D. does not justify Somalia's claim to its sovereignty.

2. If the Somalis living in the N.F.D. wish to join Somalia, let them cross the frontier and do so—nobody is stopping them; if they remain, we shall continue to treat them as our brothers, as indeed we treat all Africans.

3. The British created the idea of Greater Somalia in the first place and stirred up trouble in the N.F.D. in accordance with their policy of divide and rule; they dispatched a commission to investigate public opinion in this area which was not theirs to evaluate or give away and which is of economic importance to us.

4. The Somalis are creating conflict in the N.F.D. through the bandits who infiltrate the area, and their broadcasts from Radio Mogadiscio are trying to cause unrest inside our country.

If anyone not familiar with these two conflicts finds that the contentions and countercontentions have a familiar sound, he is not suffering from the illusion of *déjà-vu:* most of them are part of the litany or syndrome of nationalism anywhere and hence have a transnational character.[42] Sometimes the arguments are within the same frame of reference as those of the protagonist, often times they are not. Here, therefore, seem to be situations in which both sides agree on the basic economic and anthropological facts but disagree concerning the historical, political, and psychological interpretation to be placed upon those facts. Could not a workshop enable representatives of the three countries to change those interpretations and thus achieve a satisfying and innovative solution which could bring peace or at least less trouble to the Horn?

Resolving the Conflicts

Short of war, the usual way to produce the rapid changes necessary to reduce international conflict is through diplomacy or through the good offices of a third organization such as the United Nations. These devices have been tried in the Horn ever since Somalia's independence—especially at international conferences of African states—but so far without success. For example, in May of 1961, the African governments at the Monrovia Conference called upon Ethiopia and Somalia to settle their differences; in August of 1963 representatives of Britain, Kenya, and Somalia met in Rome and tried without success to reach an agreement concerning the N.F.D.; during 1964 the conflicts were discussed at the Dar es Salaam, Lagos, and Cairo meetings of the Organization of African Unity, and resolutions calling upon the countries to settle their disputes peacefully were passed, again without effect.

Evidence for the failure of these formal efforts is the continuation of the disputes. In addition, I interviewed high officials in the three countries during the summer of 1966 and found their attitudes unchanged. They quickly expressed both determination and despair: they insisted that they were fighting in behalf of a just cause and that they would never yield to their opponent. In the words of the ancient analogy: Somalia wants the window opened, Ethiopia (or

Kenya) wants it shut, and on this level neither will compromise. They have not yet come to realize that one of them wants fresh air and the other would avoid draft, and hence that a solution might be to open a window elsewhere in the house. And yet these men seem highly motivated; without doubt they realize that the fighting is tragic and the expenditure of resources useless.

The leaders in the Horn, moreover, cannot turn for inspiration to other parts of Africa: since World War II and especially the attainment of independence, African states have been almost uniformly unsuccessful in carrying on negotiations among themselves, and certainly without exception the trend has been away from federation or the unification of the separate African states. Recall simply the failures of the Mali Federation,[43] Ghana and Guinea,[44] the Federation of Rhodesia and Nyasaland (a special problem, of course), and the difficulties which the three countries in East Africa (Uganda, Kenya, Tanzania—with the strange case of Zanzibar also involved) have had in trying to retain the bare minimum of their common services.[45] In these instances available records suggest (but do not prove) that African leaders have been operating in a manner which does not permit them to change their basic sentiments or political positions. During a meeting of the three heads of state in 1961, at which a federation of East Africa was discussed, Dr. Nyerere, the leader from Tanganyika, "offered to delay his own country's independence briefly to allow Uganda and Kenya to catch up"; thus he made a personal decision, however tentative, with which, as a matter of fact, the executive of his own party back home did not agree.[46] Indeed at these and other meetings the leaders of the same countries, it seems fair to say in retrospect, beat the drum of unity without considering the political, social, and emotional currents within their own countries, which would grow in strength after independence and many of which would run counter to federation:

> [At a meeting in June 1963] the East African leaders announced their intention to federate by the end of the year . . . Several Kenyan cabinet ministers flew to Tanganyika for a few hours on a Saturday afternoon to greet a visiting West African head of state. In the course of conversations with Tanganyikan leaders, they hit on the idea of a meeting to announce their intention to federate. The missing Ugandan leader was reached by telephone. He agreed. On the following Wednesday the Ugandans and Tanganyikans flew to Nairobi and, with Kenya, agreed to federate. Their decision was announced to reporters, who quickly wired it to all three capitals . . . [The Prime Minister of Uganda had been] caught by surprise, and a conference was announced for the next Wednesday . . . The Working Party . . . first met in Dar es Salaam four days after the Nairobi declaration. After two days' discussion, the Working Party announced "agreement on every issue," and added that they had instructed lawyers to draft a constitution to be ready for a meeting in Kampala at the end of the month. . . . The era of good feeling was brief. It was over by the time the three leaders and the Working Party met in Kampala at the end of June, though no one admitted the fact publicly until August. . . . [By then] the subjects of disagreement read almost like the framework for the constitution that was supposed to have been agreed upon. . . .[47]

Even if this "final decision to federate," though sudden, had been made "not without preparation . . . every time politicians had met for the past three years they had talked about federation," it is clear that planning with respect to economic, political, social, *and* emotional details had been most inadequate.

When political leaders arrive at a meeting with

stated goals, when they follow strict agenda which compel them to discuss issues in terms of surface demands and claims, when they know that they will be compelled to issue public statements concerning the accomplishments of the meeting, and when they are never permitted to forget that they are responsible to the governments and peoples they represent, they cannot be expected to think freely or, if the word be permitted, creatively. No wonder, then, that the conclusion of a survey in 1962 of Pan-Africanism is applicable five years later: "The existing combinations of states were marriages of convenience and subject to change."[48] In passing it is impossible to repress the observation that the very African elite, who have successfully rebelled against the West and who seek, whenever possible, to solve their own problems in an African manner, are themselves victims of Western procedures in the area of diplomacy, summit meetings, and all the communication trappings of conflict in the modern world: they ape too well the world from which they ostensibly have liberated themselves.

Again, what should be done? Turning to the more general literature of social science on the subjects of international relations and the reduction of international tensions in order to discover techniques for changing protagonists rapidly and creatively has been singularly sterile. The first two sentences of a recent and very competent book called *How Nations Negotiate* sets the tone: "States have negotiated since the beginning of history—as they have fought wars. Compared with the changes in methods of warfare, however, the methods of negotiation have remained much the same."[49] An examination of that book's contents suggests that the process of negotiating is almost always a pitched verbal battle between the negotiators. Even in a section called "innovation," this scholar uses the language of competition: "it is usually quite clear which party has made the first move proposing the innovation."[50] The "three major factors" which are said to explain the outcome of all decisions, including international ones, are stated to be "the occasion for the decision; the individual decision-maker; and the organization context in which he decided." The last factor, the one related to the discussion at hand, is analyzed, however, only in terms of existing organizations such as the United Nations and the European Economic Community, which follow conventional procedures.[51] Or the process of negotiation is discussed in terms of game theory, with an effort to isolate some of the conditions influencing the outcome, such as the setting, the number participating or negotiating, the availability of information, the stresses while interacting, timing, and background factors.[52] Nowhere is there a concrete, normative program for improving the art of diplomacy, in as much as such an explicit proposal is not within the author's purview.

"The major hope" for avoiding future wars, one analyst has stated, "seems to lie in a new approach to negotiation, a new concept of what can be done around the international conference table." And he thinks that such an approach must somehow reduce rigidity, ethnocentrism, fear and distrust, and the desire to triumph over the other fellow.[53]

But the wars and the waste in the Horn continue, and the need for rapid change there remains. It was, then, in this gloomy context[54] that I considered the possibility of a workshop: could a disinterested American offer Africans the opportunity to behave like Africans in settling their disputes rather than as imitators of Western diplomacy? As this chapter is being revised, the question cannot be answered: I do not know whether the project will turn out to be feasible politically or financially. Instead I can only indicate—I hope with a light touch—some of the vicissitudes which have been endured in trying to organize the workshop. For the nasty details are part of the record: they suggest the kind of obstacles confronting the proponent of rapid change in the international sphere.

A Workshop for the Horn

The first step in planning the workshop was to enlist the help and skill of interested colleagues. Professor Robert B. Stevens, a lawyer who has been involved in legal problems facing the three East African countries as they contemplated the possibility of creating an Economic Community to replace their ill-fated Federation, was eager to co-operate; we then invited Professor William J. Foltz, a political scientist who is especially interested in the problems of federation and changes in Africa, to join us after his return from Africa. For technical assistance on workshops I immediately consulted another Yale colleague, Professor Chris Argyris, not only because he is a sociologist with wide and long experience in workshops, but also because he has been responsible for special workshops sponsored by the Department of State for members of its Foreign Service, many at the ambassadorial level.[55]

Then the concrete details for the workshop quickly emerged not out of whimsey or inspiration but as informal deductions from the nature of the technique and from various implicit principles of social science. At least three representatives from each of the three African countries would be invited. They would meet in some neutral country, probably in Africa or the Middle East, and there, having been given the opportunity to interact in a permissive atmosphere, would hopefully emerge with one or more creative ideas having political implications for the border disputes. The issue was not to be prejudged in terms of a Federation of the East African Horn or any other agreement. We from Yale would function as private individuals not wedded to particular aspects of the workshop technique but prepared to introduce any kind of arrangements which might stimulate creativity. At first the African participants would undoubtedly be given an opportunity to learn to communicate more effectively with one another in a general way before turning to the political complexities at hand. Toward the end of the period, they would discuss, perhaps even be given some instruction concerning the difficulties they would experience upon "re-entry" into their own country with respect to the transmission of decisions, criticisms directed at themselves, etc.

The participants to be invited would all be academic persons of high standing. Scholars, it was thought, would have the psychological attributes which would make unconventional change more probable. By virtue of their superior education they would possess, hopefully, some degree of perspective concerning the problems of the Horn. They would not officially represent their governments and hence would not be constrained to uphold a position previously established by the leaders of their country. It would be extremely simple to find men with a fluent knowledge of English and thus the problem of language and of any possible emotional or conventional complications resulting from the presence of women could be eliminated. As academic persons in Africa, they undoubtedly belong to the small group of elite and hence have some or great influence informally both within government and among their own peers. Were a decision of significance to be reached at the workshop, therefore, they would have access to the channels along which those decisions could be communicated to men in power; but of course there could be no guarantee that those men would be willing and able to transmit the information when they returned home or that, if they did so, they would be heeded.

Other reasons could be advanced for inviting African scholars. If, as seems probable but as yet undemonstrated, the two-step theory of communications is applicable to these African societies—most Americans are influenced not directly by the mass media but by informal "opinion leaders" who are attentive to the media and pass on the messages[56]—then the views of the returning participants might also have greater influence throughout the population. Scholars who were also social scientists might be additionally motivated to attend the workshop if their interest in the Horn had a professional tinge; and they might welcome the opportunity to become acquainted with the techniques of the workshop by actually participating in one. Academic persons flock to meetings, especially if expenses are paid and travel is involved—actually the plan called for the paying only of expenses without an honorarium. Although, being by and large strangers from different countries, the participants would not constitute a "natural" group, they would at least share certain scholarly and university traditions and hence the preliminary basis for interacting. Finally, it was thought to be relatively easy for an academic person from America to establish contact with his African counterparts in the three countries: in some instance he had previously known people attached to universities, and he would perhaps be trusted as someone also working in the scholarly vineyard.

In short, the proposal involves a preliminary attempt to determine whether a very select group who are not committed professionally to political power can reach some kind of creative consensus. Perhaps the next step thereafter could be to conduct a similar workshop among minor or major officials from the three countries. These men would suffer from their commitment to a political position, but they might be psychologically liberated by their knowledge of the gains from the previous workshop. And if they could reach consensus and if that consensus could facilitate a formal conference of heads of states—why, then, the Horn might become a happier place and the workshop might find favor elsewhere as a tool to diminish international tension! It is this kind of pure fantasy which I have had to use from time to time to reinforce my faltering interest in the plan.

In Pursuit of the Workshop

In order to realize the plan, it was then necessary to raise money and to invite potential participants to attend the workshop. At this point the tale of woe begins: rapid social change also requires patience and perseverance. First, major foundations in the United States were approached. While responding with some enthusiasm to the idea, they refused to lend their support because, they maintained justly, the idea was too politically tricky. They were convinced, moreover, that we could secure the co-operation neither of the governments nor of potential participants. One foundation believed that it might jeopardize its "investment" in one country by involving itself, however indirectly, in the affairs of its protagonist.[57]

These objections could be met only by proving the feasibility of the plan, the first step of which demanded a gamble in time, viz., visiting the countries.[58] The purpose of the trip in the summer of 1966 was clearly formulated in advance: to find at least three and preferably more scholars in each country (more, to provide for avoidable and nonavoidable contingencies), to explain the proposal to them, to outline the general and specific nature of the workshop, to indicate the kind of travail that the experience might entail, to have them trust me as a person, and in short to persuade or induce them also to gamble some of their time. Each country, of course, presented different problems, and so the account of this wearying, boring, exciting, frustrating, gratifying venture is first broken down country by country and, mercifully, abbreviated. But the details are perhaps worth giving, I say again without apologizing—and thus in effect apologize—because they vividly illustrate the kinds of problems which arise when a private citizen seeks in a complex set of relationships to initiate rapid social change.

Ethiopia

Before leaving America, I was advised by an American who had held a high position in the university at Addis Ababa that my only chance of succeeding lay in going as high as possible in the university to secure permission and to obtain very influential scholars. The president of the university, a very important Ethiopian, was not available; hence contact was established with the academic vice-president, who, being an American and having just arrived at his post, could provide only mild encouragement and the names of various academic officials. Eventually five people were seen at least once and they enthusiastically agreed to attend if invited and if they had the time: two from the field of education and one each from economics, geography, and linguistics. One man refused on the grounds that a workshop would accomplish very little or nothing either from a political or research standpoint; but he claimed that he would attend without consulting the government if he were so inclined.

The interested ones, however, insisted that the government's permission would be needed because otherwise they might not be granted passports and they could not afford to jeopardize their academic careers. They and others used the phrase "academic freedom" again and again, sometimes by asserting that the university enjoyed such freedom, sometimes by asserting that at this stage of the country's development complete freedom was neither possible not desirable. The idea seemed to be that, although academic persons have the right to attend an international conference, somehow this workshop would involve Ethiopian prestige as a result of the presence of the Somalis; if the Ethiopians were permitted to attend, one high official said, it was presumed that they would not express "un-Ethiopian ideas" upon their return.

It was not at all easy for me as a private person to approach "the Ethiopian Government." Through the helpful offices of some of the academic people, I eventually saw the legal adviser to the Prime Minister, the legal adviser to the Minister of Foreign Affairs, and then the Foreign Minister himself. They agreed that a confrontation with the Somalis would be desirable but that the Somalis would have to make concessions since the Ethiopian cause is just and nonnegotiable. No decision, however, could be reached during my stay in Ethiopia: the president of the university and the Emperor were touring in the provinces and no meeting with them could be arranged. Right before leaving for Kenya, however, I was told that the decision would be communicated to me through the Ethiopian Ambassador in Nairobi or through him I would hear whether I should return to Addis to see the president or, possibly, the Emperor.

No word ever came to me in Kenya, though I plagued the switchboard of the Ethiopian Embassy. Through intermediaries I learned after my return to Yale that the project had probably been described to the Emperor and that his decision eventually would be a function of whether the timing of the workshop appeared propitious from the standpoint of his country's best interest. Exactly three months later the president of the university wrote me that the men "will not be able to participate in your proposed research" since "the University is under considerable pressure of work." From time to time, nevertheless, there have been indications that this decision might be reversed and that clearly it was up to us first to set a date for the workshop. Undoubtedly the riot of the Somalis when President de Gaulle visited French Somaliland in 1966, the disturbances during and after the plebiscite there, the demonstrations by the Eritreans during the visit of Haile Selassie to Cairo in 1966, and the Arab-Israel war in 1967 have not created the kind of atmosphere likely to induce the Emperor to grant permission—although such tension-producing events ought really to make a workshop appear all the more pressing.

Kenya

Again the first contact was attempted with the highest official of the university then in Nairobi, the deputy principal. While awaiting a conference with him, I was able to see a number of scholars I knew or who had been recommended to me. In comparison with their counterparts in Ethiopia and later in Somalia they seemed only mildly interested in the conflict on the border of their country: the N.F.D. from their standpoint is a remote area and not a very pressing problem; of course, however, they knew of the struggle. It was possible, then, to secure the lukewarm assent of the following: three geographers, a historian, an economist, and a political scientist. Again one man refused: an American, he said, should not try to interfere in African affairs.

Many of the potential participants, and also the deputy principal when he finally consented to see me, laid down two conditions. First, the Kenyan government had to be informed. Again this was no easy task to inform a government, for there was no agreement as to which division should be informed; for example, was the matter of the N.F.D. of greater concern to the Foreign Office than to the Ministry of Defense? No one, whether African or European, moreover, was eager to arrange an appointment for me; and the secretaries to permanent secretaries of the relevant ministries seemed to have, as their principal function, the protection of their chiefs from seeing visitors, especially Americans. Two permanent secretaries in the relevant ministries flatly refused to see me. Finally, therefore, I visited an African acquaintance, a very capable man having a high position in Kenyan journalism. In minutes he was able to speak with the Attorney General—by long-distance telephone, because President Kenyatta at the time was vacationing at Mombasa—who asked me to telephone him directly. Without difficulty I reached him and briefly explained the project. That evening, he indicated to the journalist the next day, he spoke with Mr. Kenyatta, who apparently had no objection to the scheme. Thus government was informed but, alas, a misunderstanding arose at this point: the Attorney General somehow felt that the workshop was about to occur and hence suggested that the men at the university telephone his office to verify the government's attitude. How, then, could this consent be preserved for some point in the indefinite future? I wrote a long letter to the Attorney General, outlining the project and summarizing our conversations; this, it was hoped, would constitute the "record" in his office to which reference in the future could be made.

The second requirement of the scholars and of the deputy principal was that a few men from the two other East African universities be asked to participate, because in theory—but less so in practice as time goes on—all three institutions are part of the same university system. My colleague Foltz, then in Uganda, invited a political scientist; making a quick trip to Tanzania, I located two political scientists and a historian, all of whom accepted with enthusiasm and alacrity; and the vice-principals of both institutions gave their consent. The government's permission was not considered necessary: the countries are not directly involved in the disputes and have only a friendly interest in seeing them settled.

Somalia

Since Somalia has no university, another route to participants had to be employed. Fortunately I had no difficulty establishing contacts in Mogadiscio, the capital: I had spent part of the previous summer in Somalia, was known by important officials, and had the active support of a very influential and understanding individual. I decided, therefore, to invite persons who had studied abroad and who were in strategic positions, if possible of a research nature, either in the community or in divisions of government not directly concerned with foreign policy. All the Somalis I approached eagerly responded; whatever hesitation they exhibited clearly stemmed from uncertainty as to whether they could afford the time away from their regular jobs. The men who seemed suitable to me are two lawyers, a museum official, an editor, an accountant, an economist, and an official from the Information Office. Even before I left Somalia, as so often happens with elite in Africa, one man had his position shifted abroad and hence might not be able to attend. Co-operation from Somali officials was complete, I discovered, as I conferred informally with the Minister of Foreign Affairs and with the Prime Minister. Permission for government employees to leave the country and to be on leave, with full pay, during the workshop was quickly granted. Only in Somalia did I visit the American Embassy, and then for reasons not connected with the workshop.

Certain obstacles were always encountered in enlisting the African scholars, regardless of their country. First, they are all very busy, and many hesitated to commit so much time to the workshop. Then university calendars vary in Africa and are also different from Yale's; hence it was impossible to find a time completely satisfactory to everybody. Many features of the project, especially the unstructured character of the workshop, were not readily grasped. Perhaps the flavor of the conversations can best be recaptured by translating my notes into a sequence which, though hypothetical, reflects my responses most accurately and also the actual questions posed by at least three and usually many more Africans.

You mean to say there will be no agenda for the conference?

No, we are not going to have agenda, for this is not a conference. You, you Africans, you will have to decide what to talk about.

Without any help from you?

Yes, without any help, except that we shall welcome you at the beginning and tell you to run your own affairs. If you ask us, we may make a suggestion from time to time, but only with reference to procedure. For example, for a given session we might propose that our Somali friends present the Ethiopian case for the Ogaden, that is, they will play the role of Ethiopians and we all will listen to them.

Why do that?

So that you can understand, deep inside yourselves, how your protagonists feel; you won't want to make a fool of yourself in front of us, even if you are acting.

But how can you be sure we shall talk about the disputes in the Horn?

We cannot be, but all of you we are inviting know why we want the workshop, and all of you are interested in the disputes, and in settling them. And of course everybody is bound to realize that his colleagues in the other countries will be thinking of what they are going to say from their political standpoints; hence each person will alert himself to his own case. Under these circumstances I think it will be impossible for you not to devote most of your time to the problem.

Should I read anything about workshops beforehand?

That is up to you; I shall send you a bibliography and literature if you wish. But perhaps the best way to find out about a workshop is to participate in one; and you may also learn something about yourself as a result of the experience.

But why invite me? I am not an expert.

That does not matter: you are a citizen of your country; you have loyal feelings which you will express.

What will all this accomplish?

That question is hard to answer. The most honest answer is: I do not know, but I have hopes. At the very least we shall discover how the technique of the workshop functions among scholars coming from countries where there is tension; we may publish a scholarly article describing the experience. In research terms we may also learn something about attitudes and how they are expressed and hence can be investigated in such a group setting. And at the very most you Africans may hit upon a new, perhaps an African solution to your territorial disputes. . . .

And if we do?

Again I do not know except for one thing: toward the end of the workshop it will be you and not we outsiders who decide what the next step should be. Perhaps you may wish to make known to your governments any new ideas you have. Perhaps you may advise us to stage another workshop with representatives of your governments being the participants. Perhaps, I sometimes tell myself late at night when I try to comfort myself for going on this wild trip which I am not enjoying, perhaps we might suggest to everybody that here is a tool—the workshop—which could be used to help resolve other international conflicts, much bigger ones.

Will the workshop be secret?

No, there is nothing secret about it, or for that matter about our conversation. Tell anybody you like what we are trying to do. Naturally when we come together there will be no publicity, and journalists will not be present.

Do I personally run a risk by attending?

Perhaps you do, but you must make that judgment. All I am doing is to invite you, you know the risks better than I.

Where is the money coming from for the workshop?

I wish I knew, but I promise you one thing: the money will not come from the government, the United States government. I shall try to raise it from private foundations, from private companies, from private individuals.

Why should you as an American be doing this; have you any connection with the American government, with the CIA?

The reply to these last questions could only be trite: an appeal to the tradition of increasing knowledge and also an expression of idealism.

As already indicated, no effort was made to minimize the psychic pain that can be experienced during the give-and-take of a T-group or at other times as a workshop sets about its task. In the course of the interview each person usually expressed his own country's viewpoint regarding the boundary—"those people cannot be trusted." The neutral silence I then tried to maintain sometimes did create tension or embarrassment, but I could not depart from my own role of the impartial organizer of the workshop.

Most disturbing to me, both at the time and in retrospect, was the uncertainty as to whether my African acquaintance was being pleasant or polite concerning the proposal or whether he was genuinely interested. It seemed so easy to promise to attend with no date set. In fact, one foundation official maintains even now that in one of the countries I was thoroughly duped; he thinks I was referred only to the opponents of the regime. In short, as an eloquent Ethiopian metaphor would state, were people offering me wax or gold?

A Sad Anticlimax?

I returned to Yale, then, with the names of potential participants in my notebook, with official permission from two of the governments, and with encouragement but no final word from Ethiopia. The feasibility of the project, so far as it could be ascertained during the planning stage, had virtually been demonstrated. In the course of the next few months, we tried one other way to appease timid donors: informally I discussed the project with various officials of the Department of State, most of whom play extremely important roles in helping to formulate and to carry out American foreign policy with reference to Africa. A high official suggested that he would indicate his approval—presumably on an informal level—to any foundation or person communicating with his office. Another wrote and said that "I hope very much that you are successful in finding an 'angel,' since I do think the idea has possibilities for real accomplishment."

Even when we reported the results of my trip and the attitude of the Department of State, we could obtain no financial support. The three of us underwent the humiliating experience of soliciting funds from a wide variety of foundations and private individuals. We had neither the patience nor the fortitude to grovel at all conceivable doors. With one exception—"I am sorry I cannot become more sanguine over the idea" —the project has aroused what appears to be unrestrained enthusiasm—in fact, I say with a trace of a blush, the word "brilliant" has been hurled at the idea. *But,* but, but: funds are low; this is not in line with our charter; this is too politically sensitive; we must wait until the reorganization is complete; we cannot invest in a high-risk, high-return proposition; etc. Sometimes I feel paranoid: maybe these people are being pleasant because they think me insane and

then wish gently to push me toward reality by turning
me away.

As we reflected upon the project while seeking to
raise funds, we introduced a number of modifications
or additions. First, we became convinced that another
professional workshop expert besides our colleague
at Yale, Chris Argyris, should be added to the American corps. For if there were a dozen or more African
participants, it would be better to divide them into
two T-groups, each under the supervision of an expert: the size would thus be kept small and, after the
hectic give-and-take of such a group each day, all the
participants would come together with the Americans
and thus form a community in which there could be
some relaxation and a partial healing of psychic
wounds. Then, secondly, the tentative procedure to
be followed might be more easily anticipated by first
conducting at Yale a miniature workshop, during a
long weekend, composed of graduate students from
the three countries. How quickly, for example, could
members of T-groups learn to communicate with one
another in general terms and then turn from gaining
insight into themselves to the critical substantive problems of the boundary disputes? It would also be well
to try to anticipate in detail the kinds of specific questions most likely to arouse powerful emotions. Next
we began to wonder whether we could cut down on
costs and simultaneously eliminate the responsibilities
associated with housing and feeding the participants;
in this connection we considered making an application to one of the foundations to use a villa of theirs
in Europe which efficiently and comfortably provides
the physical setting for small conferences.

Finally, it began to seem desirable for my two Yale
colleagues, Foltz and Stevens, to retrace my route in
the three countries before the start of the workshop.
A meeting between them and the African scholars
would reinforce trust and rapport. Some of the poten-

tial participants, moreover, may have possibly grown unwilling or have found themselves unable to participate as a result of circumstances arising in the interim—a danger we had recognized from the outset; if this were so, then new men would have to be recruited. It would be well to explain to them why the financing had been delayed and to renew their interest in the project.

That trip appeared to us absolutely essential as a result of another decision we made: to apply to the United States Government for financial support. Two departments in Washington had in fact indicated their willingness to consider an application from us. After hesitation, vacillation, and consultation and with no feeling of satisfaction, we submitted first an informal and then, before Christmas, a formal application to the Advance Research Projects Agency of the Department of Defense. We were of the opinion that no strings would be attached to their money which could be administered by Yale University; and we knew from public statements that the agency had previously been interested in the general problem of conflict resolution. As indicated above, I had promised the African scholars that we would not accept money from the government, and so the reason for the shift would have to be thoroughly explained to them: we believed the money would be clear and free and that, therefore, the workshop could function exactly as we had envisioned it would under private funding.

Individual members of the State Department's board which reviews overseas projects directly financed by the federal government—the Foreign Affairs Research Council—had on more than one occasion expressed informally their support of our project and their belief that it could win approval of the council if government funds were involved (one man was rash enough to whisper that maybe funds might even be made available from State); nevertheless, members of the council, when approached informally by the agency in January 1967, indicated that the proposal would be turned down. Half-heartedly, we tried to determine whether this ban could or should be lifted. We were painfully aware of the exposure of the CIA which occurred at the time and we anticipated understandable suspicion among our African scholars. In fact, the Department of State formed its "basic views" on our project "before" the "recent publicity on subsidies," as one official wrote us; they feared that any kind of official sponsorship would damage our plan. Under these circumstances, it was easy for us to agree with State and to shift back to our original position: no government subventions for the actual workshop.

In the spring of 1967, we had grown weary of being rebuffed, but we discovered that the wild idea could not be buried—or at least we could not tolerate its burial. We again visited foundations and then, in June of 1967—fourteen months afterwards—one small, adventurous, private foundation voted us about one-fourth of the money we need; another has been showing keen interest in the idea; and officials of the United Nations have said that they may be willing to co-sponsor the workshop and also contribute to its financing.

Personally, however, I remain pessimistic. For the experience so far has clearly shown that a technique which conceivably could produce rapid change meets with verbal acclaim and then probably perishes. It *is* so easy to find ways of criticizing an idea, and I myself am quite capable of outlining objections to this particular idea more trenchantly than any of the sources which have rejected our pleas. The Africans enrolled as potential participants might decide at the last moment not to attend the workshop, or their governments could suddenly withhold permission. They might appear, but simply engage in a fruitless give-and-take. They might evolve creative proposals, but feel differently when they return to their usual routine and are there subject to pressures from other groups. They might survive this dampening effect and transmit their novel decisions to political leaders who then could respond unenthusiastically or not at all. Some of the leaders might begin executing a new policy involving the disputed border lands and be unable to persuade the masses of the people to co-operate; perhaps, too, they might be overthrown by a ghastly, bloody revolution. Or unfavorable publicity might descend upon the preparations for the workshop, its actual sessions, or the outcome. Yes, one or more of the airplanes carrying us to the site of the meeting could crash, and we might all catch hepatitis. And so on.

There are two answers to such negativism. The first is unacademic. No idea is perfect, no decision can ever be foolproof. The second is very academic. If we possessed a tape or some sort of record of the proceedings, a research door—not a Pandora's lid—would swing open: we might begin to know whether the workshop in some modified form could assist in helping to diminish the scourge of war. Any man in his senses ought to be willing to risk time, energy, or even money to facilitate rapid change of that kind, in Africa or anywhere.

Footnotes

1. Africans and non-Africans are so friendly and helpful that it is always difficult, short of producing a directory, to discharge one's emotional and intellectual debts by footnoting nonperfunctory gratitude. In this instance, moreover, the list is longer than usual and, in addition, for reasons that become painfully clear later in this chapter many persons must remain anonymous— for their own good. Otherwise I would mention the Carnegie Corporation of New York, which enables me to remain perplexed about problems involving rapid change; the Concilium on International Studies, particularly its chairman, Leon Lipson, and the President of Yale University, Kingman Brewster, Jr.,

for permitting me to pursue a wild dream in Africa during the summer of 1966; and Donald Nylen and J. Anthony Stout for wisdom concerning workshops in Africa. Paul Proehl encouraged me to prepare this unlikely account for a colloquium at the University of California, Los Angeles.

2. William J. McGuire and Demetrios Papegorgis, "Effectiveness of Forewarning in Developing Resistance to Persuasion," *Public Opinion Quarterly,* Vol. 26 (1962), pp. 24–34.

3. Daniel Katz, "The Functional Approach to the Study of Attitudes," *Public Opinion Quarterly,* Vol. 24 (1960), pp. 163–204.

4. Gordon W. Allport, *Personality* (New York: Holt, 1937), p. 263.

5. Margaret Mead, *New Lives for Old* (New York: Morrow, 1956), p. 172.

6. George Delf, *Jomo Kenyatta* (New York: Doubleday, 1961), pp. 32–33.

7. Alan Rake, *Tom Mboya* (Garden City: Doubleday, 1962), pp. 33–34.

8. Kwame Nkrumah, *Ghana* (New York: Nelson, 1957), p. 16.

9. Peter Du Sautoy, *The Organization of a Community Development Programme* (London: Oxford, 1962), p. 78.

10. R. N. Ablett, "Community Development in the Former Somaliland Protectorate," *Community Development Bulletin,* Vol. 12 (1961), pp. 74–77.

11. Margaret Mead (ed.), *Cultural Patterns and Technical Change* (New York: Mentor Books, 1955), p. 285.

12. Philip Mayer, *Townsmen or Tribesmen* (Capetown: Oxford, 1961).

13. David E. Apter, *The Politics of Modernization* (Chicago: University of Chicago, 1965), pp. 85–86.

14. David C. McClelland, "Toward a Theory of Motive Acquisition," *American Psychologist,* Vol. 20 (1965), pp. 321–35.

15. Gilbert Kushner *et al., What Accounts for Sociocultural Change?* (Chapel Hill: Institute for Research in Social Science, 1962).

16. Leonard W. Doob, "Psychological Aspects of Planned Developmental Change." In Art Gallaher, Jr., *Perspectives in Developmental Change* (Lexington: University of Kentucky Press, 1967).

17. Irving L. Janis and M. Brewster Smith, "Effects of Education and Persuasion on National and International Images." In Herbert C. Kelman (ed.), *International Behavior* (New York: Holt, Rinehart and Winston, 1966), pp. 190–295. P. 227.

18. M. R. Jellicoe, "An Experiment in Mass Education Among Women." In East African High Commission, *Occasional Papers on Community Development* (Kampala: East African Literature Bureau, 1962), pp. 1–46. Pp. 24–37.

19. Robert R. Blake and Jane S. Mouton, *Group Dynamics* (Houston: Gulf Publishing, 1961).

20. Leland Bradford *et al.*, *T-Group Therapy and Laboratory Method* (New York: Wiley, 1964).

21. Chris Argyris, *Organization and Innovation* (Homewood: Richard D. Irwin and Dorsey Press, 1965); Daniel I. Malamud and Solomon Machover, *Toward Self-Understanding* (Springfield: Charles C. Thomas, 1965); James G. March (ed.), *Handbook of Organizations* (Chicago: Rand McNally, 1965).

22. Janis and Smith, *op. cit.*

23. Barry E. Collins and Harold Guetzkow, *A Social Psychology of Group Process for Decision-Making* (New York: Wiley, 1964).

24. William A. Scott, "Psychological and Social Correlates of International Images." In Kelman, *op. cit.*, pp. 71–103. P. 93.

25. Donald Nylen and J. Robert Mitchell, *Staff Development and Human Relations Training* (New York: mimeographed, Ford Foundation, ca. 1962), p. 54.

26. Theodore Sarbin, "Role Theoretical Interpretation of Psychological Change." In Philip Worchel and Donn Byrne (eds.), *Personality Change* (New York: Wiley, 1964), pp. 176–219.

27. Eugene T. Gendlin, "A Theory of Personality Change." In Worchel and Byrne, *op. cit.*, pp. 100–48. P. 105.

28. Leon Festinger and Jonathan L. Freedman, "Dissonance Reduction and Moral Values." In Worchel and Byrne, *op. cit.*, pp. 220–43.

29. Nylen and Mitchell, *loc. cit.*

30. Collins and Guetzkow, *op. cit.*, pp. 45, 119.

31. Donald Nylen, J. Robert Mitchell, and Thomas Wickes, *Five Training Institutes in Staff Development and Human Relations in West Africa* (New York: mimeographed, Ford Foundation, 1961), p. 1.

32. Nylen and Mitchell, *op. cit.*, p. 1.

33. Nylen, Mitchell, and Wickes, *op. cit.*, pp. 35–40.

34. *Ibid.*, p. 32.

35. *Ibid.*, p. 34.

36. Charles Seashore, *An Evaluation of Staff Development and Human Relations Workshops Conducted by the Ford Foundation in West Africa 1961–1963* (Washington: mimeographed, National Training Laboratories, 1965).

37. Nylen, Mitchell, and Wickes, *op. cit.*, pp. 45–47.

38. Ford Foundation, *Workshops in Staff Development and Human Relations* (Lagos: Ford Foundation, no date), p. 7.

39. Kenya Delegation, "Pan African Unity and the N. F. D. Question in Kenya." In Carnegie Institute in Diplomacy, *The Ethiopia-Somalia-Kenya Dispute, 1960–65* (Dar Es Salaam: mimeographed, University College, 1965), pp. 40–44. Also: I. M. Lewis, *The Modern History of Somaliland* (New York: Praeger, 1965); Mesfin Wolde Mariam, *The Background of the Ethio-Somalia Boundary Dispute* (Addis Ababa: Berhanena Selam, 1964); Saadia Touval, *Somali Nationalism* (Cambridge: Harvard, 1963).

40. Touval, *op. cit.*, p. 12.

41. Colin Legum, *Pan-Africanism* (New York: Praeger, 1965), p. 69.

42. Leonard W. Doob, *Patriotism and Nationalism* (New Haven: Yale, 1964), pp. 161–98.

43. William J. Foltz, *From French West Africa to the Mali Federation* (New Haven: Yale, 1965).

44. Legum, *op. cit.*, p. 46.

45. Thomas M. Franck, *East African Unity Through Law* (New Haven: Yale, 1964).

46. *Ibid.*, p. 72.

47. Joseph S. Nye, *Pan-Africanism and East African Integration* (Cambridge: Harvard, 1965), pp. 59, 60, 183, 184, 185, 186.

48. Vernon McKay, *Africa in World Politics* (New York: Harper & Row, 1963), p. 132.

49. Fred Charles Iklé, *How Nations Negotiate* (New York: Harper & Row, 1964), p. ix.

50. *Ibid.*, p. 36.

51. James A. Robinson and Richard C. Snyder, "Decision-Making in International Politics." In Kelman, *op. cit.*, pp. 435–63. Pp. 439, 455–56.

52. Jack Sawyer and Harold Guetzkow, "Bargaining and Negotiation in International Relations." In Kelman, *op. cit.*, pp. 466–520.

53. Otto Klineberg, *The Human Dimension in International Relations* (New York: Holt, Rinehart and Winston, 1964), pp. 145–46.

54. That context in turn was affected by a series of events. In April 1966 officials of one of the countries approached us at Yale University through E. A. Bayne of the American Universities Field Service and suggested that we organize a research team to investigate the feasibility of a federation of the East African Horn. I discussed the request with two of my colleagues, Joseph LaPalombara and Robert B. Stevens, and we rejected it: it seemed too policy-oriented and unrealistic, and we suspected that the basic data were already available. During one of our discussions the idea of the workshop arose. And I suppose I must consider relevant my own, unoriginal conviction that social science ought to make some sort of contribution to the avoidance of international catastrophe.

55. Chris Argyris, *Some Causes of Organizational Ineffectiveness Within the Department of State* (Washington, D.C.: Department of State, 1967).

56. Elihu Katz and Paul F. Lazarsfeld, *Personal Influence* (New York: Free Press, 1955).

57. It is impossible to refrain from conveying the maddening flavor of these rejections; here, then, are scattered excerpts from a glowing letter which ended by sending us on our way:

> I hate to think that I am the kind of fellow who can't respond to a good man with a bright idea in a bold and gambling spirit. There is much that I find intriguing in your idea. . . . But I find myself overwhelmed with caution and doubts. . . . I also see the step of bringing people together from the three countries as perhaps an overly delicate start. . . . I know from casual conversations with various people that there are many interesting questions here that might be explored and might have a real value in avoiding traps in negotiation or discussion. . . . It is obviously a delicate matter to do something like this on outside initiative. Even when kept in a rather academic context, it is the sort of thing which we in the foundation would approach with great caution, and in matters like this we would, I think, want the clear approval of the State Department. . . .

I am sorry I can't be more constructive and positive about your proposals. When I see the funds that are chewed up in trying to pacify Kenya's Northeast Province, and the dismaying costs to both Ethiopia and Somalia of their antipathies, I am well aware that one of the best possible forms of aid to these countries would be helping them toward peaceful mutual relations. . . .

58. Yale University, through its president and Concilium on International Studies, also agreed to gamble: it provided adequate money for travel and expenses.